Current Research in Egyptology 2015

Proceedings of the Sixteenth Annual Symposium

University of Oxford, United Kingdom
15–18 April 2015

edited by

Christelle Alvarez, Arto Belekdanian,
Ann-Katrin Gill, and Solène Klein

Oxbow Books
Oxford & Philadelphia

Published in the United Kingdom in 2016 by
OXBOW BOOKS
10 Hythe Bridge Street, Oxford OX1 2EW

and in the United States by
OXBOW BOOKS
1950 Lawrence Road, Havertown, PA 19083

Paperback Edition: ISBN 978-1-78570-363-8
Digital Edition: ISBN 978-1-78570-364-5 (epub)

A CIP record for this book is available from the British Library

For a complete list of Oxbow titles, please contact:

UNITED KINGDOM
Oxbow Books
Telephone (01865) 241249, Fax (01865) 794449
Email: oxbow@oxbowbooks.com
www.oxbowbooks.com

UNITED STATES OF AMERICA
Oxbow Books
Telephone (800) 791-9354, Fax (610) 853-9146
Email: queries@casemateacademic.com
www.casemateacademic.com/oxbow

Oxbow Books is part of the Casemate Group

Front cover illustration: Model of boat (Paris Louvre E 284). © Musée du Louvre, dist. RMN-GP/Georges Poncet.

jḥ nꜣ mꜥš swgꜣ j.dj=w jr=k

‘What are these foolish journeys which they have had you make?’

Wenamun 2.22

Contents

List of papers presented

Accetta, Kelly. University of Cambridge
Pathways to the gods: travelling through and between Theban temples of the New Kingdom.

Asbury, Beth. Pitt Rivers Museum, University of Oxford
Pitt-Rivers in Egypt and Egypt in the Pitt Rivers.

Baldi, Marco. University of Pisa
The journey to sacred experience in the Napatan-Meroitic world: pilgrimage and other expressions of popular devotion.

Bardoňová, Martina. Charles University in Prague
Curious routes of barley and emmer. The transport of cereals in the Middle Kingdom era.

Bealby, Marsia. University of Birmingham
One man's trash is another man's treasure? The aesthetics of Egyptian/ising antiques on Crete.

Bennett, James E. Durham University
Travelling through the 21st dynasty with Amenemope: archaeological reality or didactic fantasy?

Bondada, Gautam. University of Oxford
Ancient Egypt and India: the role of networks in shaping culture.

Caramello, Sara. Independent researcher
Pariamakhu and his colleagues. The role of physicians in Late Bronze Age international relations.

Carrington, Jennifer. Cornell University
Sight-seeing and state-branding: diplomatic travel in Egypt under the Ptolemies.

Chapman, Sarah. University of Birmingham
At life's crossroads: reconstructing the travels of the corpse during mummification.

Chantrain, Gaëlle. Université catholique de Louvain
Travel in space and time: between concrete realities and mental representations in ancient Egypt.

Chyla, Julia and Ejsmond, Wojciech. University of Warsaw
By ship or foot – Gebelein crossroads.

Colazilli, Alessandra. Sapienza University of Rome
Weep and laugh as demarcating points of the journey to rebirth. Textual analysis and overview.

Dal Sie, Elettra. Ca' Foscari University of Venice
Girolamo Segato: some new Egyptian documents.

De Magistris, Francesco. University of Oxford
Were the kings of the Late Bronze Age Levant able to effectively control the entire extension of the land of their kingdoms and secure their commerce?

El-Menshawy, Sherine. Qatar University
Heritage and knowledge seekers: travelling within Egypt for discovering the past.

El-Aboudy, Ola. Cairo University
The use of waterways in the warfares of the New Kingdom.

Eltze, Elizabeth. University of Auckland
There and back again: Tanutamani's travel into Egypt.

Gill, Ann-Katrin. University of Oxford
A mention of the gods Shai and Reret in the 'Great Ceremonies of Geb' or rather an important stage of the journey of the Osiris-mummy?

Hart, Cheryl. University of Wales Trinity Saint David
Travelling to the afterlife: an analysis of the rosette motif as a symbolic aspect of the journey of the deceased in the ancient Egyptian iconographic repertoire.

Jackson, Emmet. Independent researcher
'Enough danger to make it a very exciting business'*: the Egyptian travels of Lady Harriet Kavanagh.*

Kilroe, Loretta. University of Oxford
Packing the kitchen sink: accessing the identity of Nubian 'colonial' towns through their pottery in the New Kingdom.

Langer, Christian. Freie Universität Berlin
The motif of forced migration in New Kingdom sources.

Mekawy Ouda, Ahmed M. Cairo University
The writings of Ahmed Lutfi el-Sayed Pasha (1872–1963) on ancient Egypt.

Nuoffer, Cindy. Independent researcher
The journey of Egyptian art to Roman art: egyptianizing patterns in the Roman wall paintings in Rome and Campania.

Oeters, Vincent. Leiden University
A journey through time: 40 years of fieldwork in the New Kingdom necropolis at Saqqara by the Leiden Mission.

Ortiz-García, Jónatan. University of Valencia
The journey to the afterlife under the protection of the Mistress of the Sea: a 'new' funerary belief from Roman Memphis.

Rashwan, Hany. SOAS, University of London
Rethinking the role of cognates in reading ambiguous ancient Egyptian literary passages.

Rocha da Silva, Thais. Independent researcher
Egypt made in Brazil. *Challenges and possibilities.*

Schutz, Manon. University of Oxford
The metamorphosis of Anubis or: how Anubis learned to sit.

Shepherd, Sarah. University of Hull
A friendly invasion? Soldiering in Egypt c.1836–1918.

Siffert, Uta. University of Vienna.
The material culture of the Egyptian funeral and the decorative programme in Middle Kingdom tombs: a case study of representations of the deceased.

Sonbol, Hannah. Freie Universität Berlin
Medieval Arab travelers in the oases of Dakhla and Kharga.

Stienne, Angela. University of Leicester
Movement of objects in museum context. Issues related to the relocation of the Musée du Louvre stored collection.

Subramaniam, Shantanu. Independent researcher
Travelling exhibits and cultural intercourse. A cultural and contextual study of the Egyptian travelling exhibition to India.

Thornton, Amara. University College London
Flinders Petrie's periodical Egypt.

Végh, Zsuzsanna. Ludwig Maximilians University Munich
The role of Re in the Abydene Osiris-Festival.

Watt, Kimberley. University of Cambridge
From Egypt with love.

Williamson, Jacquelyn. Brandeis University/Harvard University
Haunting Amarna: new evidence for private mortuary cults in the Amarna Period.

Xu, Dongni. The Chinese University of Hong Kong
Travelling networks of precious metals: sketching wealth movement in New Kingdom Egypt.

Yoo, Justin. King's College London
Greek traders and visitors to Late Period Egypt.

List of posters presented

Cincotti, Silvana. Université Paul Valéry – Montpellier III
The journey of a collection: the British excavations in the manuscripts of Jean-Jacques Rifaud.

Diletta Pubblico, Maria. University of Naples "L'Orientale"
The role of Osiris in Italian peninsula: travels, routes and diffusion's ways.

Gentelli, Liesel,[1,2] Westmor, Colleen,[2] and Bonnette, Hal.[2]
[1]University of Western Australia, [2]Tell Timai Project, University of Hawaii
Excavation of a Hellenistic structure at Tell Timai.

Hamilton, Julia. University of Auckland
An antipodean traveller in Egypt in the 19th century: Sir John Logan Campbell.

Kapiec, Katarzyna. University of Warsaw
Travel of artifacts – objects from Hatshepsut's temple in Deir el-Bahari in the museums' collections around the world.

Kučová, Stanislava. Charles University in Prague
Roman pottery production centres and trade routes in the Egyptian Western desert.

Mushett Cole, Edward. University of Birmingham
The travel of an idea: how the environmental explanations for the end of the Late Bronze Age have spread to discussions of the political decline in twentieth dynasty Egypt.

Sadik Aly, Amira and Abdel Halim, Shereen. CULTNAT, Bibliotheca Alexandria
Crafts and professions – the permanent ambassadors of the ancient Egyptian civilization.

Takács, Dániel Viktor. University of Warsaw
A journey of conventions.

Yehia, Maha. University of Sadat City
The title *, its function on expeditions in the Middle Kingdom.*

Past conferences

Location	*Year*
University College London, King's College London	2014
University of Cambridge	2013
University of Birmingham	2012
Durham University	2011
Leiden University	2010
University of Liverpool	2009
University of Manchester	2008
Swansea University	2007
University of Oxford	2006
University of Cambridge	2005
Durham University	2004
University College London	2003
University of Birmingham	2002
University of Liverpool	2001
University of Oxford	2000

Foreword

Rather a few years ago, I attended an evening event at the British Museum as a graduate student. I was one of a small group from Oxford University, but by no means were we the only graduate students there. Before that night, none of us knew each other, or each other's work. My fellow graduate student Christina Riggs and I decided to take steps to remedy that. Our decision culminated in the first Current Research in Egyptology event held in the Ashmolean Museum in Oxford, generously supported by the Griffith Institute, on 13–14 January 2000.

Our idea was not only to create a forum in which those just starting out on their Egyptological research could get to know one another and hopefully forge personal and professional links, but also to create a platform specifically for our peers, where some of us might present papers about our work for the first time in a supportive environment. We agreed that papers should be short – 20 minutes – with time for questions. We also agreed that it would be useful to record the event with a publication, including as many of the papers presented as possible.

It was a hugely valuable experience. It gave us the opportunity to sharpen our organisational skills in the lead-up to and over the course of our symposium, and to develop editorial skills after the event had concluded. It also made us feel like part of a wider Egyptological community. Social media has no doubt stepped in to play its role now in sustaining such communities across Egyptology, but it has been gratifying to see Current Research in Egyptology continuing to go from strength to strength rather than being supplanted. At the risk of sounding terribly old-fashioned, I do believe there is something about getting together in person that makes a difference to our interactions.

Our subtitle for CRE in 2000 was 'A symposium for graduates in the British Isles'. CRE has expanded beyond those initial parameters to include independent researchers rather than just enrolled students; it has also become much more of an international event. This sixteenth incarnation of CRE, again hosted at the University of Oxford, saw participants coming from all over the world to share their ideas and the various issues they have encountered. I was very honoured to be asked to participate, for which I thank the organisers and editors of this volume, and it was a genuine pleasure to listen to the papers of those presenting, as well as having a chance to share some of my own ideas. I am honoured again to play a part in introducing the following publication of some of those papers, diverse in their scope and ranging across our shared subject. The writer and visionary Antoine de Saint-Exupéry once praised the 'zest of creating things new', but there is also great satisfaction in the appropriately

Egyptological dynamic of creating established things anew. Each year Current Research in Egyptology undergoes a re-birth, with new organisers and editors, and with them, it grows and evolves. Long may it – and the dialogue it fosters – continue.

Dr Angela McDonald
Centre for Open Studies, University of Glasgow

Editorial preface

After almost a decade, the University of Oxford hosted the sixteenth edition of Current Research in Egyptology on 15–18 April 2015. Fifteen years earlier, in 2000, the first edition of the conference was launched by two Oxford postgraduate students, Dr Angela McDonald and Dr Christina Riggs. Their idea to create a platform for postgraduate students to meet and talk about their research was then taken up by successive students committees. Over the years, the conference has been held in various universities in the United Kingdom and once abroad, in the Netherlands at the University of Leiden. It expanded considerably, improved, gained international recognition, and opened to the egyptological community worldwide.

We were delighted to welcome more than 120 participants from all around the world to Current Research in Egyptology XVI, including our colleagues from Egypt and more distant countries such as New Zealand, China, and India. Among them, 52 speakers from 21 different countries presented their research on the topic of travel in ancient Egypt from a wide range of perspectives such as concrete or abstract travels, travel in space and time, travel inside, to, or from Egypt, travel in literature, travel of beliefs and ideas, or travel of objects. The variety in the subjects of the conference papers and posters, of which a selection has been turned into articles and published in this volume, reflects the variety of the current research.

The conference took place over four days in several University of Oxford institutions and colleges, which allowed participants to experience both the city and the university and get a glimpse of its historical settings. Prof. Richard B. Parkinson welcomed the conference attendees in Merton College with an opening lecture '"Now, Voyager": the poetics of place in ancient Egypt', and we include his paper as a preface to this volume. The second conference-day was concluded by Prof. Emeritus John Baines with his presentation on 'Biographies: journeying through life and creating a memorial' at the Taylor Institution, while Dr Angela McDonald closed the third day in the same venue with her talk on 'Travelling ideas in the written world of ancient Egypt'. As co-founder of the Current Research in Egyptology, her presence at this sixteenth edition of the conference allowed for the celebration of its ongoing success, and she has kindly accepted to introduce this volume with her foreword.

As part of the event, the participants were offered visits to the archives of the Griffith Institute and tours of the Egyptian galleries at the Ashmolean Museum. The conference dinner was held in The Queen's College dining hall, giving them the opportunity to experience a typical and traditional 'formal dinner' in a renowned Oxford college. The usual Annual General Meeting was finally held on the last day and included a vote in favour of the removal of themes for conferences as well as the vote for next year's conference host, successfully won by the Jagiellonian University in Kraków.

Thanks to the dedication, hard work, and enthusiasm of its successive committees, the Current Research in Egyptology conferences have continued to run successfully. With the increasing interest in the conference, there is no doubt that it will keep running annually, promoting current research in Egyptology. We wish all the best of luck to future committee members!

CRE XVI editing committee
Christelle Alvarez, Solène Klein (principal editors), Arto Belekdanian,
Ann-Katrin Gill (co-editors)
Oxford, February 2016

Acknowledgements

The sixteenth edition of Current Research in Egyptology would not have been possible without the support of many institutions and individuals throughout the process.

We would like to thank the Faculty of Oriental Studies at the University of Oxford, the Griffith Institute, Merton College, the Taylor Institution, the Ashmolean Museum, the Ioannou Centre, and The Queen's College for facilitating the organisation of the conference and allowing us to host this edition in Oxford. We are extremely grateful to the Griffith Egyptological Fund, the Egypt Exploration Society, the Institute of Classical Studies, and the London Centre for the Ancient Near East for renewing their financial support through bursaries and funding.

We would also like to acknowledge the invaluable help of the University of Oxford administrative and academic staff. We would like to thank Assoc. Prof. Elizabeth Frood for her initial input and Prof. Richard B. Parkinson for his precious advice. Our sincere thanks go to Sarah Ballstadt, finance officer at the Faculty of Oriental Studies, for her cooperation and patience with our regular requests, and to Sarah Daley, conference and events officer at The Queen's College, for her kind assistance with the organisation of the conference dinner. We would also like to express our gratitude for the managers of our venues: Richard Stayt at the Taylor Institution, Ilaria Perzia and Claire Burton at the Ashmolean Museum, Kate Del Nevo at the Ioannou Centre, and Caroline Massey at Merton College. We are thankful to Charmian Maskell and Linda McCluskey, administrative officers at the University of Oxford, who were most helpful with the management of the online registrations.

We are indebted to Liam McNamara, curator of the Egyptian Department at the Ashmolean Museum as well as Elizabeth Fleming and Catherine Warsi from the Griffith Institute Archives for offering visits in both institutions. We also wish to thank our keynote speakers Prof. Richard B. Parkinson, Prof. Emeritus John Baines, and Dr Angela McDonald for agreeing to take part in Current Research in Egyptology XVI and for their fascinating lectures.

Many students from the department have shown their support and volunteered in various tasks before and during the conference: Ambrose Boles, Francesco De Magistris, Marwan Kilani, Loretta Kilroe, Thais Rocha da Silva, Chiara Salvador, Manon Schutz, and Elsbeth Van der Wilt. We are really thankful to all of them. Finally, we are grateful to Justin Yoo who advised and offered his help all along.

The edition and publication of the proceedings benefited from the expertise and support of a number of people. We are extremely grateful to our reviewers for their time with the selection and improvement of the articles submitted. We are also indebted to Prof. Emeritus John Baines and Prof. Richard B. Parkinson for their editing advice. We would also like to thank the authors for their articles as well as their kind cooperation during the process. We are equally thankful to the team at Oxbow for their work on this manuscript.

Last but not least, we would like to thank all the participants who contributed to the success of this edition of Current Research in Egyptology in Oxford.

CRE XVI editing committee
Christelle Alvarez, Solène Klein (principal editors), Arto Belekdanian,
Ann-Katrin Gill (co-editors)

CRE XVI organising committee
Christelle Alvarez and Solène Klein (co-chairs), Ann-Katrin Gill, Marwan Kilani
Oxford, February 2016

Chapter 1

'Now, Voyager': a preface on the poetics of place[1]

Richard B. Parkinson
University of Oxford, United Kingdom

Are you for magic? I am. ... I am for magic. For dream. For love.

–Patrick White, *Shepherd on the rocks*, xiv (1994, 229)

Approaching literary landscapes

This meditation acts as a preface for the following papers, just as it welcomed the conference participants to the opening of Current Research in Egyptology XVI at Oxford in April 2015. All of those present were fully aware that they were in Oxford, but the question remained, and remains, *which* Oxford were they actually visiting? There are many possible Oxfords: the teddy-bear-infested playground of Evelyn Waugh's *Brideshead revisited*; the corpse-strewn locality of Inspector Morse; the snobbish city so fatally visited by Max Beerbohm's *Zuleika Dobson*; the alternative world of Phillip Pullman's Lyra and Asriel; or even simply the kitsch backgrounds for the Harry Potter films. There are many alternatives to the narrowly academic 'Oxford' that is named on the title page of the Griffith Institute's publications. Questions of locality are often not as simple as one might assume, and the direct experience of Oxford during CRE may have varied from, and will certainly have interacted with,

[1] My thanks are due to the conference organisers for their kind invitation and impressive effectiveness. The paper retains its character as a light-hearted, oral and non-theorised entertainment before the welcome-drinks, and references have been kept to the barest minimum accordingly. A version of this paper was delivered in Florence at the 11th International Congress of Egyptologists in August 2015. The contents derive from an ongoing project to write a new commentary on *Sinuhe*; references to Middle Kingdom compositions follow the conventions of Parkinson 2012, 331–3. In several places I cite films, since the process of creating a film from a fictional work of literature in authentic locations also embodies the interpretative dialogue between the actual and the imaginary and offers parallel dilemmas to those of the textual commentator on poetic places. I am thankful to Katherine Hunt and Simon Smith for early modern advice, to Hisham el-Leithy and Heba Ibrahim for arranging a much appreciated trip to the Wadi el-Natrun in 2012, and to my husband Tim Reid for walking through various literary landscapes with me.

the participants' own internal imaginings and the cultural representations to which they have been exposed.

Over the past half century, academics have become increasingly aware of the extent to which landscape is a cultural construct, and many subject areas have seen the rise of landscape history (e.g. Alexander and Cooper 2013; Prieto 2013), as exemplified by scholars such as the great Oliver Rackham (1939–2015; e.g. the classic account of 1986), and even extending to such approaches as Jeremy Mynott's *Birdscapes* (2009); in intertextual terms, these often draw on a long English tradition of prose writing about landscape (e.g. Macfarlane 2013, 13–33). In Egyptology, there has been a turn to landscape studies with GIS (Geographic Information Science) projects providing a new vision of the changing historical landscape (e.g. Bunbury and Jeffreys 2011). Archaeologists have led the way with studies of phenomena such as desert roads (e.g. Riemer and Förster 2013), but philologists also should be aware of these factors, especially given that one classic example of such a shifting literary landscape is Alexandria – the city of the Ptolemies, but also subsequently of writers such as Constantine Cavafy (1833–1933), Edward Morgan Forster (1879–1970), and Laurence Durrell (1912–1990; e.g. Haag 2004).

The significance of locations can be highly contingent and intense. The Egyptian 'marsh' landscape is now largely lost to us by environmental changes, but was once highly charged with value and meanings, being celebrated in both visual art and Middle Egyptian poetry such as the courtly *Pleasures of fishing and fowling* and *The sporting king* (e.g. Parkinson 2002, 226–32, 311–12). To take a more directly accessible example of a highly valorised landscape, CRE XVI took place in England in the month of April. So much has been written about the English spring landscape but the reactions of a reader of English literature are somewhat restricted if he/she lacks direct experience of what this spring involves (I think here of my father-in-law as an Australian school-boy puzzled by English literary landscapes). Here is a passage from an early 20th century novel:

> The hedge was a half-painted picture which would be finished in a few days. Celandines grew on its banks, lords and ladies and primroses in the defended hollows; the wild rose-bushes, still bearing their withered hips, showed also the promise of blossom. Spring had come, clad in no classical garb, yet fairer than all springs; fairer even than she who walks through the myrtles of Tuscany with the graces before her and the zephyr behind. (Forster 1973, 266)

To understand this text in any full sense, we need not only to identify the flowers lexicographically and botanically but also to identify the allusion to Botticelli's *Primavera* (*c.*1482). Beyond these allusions, however, are the physical glories of the Tuscan spring, which are implicitly contrasted (ironically and anti-heroically) with the actuality of the uncertain early phases of the season in Hertfordshire. The passage creates its meaning in multiple and mixed ways – not only through a reader's awareness of the lexicography and cultural allusions, but also through his/her direct experience of the season and flowers that are mentioned. In a similar manner, how can one fully understand – or feel – the cultural weight of an Indian rainy season raga, such as *rag Megh*, without knowing a little of what the rainy season means in India? What variations and emotions that the ancient texts contained for their original readers have now been lost to us?

Topography is not only a matter of fact, and even simple toponyms can be deceptive. As a preface to the academic papers that follow, I here (playfully) suggest some ways in which travel and locality can be more ambiguously poetic than is often assumed, in line with the turn to a more embedded, visceral 'Material Philology' that has been advocated elsewhere (Parkinson 2009). I discuss a few examples which I hope will throw some indirect light on three famous Middle Kingdom poetic travellers, the eloquent peasant, Sinuhe, and the shipwrecked sailor. These 12th dynasty fictional figures travel to some 'real' locations. One of the most discussed of these is the pyramid where Sinuhe is buried in the royal enclosure of Senwosret I at el-Lisht (B 300–1). This location is demonstrably actual, since the pyramid enclosure was excavated in the early 20th century (Arnold 1992, esp. 34). Gerald Moers, however, has argued that Sinuhe's burial in one of these actual pyramids is a consciously fictionalised act, contradicting known or expected reality for the original audiences (2001, 42–4, 79–105; see Parkinson 2009, 244–5). Sinuhe's fictional burial in an actual place provides the poem with an impossibly happy ending – a courtier buried as a royal prince – and its unlikeliness is integral to its role as an ending. The meaning is arguably created by the dialogue between the actual and the imaginary, and the later textual history of the poem may in part embody this tension (as suggested by Parkinson 2009, 185). One can speculate whether the unknown author(s) of the poem had ever visited the actual pyramid complex, or cited it only from viewing it from nearby Itj-tawi or from repute? It is of course impossible to know and probably irrelevant; it seems that the Theban scribe of the 12th dynasty manuscript of the poem was probably less concerned with factual precisions than with reading impressionistically (Parkinson 2009, 113–19). The same may also be true of the poem's representation of foreign localities such as Retjenu. Although this is a location attested in contemporaneous 'historical' inscriptions, it remains uncertain how the original audiences were intended to assess the poem's account of the Bronze Age Levant (e.g. Hinson 2014). They may have recognised the account as referring to a historical reality, albeit ideologically reshaped, but the representation could also have been more complex, mediated, subtle, and fuzzy than modern historians might wish (e.g. Parkinson 2002, 87–91).

English and Italian places

I outline three cases from comparatively recent English literature, partly because they are familiar to me at first hand. With modern works it is comparatively easy to document the context and the author's intentions, and so they can serve as a reminder of the possibilities of complexity that we should envisage for ancient texts if we are to produce a methodologically plausible analysis. However, I also intend it as a reminder that Egyptology should look outside its own specialism, despite our increasing insistence on our own professionalism and scientificity.

Fig. 1.1: Rooksnest/Howards End *in 2013. © R. B. Parkinson.*

First is an actual place that is transfigured by emotional resonance in literature. In E. M. Forster's *Howards End* of 1910, there are several journeys to a house that 'carries as great a structural load of values as any house in fiction' (Stallybrass in Forster 1973, vii). This semi-mystical place is modelled on the Forster's childhood home, Rooksnest, on the outskirts of Stevenage (Fig. 1.1). It is a surprisingly normal red-brick dwelling, and is still a family home, although the landscape is increasingly threatened by urbanisation (Ashby 1991; photograph: 1991, 17; Friends of the Forster Country 2015) – so much so the Merchant Ivory film of 1992 had to use another location in Rotherfield Peppard, Oxfordshire, in order to evoke the unspoiled landscape of 'the house and the tree that leans over it' (Forster 1973, 311).[2] A visit to the actual house and garden in Stevenage reveals how precise the physical correspondences between the original and the fictionalised house are. The author's emphasis on certain aspects of the building (such as the small rooms) make immediate sense, and the atmosphere is

[2] The surrounding landscape now has electricity pylons, and the tree has been felled, apparently in the interwar years (noted by Stallybrass in Forster 1973, viii), although the historian Margaret Ashby had the impression from the house's then owner, Elizabeth Poston, that the tree became unsafe and had to be felled only after Poston was the sole owner, i.e. in the 1960s (Ashby 1991, 17; pers. comm. 2014). On the Merchant Ivory film, see e.g. Pym 1995, 91–2.

palpable to a visiting reader: here Leonard Bast fell, here Mrs Wilcox walked with her wisp of hay. But who among future readers would realise that the symbolic house was an actual building without knowing the context? Who among future archaeologists would feel any of the intense significance of the actual building without knowing the fictional text? Fact and fiction are hopelessly interwoven here, and literary emotion effects an apotheosis of topography.

Second is an example of the complicated tricks that texts can work on readers; again, I cite Forster, but this time *A room with a view*, published in 1908. The novel's Italian locations are (on the whole) accurately mentioned and are easy to chart with the notes by Oliver Stallybrass in the Abinger edition of the novel (1977). The Florentine sights mentioned in this novel of social comedy were familiar to many of the intended readers, and presumably had to be cited realistically in order to create a sense of familiarity and recognition. The famous hillside near Fiesole in chapter 6 (Forster 1977, 58–68) appears to have been actual, and can still be located as being off the Fiesole road to Settignano, slightly above the Castello di Vincigliata, although the 'bare' hillside of the 1908 novel is now cultivated with olives (Stallybrass note to p. 64: Forster 1977, 230). This hill and the valley below are the (characteristically authentic) locations in the Merchant Ivory film of 1987, shot partly on the estate of the Villa Maiano (Merchant 1994, 16–19). Forster's fictional characters visited the hillside because, as the Rev. Cuthbert Eager says:

> The view thence of Florence is most beautiful – far better than the hackneyed view of Fiesole. It is the view that Alessio Baldovinetti is fond of introducing into his pictures. That man had a decided feeling for landscape. Decidedly. But who looks at it to-day? Ah, the world is too much for us. (1977, 49–50)

Indeed it is. The painter is real – he is Alesso/Alessio Baldovinetti (1425–1499) – but his surviving paintings apparently lack any such views (Stallybrass note to p. 64: Forster 1977, 230), although the view of Florence from the actual hillside is indeed 'most beautiful' (Fig. 1.2). This discrepancy is just possibly a mistake by the author for Benozzo Gozzoli (as suggested by Harold Acton; see Stallybrass note to p. 64: Forster 1977, 230), or a conscious 'wilful' confusion (Stallybrass note to p. 64: Forster 1977, 230). It is, however, arguably more complex, since another view existed in an earlier draft of the novel, where a pretentious young man says that he has visited 'one of those hills beyond Bagno a Ripoli, and to my astonishment I had the very view of the Arno valley that Alesio [sic] Baldovinetti introduces into his pictures' (Forster 1977a, 31).[3] Later in the same conversation, the young man remarks that 'the view occurs in the undoubted Alesio [sic] in the Annunziata' (1977a, 32), which refers to the actual view of a city in a valley in Baldovinetti's nativity fresco of 1460–1462 in the Chiostrino dei Voti in

[3] In this draft of the novel, there were multiple excursions: the characters apparently intended to visit Bagno a Ripoli (Forster 1977a, 55), and an excursion to Fiesole was intended to feature in a planned but unwritten episode (Forster 1977a, 4).

Fig. 1.2: The actual view of the city in 2013 from the hillside near Fiesole visited in chapter 6. © R. B. Parkinson.

SS. Annunziata in Florence (Fig. 1.3).[4] In the published novel, the author has moved an actual hill with the actual view across the valley to a new (and actual) location in Fiesole, but has also transposed Baldovinetti's painted view to a new location in which it is no longer recognisable and no longer actual.

The surviving drafts and sketches of this novel document a transformation within the text's composition, and the author apparently retained his original (actual) view of the city for its metaphorical meaning, even though its literal accuracy became irrelevant as the text evolved, producing a discrepancy that was of course very appropriate for a novel about travellers' pretensions. Such subtleties and complexities are not necessarily phenomena that are restricted to modern literature.

Third is an example of how modern readers can be deceived by fictionality: 'Shakespeare Cliff' near Dover. This toponym features on the Ordinance Survey, and was in place by at least the early 19th century (as in a print after Samuel Owen, *Shakespeare Cliff Dover* of 1816: Tate 2015). The name derives from the scenes in the

[4] The implications of this are un-noted by Stallybrass. The actual fresco is badly damaged, which perhaps accounts for the subsequent comment 'And a fright it is' (Forster 1977a, 32).

Fig. 1.3: 'The undoubted Alesio in the Annunziata' with a damaged view of a city in a valley to the left. © R. B. Parkinson.

(fictional) *Tragedy of King Lear*, where the doomed king's enemies and allies gather at Dover to face a French rescue mission. The blinded Gloucester wants to be taken to a specific 'Cliffe, whose high and bending head: /Lookes fearfully in the confined Deepe' ([Folio text] IV.i l. 67–8). This could very well be referring to an actual cliff near Dover. His son then tells him that he has taken him to the cliff edge, and he famously describes the cliff to his father ([Folio text] IV.v l. 11–24), so as to trick him into believing that he is throwing himself off the top of 'this Chalkie Bourne' ([Folio text] IV.v l. 57); in this way the blinded Gloucester's suicide attempt is rendered harmless. For the original audiences, the vividly described cliff was part of a flat stage, although the scene significantly – and painfully – plays with the ambiguities of early modern stage conventions (e.g. Kott 1967, 112–16; Nuttall 2001, 98–100). The described cliff is confirmed in the play to be fictional and non-existent; nevertheless, imagination has worked not only on Gloucester but also on modern audiences – not so as to evoke a

Fig. 1.4: 'Shakespeare Cliff' looking towards Dover port in 2011. © R. B. Parkinson.

sense of deeply felt agony, but so that they have identified this improvised cliff from the fictionalising description and named it on maps. An ambivalent emotionally charged fictional evocation of a cliff has become an unequivocally actual locality (Fig. 1.4).

Two Middle Kingdom journeys

A close ancient parallel to the modern reception of Shakespeare's Dover cliff is the 'island of the *ka*' in *The shipwrecked sailor*. In this fictional expedition report about an exotic locale 'in a far land, unknown to mankind' (l. 148), a paradisal island is inhabited by a divine serpent and will vanish (l. 154–5). Gerald Averay Wainwright proposed that the island could be identified with the barren, serpent-less Zeberged or St John's Island, described by Strabo and Pliny, off the shore from the ancient port of Berenike in the stormy Foul Bay (Wainwright 1946). Ancient accounts of an actual island, once infested with serpents, in the Red Sea could conceivably have fed into the poem in some way, like the list of actual exotic imports that are mentioned as the produce of the fantastic island (l. 162–5). It seems difficult, however, to identify the poetic and actual islands directly, given that the island of St John is (rather awkwardly) still there, contradicting the serpent's prophecy that 'you will never see this island again, which will have become water' (l. 154–5; see, however, Allen 2015, 42). The fictional report does feature actual islands in the opening verses, where the narrator says that they have passed the cataract island of Biggah and have just moored at home, presumably at Elephantine (l. 9–11). This ambivalent complex relationship with actuality should not surprise us: there is stylish wordplay with the word *ẖnw* as the 'interior' of the island, the distant 'Residence', and 'home' (e.g. in l. 172–5), producing a dialogue of places in a shifting world that destabilises the audience's sense of location. The interplay between the actual and the imaginary is an integral part of the poem, in which even a remote fantastic island becomes uncomfortably familiar, since the loss and grief experienced there gradually suggest that it is a metaphor for the audience's own cosmos (e.g. Parkinson 2002, 188–9). As often, instead of dealing with a binary opposition of fact and fiction, readers find themselves inhabiting the uneasy ground of what Ahdaf Soueif would call the *mezzaterra* (2004). Imaginative literature rarely offers a simple 'altogether elsewhere' (in W. H. Auden's phrase from 'The Fall of Rome': 1991, 333). Where exactly, for example, is Sinuhe's 'real' life located: in Upper Retjenu or at home in Itj-tawi? At the end of that poem, external geography is less important than subjective closeness to the king, and the physical location is meaningless compared to a psychological sense of belonging:

> Whether I am at home,
> whether I am in this place –
> it is you who veils this horizon of mine. (B1 232–3)

Sinuhe's flight to the Levant has been much discussed (e.g. Goedicke 1957; Hinson 2012). Traditionally, the emphasis has been on an assumed referential topographical reality; I focus instead on the process of experiencing the poem. The journey is precisely narrated both in terms of motivation and topography by the fugitive narrator, and this level of detail (whether real or imagined) has various effects on the audience. It creates a sense of an actual lived event; it also increases, through contrast, the audience's sense that the moment of panic that caused this carefully executed flight is beyond rationalisation. In a similar manner, the irrational panic itself is described in precise medical-like terminology, as Hans-Werner Fischer-Elfert has noted (2013). The narration of the journey is arguably patterned on multiple levels: that of real geography that embeds the narrative in a known world, but also that of the psychological state of the fictional hero. He moves in a manner intended to conceal his flight through a sequence of locations whose significant names suggest that they are intended to evoke more than physical locality alone. The itinerary is thus perhaps simultaneously outer and inner, real and metaphorical, actual and imaginary, and it is hard to disentangle these various aspects, partly due to our fragmentary knowledge, but also due to the complex nature of the narration itself.

The stanza of his flight across the Nile valley reads, in the version preserved in a 12th dynasty Berlin papyrus (B 5–13; Fig. 1.5):

jrt=j-[6]*šmt m-ḫntyt*
n-kꜣ=(j)-spr r-ẖnw-[7]*pn ḫmt.n=j-ḫpr-ḥꜣꜥyt*
n-ḏd=j-ꜥnḫ r-sꜣ=f
[8]*nmj.n=j-mꜥꜣtj m-hꜣw-nht*
[9]*smꜣ.n=j m-jw-snfrw*
wrš.n=j <jm> m-ꜥḏ n-[10]*sḫt*
ḫḏ.n=j wn-hrw
ḫp.n=j-s(j) ꜥḥꜥ [11]*m-rꜣ-wꜣt=(j)*
tr.n=f-wj snḏ.n=f
ḫpr.n-[12]*tr n-msyt*
sꜣḥ.n=j r-dmj n[13]*-[ng]ꜣw*
I made [6]my way southwards.
(I) did not plan to reach this [7]Residence, expecting strife would happen;
I did not think to live after him (the dead king).
[8]I crossed Maaty in the region of the Sycomore.
[9]I came to the Island of Sneferu.
I passed a day <there> on the edge of [10]a field.

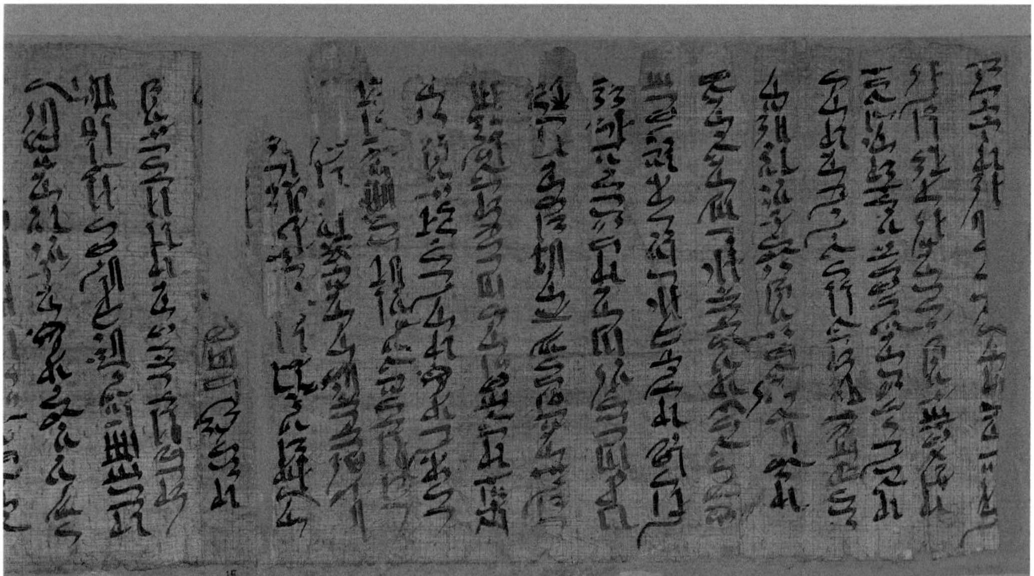

Fig. 1.5: P. Berlin P 3022, with the narration of Sinuhe's flight (B 1–18). © Ägyptisches Museum und Papyrussammlung, Staatliche Museen zu Berlin; photographer: Lisa Baylis, The British Museum.

When it was day again, I made an early start.
I met a man standing [11]in (my) way.
He saluted me, and was afraid.
When it was [12]supper-time,
I had arrived at [13][Wild]-bull Harbour.

The first place name, Maaty (B 8), is highly resonant, and with this toponym, the poet signals that this flight is potentially symbolic (there is no reason to take the word as *šwtj*, designating the pyramids at Giza, as Goedicke 1957, 82–4). From the determinative showing a body of water (Sign N47), Maaty could be a pool, similar to 'lake of Truth (*š n-mꜣꜥt*)' in *The eloquent peasant* B1 85–6. That is an obviously metaphorical pool, but it also alludes to an apparently actual sacred lake in the temple at Herakleopolis, called Maat (*mꜣꜥt*), suggesting an interplay of the metaphorical and the actual (Parkinson 2012, 70–1). The scribe of the 12th dynasty manuscript of *Sinuhe* added a man determinative (Sign A1) to the toponym, perhaps by confusion with *mꜣꜥty* 'just man', which suggests that he was fully aware of the symbolic overtones as he copied. Was such a meaningfully named place an actual body of water, and how was the audience meant to react to it? Attempts to locate Maaty in known topography have reached various conclusions. There is later evidence for a place or settlement in the neighbourhood of Giza named *mꜣꜥty* or *mꜣꜥt* (Zivie 1976, 239–40 [NE 92], 301; Gomaà 1987, 57, n. 10–11) and perhaps even a canal (Gomaà 1987, 57, n. 12). Sedimental evidence shows that in the Middle Kingdom there were two branches of the Nile in the valley north of Memphis, suggesting to Judith Bunbury and David Jeffreys that 'Maaty' here could designate the shallow fordable western branch, located close to the modern Bahr Libeini, which Sinuhe must have negotiated before crossing the main branch in B 13–4 (Bunbury and Jeffreys 2011, 69–71). This is highly plausible, but not fully verifiable, and Maaty could also have been a smaller stretch of water or a pool. Regardless of these uncertainties, I wonder how far any actual location mattered to the original audiences beyond the resonance of the name. Any full topographical data was not necessarily accessible to all the poem's original audiences as it had been to the poem's creator(s): even assuming Maaty was a real place, would an audience in Elephantine have recognised it as such or been able to locate it very precisely?

A consideration of the experience of reading these verses suggests that the now unverifiable exact location of Maaty is not entirely essential in itself for any reading, ancient or modern. The poet immediately elaborates the toponym with the clarifying phrase 'in the region of the Sycomore'. Surviving evidence suggests that this sycomore was an actual and well-known place (see discussion of Gomaà 1987, 57–8; Baum 1988, 25, n. 29 on related toponyms). The 12th dynasty scribe's house determinative (Sign O1) in B 8 suggests that he was thinking of a building – i.e. a sanctuary of a sacred tree – and not just a prominent *ficus sycomorus*, such as was referred to as a landmark by 19th century visitors to the west bank at Luxor (e.g. Wilkinson 1843, II, 134). At Giza there was a cult of Hathor, 'the Lady of the Sycomore' (e.g. Leitz 2002, IV, 79–81), and the description of the sphinx on the 26th dynasty 'Inventory Stela' of Kheops' daughter at Giza mentions the 'mound of the Sycomore (*jꜣt-nht*)' being struck by lightning (l. 5: Jansen-Winkeln 2014, 765). In the mid-20th century, Selim Hassan even noted a sycomore 'of immense age, still flourishing a little to the south of the sphinx' (1949, 226), which may be visible in an aerial photograph showing 'the Pyramids of Gizeh near Cairo from an altitude of approx. 600 m, 21 February 1904' by Eduard Spelterini (Harpers 2013). This phrase describing Maaty as being near the well-known sycomore at Giza might have indicated to the audience which part of the extensive Nile branch Sinuhe crossed, or it might have indicated the location of a little-known (or even fictional) place, which would otherwise have been unknown to them (as is perhaps the case with the similarly qualified toponym 'Estate of Fefi' in *The eloquent peasant* B1 17–18, e.g. Parkinson 2012, 36–7). The fact that the Sycomore was an actual place does not negate its literary resonance or its emotional impact on the audience. These verses describe more than physical movement: in terms of the audience's experiential reality, the evocative toponym Maaty leads into the equally evocative 'sycomore', the tree that gives the protagonist his name 'Sycomore's son'. This name is both intensely meaningful in characterising the fictional protagonist and is also an actual, historically attested personal name of the period (e.g. P. UCL 32163 l. 19: Collier and Quirke 2004, 110–11), so it too is in a sense simultaneously imaginary and actual. This pairing of two resonant place-names creates a sense of an Egyptian who is abandoning his true cultural identity: Sinuhe flees past locations that evoke Truth and his own identity.

The next named location, the 'Island of Sneferu' (B 9), is almost certainly not a fictional place, since the same phrase is attested as an official toponym among the personified estates on the north wall of the mastaba of the 5th dynasty official Seshemnefer III at Saqqara (Junker 1938, 209, pl. 4; PM I^2, 154 [4]), without any indication of its location (Zibelius 1978, 32–3; Gomaà 1987, 58–9; I see no reason to take the 'Island of Sneferu' as a colloquial term, as Hinson 2012, 66–8). The name indicates that it is a *gezira* in the river valley, and also associates it with Sneferu's funerary complex at Dahshur, although it need not point to it being located there. Regardless of whether anyone in the 12th dynasty would have known where the agricultural estate had been or still was, the name evokes a king with positive overtones in other Middle Egyptian poems (e.g. Parkinson 2002, 182–5, 194–5), suggesting that another good is being abandoned. The resonant association with the good old king does not negate any possible actuality – like Rooksnest and Howards End, the different aspects interact to create meaning and are not mutually exclusive. The various locations create an impression of a precise and emotionally charged itinerary in which Sinuhe, having come down from the desert close to Giza, crosses to a *gezira*, abandoning his identity and home. Through specific and in part actual verifiable details, topography is fused with meaning and emotion.

After hiding as much as possible and with only partial success (B 9–11), Sinuhe finally arrives at dusk to '*dmj n-ngꜣw*' (B 12–13; on the significance of nightfall here, see e.g. Parkinson 2002, 154–5). This phrase could be the name of an inhabited settlement named 'Wild-bull Harbour' (either actual or imaginary), or 'a wild-bull harbour' designating an un-inhabited area of the riving bank used for crossing *ngꜣw*-cattle (Goedicke 1957, 80), which would have been suitable for a fugitive to attempt to cross the Nile unnoticed in the evening. The 12th dynasty B-scribe opted for a town determinative (Sign O49), suggesting that he understood it as a toponym, 'Wild-bull Harbour', while the 13th dynasty R-scribe omitted any determinative, suggesting that he understood the phrase as 'a wild-bull harbour' (see Gomaà 1987, 59–60), although this omission may have been affected by a line break just after the phrase (at the end of R 37). The choice of phrase is thematically appropriate, given that the poem later includes imagery of bulls (e.g. *ngꜣw* in B 120). There may even be an allusion to the locality as 'an abandoned harbour' (Green 1984, 27–8); although this is unlikely to be the primary meaning, given the orthography, it does add to the sense of alienation in this stanza. These dilemmas for the reader indicate the extent to which interpretation is inherently contingent, and these are not due to just modern ignorance: the ancient scribes felt them too, and perhaps even the poets.

Regardless of whether the cattle quay was a specific and actual locality that the audience was expected to recognise, it is now not locatable. Once again, the audience can deduce enough about the location from the words of the text, and they need not refer to any external known topographical reality to understand the passage. The word 'harbour' indicates that Sinuhe has reached the Nile, and the following verses narrate how he passes 'east of the quarry, [above the Lady] of the Red Mountain' (B 14–15), referring to the well-known actual 'Red Mountain', still known in Arabic as Gebel Ahmar (see e.g. Klemm and Klemm 2008, 216–19), east of modern Cairo. This location is presented to the audience in such a way that it is associated with its 'Lady', Hathor, the hero's patroness, who is also evoked by the Sycomore (e.g. Zivie 1978, 151). Once again, the sequence of locations implies that Sinuhe is moving secretly, passing beside the mountain's quarries (B 14–15) and avoiding the populated agricultural land of the valley, as he abandons his home. It is consistently presented as an emotionally charged landscape.

The subsequent verses will pose further interpretative dilemmas for modern readers: presumably the 'Walls of the Ruler' (B 17) and 'Peten' (B 20) were actual locations, but we lack any conclusive historical or archaeological confirmation (e.g. Gomaà 1987, 129–30), and doubts have been raised about the real-world referentiality of the former (Stauder 2013, 340–2). There is, ironically, no escape from indeterminacy or uncertainty for us as well as for Sinuhe.

Readers in the landscape

How then do we travel as modern scholars through these poetic locations, and how do we deal with this dilemma in pragmatic terms? Modern readers cannot access fully the psycho-geography of ancient Egypt, but by gathering up surviving parallels, we can intuit some of the rules of the game, gaining a sense of what the range of different attestations of a toponym might imply, regardless of whether it is actual or imaginary. In this way we can try to reconstruct the resonances of a location, such as 'the Sycomore', drawing on the cultural significance of this sanctuary, its actual environment, and the tree in general (e.g. Baum 1988, 18–87). A consideration of the experiential reality of reading avoids any exclusive focus on the problematic binary dichotomy of 'actual' versus 'imaginary'. When a place in a poem is demonstrably an actual one, however, this academic strategy is not the only option. If we ourselves set foot in the reality of the known places wherever we can – as with Rooksnest, Fiesole, or Dover – we can perhaps get a better grasp of their possible meanings and resonances in a text. In an academic study on *The eloquent peasant*, it is easy to note from maps that the Wadi el-Natrun is remote, and that the location characterises the peasant who comes from there as a marginal figure (e.g. Parkinson 2012, 24–5). There is no philological or scientific need to visit the Wadi in order to understand this, but if one does visit it, the matter seems clearer – not only its relative remoteness, but also the sheer strangeness of its landscape that sets it apart from the rest of Egypt (Fig. 1.6).

On location, one can feel with immediacy something of the resonance that the place could have had in the minds of the ancient poet and his audiences (Parkinson 2012, xi). As Marguerite Yourcenar noted in *En pèlerin et en étranger*,

> le déplacement dans le temps n'est souvent jamais mieux obtenu que par le déplacement dans l'espace . . . qui descend les escaliers souterrains de Mycènes plonge au puits des siècles. (1991, 532)

On a purely personal note, I must admit that I am very happy to have gathered reeds and salt in the Wadi as I did in 2012 (Parkinson 2012, xi), just as I am to have walked through the landscapes of Fiesole, Dover, and Rooksnest. My own memories of a disrupted journey back to Cairo from the Wadi with Tim Reid and Heba Ibrahim add to these personal resonances as I now (re-)read the ancient poem: our group of three modern fellow-travellers was not delayed by a villainous Nemtinakht armed with sheets, but by a puncture from which we were rescued by two young farmers and their tractor (Fig. 1.7). These memories shape my reactions to the ancient toponym.

All of this is irrelevant to philological science, and the memories only concern the feelings of an individual person reading the poem. But that is arguably what the experiential reality of a poem is all about.

Fig. 1.6: Salt and reeds in the Wadi el-Natrun in 2012. © R. B. Parkinson.

Such direct experience can provide us with a 'touch of the real' (e.g. Greenblatt and Gallagher 2000, 20–48) that can allow us to sense a little of how places might have shaped the reactions of a poem's original audiences. In these poems, the peasant's wadi or the sailor's mention of Biggah were – and still are – not simply toponyms, as they might well be in another less imaginative type of text such as an Onomasticon, whether the 13th dynasty Ramesseum Onomasticon or a modern academic commentary (Gardiner 1947, II, 1–2* [A 314]; III, pl. 2–2a [R 183]). Instead, these were place-names that had a visceral emotional impact through their cultural resonances, which we as modern readers should attempt in part to reconstruct and feel. Even when a toponym is simply an illustrative image, such as Dante's comparison of the frozen giants in the final circle of hell with the towered town of Montereggione (*Inferno* XXXI, 40–1: Singleton 1989, I, 328–9; II, 567, pl. 7), it is not generic, but a particular place chosen to create a particular reaction. A toponym in a poetic text is never 'only the name', to use a phrase from Edward Thomas's famous poem about 'Adlestrop' in Oxfordshire (l. 8: 1981, 24–5). Outer geography shapes and is shaped by the inner world, and the travels that

Fig. 1.7: A disrupted journey from the Wadi el-Natrun to Egypt in 2012. © R. B. Parkinson.

were experienced by ancient authors and readers inevitably move between these spheres – alarmingly, confusingly, wonderfully.

I conclude by making two further general observations. Any actual visit to a place in Egypt reminds us that, whether interior or external, these places were living landscapes for the poems' original audiences, just as the landscape is now. It has been easy for academics to forget this immediacy, and to overlook what Philippe Derchain termed 'une Egypte qui n'est pas dans les livres savants' (1996, [1]). Direct experience of a physical environment can bring us a little closer to the experiential reality of even a distant, fictional poem. From this, I would suggest that in some ways the real issue of travel for modern Egyptologists is how we can travel ourselves, in terms of both imagination and actuality, beyond our own (often highly restrictive) institutional and intellectual frames. Such a journey will perhaps take us like the shipwrecked sailor to a place that we cannot entirely define, as we try to find a strategy with which to imagine the experiences of an ancient culture. What else (in some sense) are these Middle Kingdom poems but *vade mecums*, urging their audiences onwards to imagine experiences elsewhere? Such aspirations are of course ultimately impossible, but we should not be deterred from undertaking intellectual journeys just because they are difficult, endless, or impossible. Rather, as Walt Whitman exhorted us in the short poem of 1891–1892 (2008, 379) that gave me my title:

> The untold want, by life and land ne'er granted,
> Now, Voyager, sail thou forth, to seek and find.

References

Alexander, N. and Cooper, D. (eds.) 2013. *Poetry and geography. Space and place in postwar poetry.* Liverpool: Liverpool University Press.

Allen, J. P. 2015. *Middle Egyptian literature. Eight literary works of the Middle Kingdom.* Cambridge: Cambridge University Press.

Arnold, D. 1992. *The pyramid complex of Senwosret I. The south cemeteries of Lisht* III, Publications of the Metropolitan Museum of Art Egyptian Expedition 25. New York: Metropolitan Museum of Art.

Ashby, M. 1991. *Forster country.* Stevenage: Flaunden Press.

Auden, W. H. 1991. *Collected poems*, ed. E. Mendelson. London: Faber and Faber.

Baum, N. 1988. *Arbres et arbustes de l'Egypte ancienne. La liste de la tombe thébaine d'Ineni (no 81)*, Orientalia Lovaniensia Analecta 31. Leuven: Peeters.

Bunbury, J. and Jeffreys, D. 2011. 'Real and literary landscapes in ancient Egypt'. *Cambridge Archaeological Journal* 21 (1): 65–75.

Collier, M. and Quirke, S. 2004. *The UCL Lahun papyri* [2]: *religious, literary, legal, mathematical and medical*, BAR International Series 1209. Oxford: Archaeopress.

Derchain, P. 1996. *Le souvenir imaginaire.* Verviers: La Dérive.

Fischer-Elfert, H.-W. 2013. 'Magische Poesie: der altägyptische Sinuhe als sprechender Patient'. *Ströme: Journal der Sächsischen Akademie der Wissenschaften* 11: 9–27.

Forster, E. M. 1973. *Howards End,* ed. O. Stallybrass, Abinger Edition 4. London: Edward Arnold.

Forster, E. M. 1977. *A room with a view,* ed. O. Stallybrass, Abinger Edition 3. London: Edward Arnold.

Forster, E. M. 1977a. *The Lucy novels. Early sketches for A room with a view,* ed. O. Stallybrass, Abinger Edition 3a. London: Edward Arnold.

Friends of the Forster Country 2015. [online] ⟨http://www.forstercountry.org.uk/⟩, accessed 18 May 2015.

Gardiner, A. H. 1947. *Ancient Egyptian onomastica* I–III. London: Oxford University Press.

Goedicke, H. 1957. 'The route of Sinuhe's flight'. *Journal of Egyptian Archaeology* 43: 77–85.

Gomaà, F. 1987. *Die Besiedlung Ägyptens während des Mittleren Reiches* II. *Unterägypten und die angrenzenden Gebiete,* Tübinger Atlas des Vorderen Orients, Beiheft B 66 (2). Wiesbaden: Ludwig Reichert.

Green, M. 1984. 'The word *ngꜣw* in Sinuhe B 13'. *Göttinger Miszellen* 70: 27–9.

Greenblatt, S. and Gallagher, C. 2000. *Practicing New Historicism.* Chicago: Chicago University Press.

Haag, M. 2004. *Alexandria. City of memory.* New Haven: Yale University Press.

Harpers 2013. [online] ⟨http://harpers.org/blog/2013/12/the-pyramids-of-gizeh-near-cairo-from-an-altitude-of-approx-600-m-21-february-1904//⟩, accessed 13 May 2015.

Hassan, S. 1949. *The sphinx. Its history in the light of recent excavations.* Cairo: Government Press.

Hinson, B. 2012. 'Locating the *mꜣꜥ.ty* – notes on B,8 and 9 of Sinuhe'. *Göttinger Miszellen* 234: 65–8.

Hinson, B. 2014. 'Sinuhe's life abroad: ethnoarchaeological and philological reconsiderations'. In K. Accetta, R. Fellinger, S. Musselwhite, P. Lourenço Conçalves, and W. Paul van Pelt (eds.) *Current Research in Egyptology 2013. Proceedings of the fourteenth annual symposium, University of Cambridge, March 19–22, 2013*: 81–93. Oxford: Oxbow Books.

Jansen-Winkeln, K. 2014. *Inschriften der Spätzeit* IV. *Die 26. Dynastie*. Wiesbaden: Harrassowitz.

Junker, H. 1938. *Gîza* III. *Bericht über die von der Akademie der Wissenschaften in Wien auf gemeinsame Kosten mit Dr. Wilhelm Pelizaeus unternommenen Grabungen auf dem Friedhof des Alten Reiches bei den Pyramiden von Gîza. Die Mastabas der vorgeschrittenen V. Dynastie auf dem Westfriedhof*. Vienna: Hölder-Pichler-Tempsky.

Klemm, R. and Klemm, D. D. 2008. *Stones and quarries in ancient Egypt*. London: The British Museum Press.

Kott, J. 1967 [1964]. *Shakespeare our contemporary*, trans. B. Taborski. London: Methuen and Co.

Leitz, C. (ed.) 2002. *Lexikon der ägyptischen Götter und Götterbezeichnungen* IV, Orientalia Lovaniensia Analecta 113. Leuven: Peeters.

MacFarlane, R. 2013. *The old ways. A journey on foot*. London: Penguin.

Merchant, I. 1994. *Ishmail Merchant's Florence. Filming and feasting in Tuscany*. New York: Harry N. Abrams.

Moers, G. 2001. *Fingierte Welten in der ägyptischen Literatur des 2. Jahrtausends vor Christus: Grenzüberschreitung, Reisemotiv und Fiktionalität*, Probleme der Ägyptologie 19. Leiden: Brill.

Mynott, J. 2009. *Birdscapes. Birds in our imagination and experience*. Princeton: Princeton University Press.

Nuttall, A. D. 2001. *Why does tragedy give pleasure?*. Oxford: Oxford University Press.

Parkinson, R. B. 2002. *Poetry and culture in Middle Kingdom Egypt. A dark side to perfection*, Athlone Publications in Egyptology and Ancient Near Eastern Studies. London: Continuum.

Parkinson, R. B. 2009. *Reading ancient Egyptian poetry. Among other histories*. Chichester: Wiley-Blackwell.

Parkinson, R. B. 2012. *The tale of the eloquent peasant: a reader's commentary*, Lingua Aegyptia Studia Monographica 10. Hamburg: Widmaier Verlag.

Prieto, E. 2013. *Literature, geography, and the postmodern poetics of place*. Basingstoke: Palgrave Macmillan.

Pym, J. 1995. *Merchant Ivory's English landscapes. Rooms, views, and Anglo-Saxon attitudes*. New York: Harry N. Abrams.

Rackham, O. 1986. *The history of the countryside*. London: Dent.

Riemer, H. and Förster, F. 2013. 'Ancient desert roads: towards establishing a new field of archaeological research'. In F. Förster and H. Riemer (eds.) 2013. *Desert road archaeology in ancient Egypt and beyond*, Africa Praehistorica 27: 19–58. Cologne: Heinrich-Barth-Institut.

Singleton, C. S. 1989. *The divine comedy. Inferno*. Bollingen Series 80. Princeton: Princeton University Press.

Soueif, A. 2004. *Mezzaterra. Fragments from the common ground*. London: Bloomsbury.

Stauder, A. 2013. *Linguistic dating of Middle Egyptian literary texts*, Lingua Aegyptia Studia Monographica 12. Hamburg: Widmaier Verlag.

Tate 2015. [online] 〈http://www.tate.org.uk/art/artworks/owen-shakespeare-cliff-dover-t05253〉, accessed 20 May 2015.

Thomas, E. 1981. *The collected poems of Edward Thomas*, ed. R. G. Thomas. Oxford: Oxford University Press.

Wainwright, G. A. 1946. 'Zeberged: the shipwrecked sailor's island'. *Journal of Egyptian Archaeology* 32: 31–8.

White, P. 1994. *Collected plays* II, Australian Dramatists. Sydney: Currency Press.

Whitman, W. 2008 [1891–2]. *Leaves of grass*, ed. J. Loving, Oxford World Classics. Oxford: Oxford University Press.

Wilkinson, J. G. 1843. *Modern Egypt and Thebes: being a description of Egypt, including the information required for travellers in that country*. London: Murray.
Yourcenar, M. 1991. *Essais et mémoires*, Bibliothèque de la Pléiade 378. Paris: Gallimard.
Zibelius, K. 1978. *Ägyptische Siedlungen nach Texten des Alten Reiches*, Beihefte zum Tübinger Atlas des Vorderen Orients, Beiheft B 19. Wiesbaden: Ludwig Reichert.
Zivie, A. 1978. 'Les carrières et la butte de Yak'. *Revue d'Égyptologie* 30: 151–62.
Zivie, C. M. 1976. *Giza au deuxième millénaire*, Bibliothèque d'Étude 70. Cairo: Institut Français d'Archéologie Orientale.

Chapter 2

An epigraphical journey in the pyramid of Ibi: between textual transmission and mistakes

Christelle Alvarez
University of Oxford, United Kingdom

Introduction

The texts of the pyramid of king Qakare Ibi (8th dynasty) at South Saqqara – published by Gustave Jéquier in 1935 – are usually considered corrupt and outside the main tradition of the Old Kingdom (e.g. Allen 2015, 3). The inscriptions show signs of carelessness in execution, contain mistakes, and display unusual features such as whole sections copied in the wrong order. The arrangement of the texts on the walls is also singular: while spell sequences in the pyramids of the 5th and 6th dynasties are, overall, consistent (Hays 2012, 120), they diverge significantly in Ibi's case. Those observations led scholars to assert that the order and choice of spells in the pyramid of Ibi were indiscriminate and follow no recognisable pattern (Jéquier 1935, 6; Theis 2010, 328); they have therefore mostly been disregarded in studies on the Pyramid Texts (e.g. Allen 2015, 3; Hays 2012, 14).

Yet Ibi's texts are a meaningful source for understanding the transmission of mortuary literature, not least because little evidence survives from the period between the late Old Kingdom and the Middle Kingdom. The only other source of royal mortuary texts is the indirect one of the 12th dynasty wooden coffin of the *jmj-r pr* Neferi (Allen 1976, 1), which is inscribed with spells bearing the cartouche of the Herakleopolitan king Khety III of the 9th dynasty (see Mathieu 2004, 256). The amount of texts is, however, significantly smaller than Ibi's, because it derives from the restricted space of a coffin. Despite the damaged state of preservation of the texts of Ibi, they are of appreciable extent, and many of them remain unidentified. Furthermore, the reopening of the pyramid of Ibi during the 2015 season of the Mission archéologique française de Saqqâra (MafS) has brought to light hundreds of unpublished fragments that will certainly contribute to a better understanding of this corpus.

The aim of this article is twofold: first, I reassess the supposedly random arrangement of texts of Ibi's wall through an examination of one section on the fifth register of the south wall of his pyramid; second, I address issues of disorder and miscopy in these texts. This preliminary research based on two case studies – Ibi/S/S V 1–25[1] and *PT* 1002 – attempts to shed light on the way spells were combined and inscribed in the pyramid, and also to hint at redactional practices in the transmission of mortuary literature of this period.[2]

Description of Ibi/S/S V 1–25[3]

The section Ibi/S/S V 1–25 (Fig. 2.1) consists of 25 columns of text containing three spells belonging to the known corpus of the Pyramid Texts – *PT* 407 (cols. 1–2), *PT* 268 (cols. 2–13), and *PT* ^{N}627B (cols. 13–17) – followed by eight more columns of an unknown text (cols. 18–25). Two of the three spells are shortened (*PT* 268 and ^{N}627B), but in other respects all three follow the versions of the Old Kingdom Pyramid Texts strictly. In contrast, the eight additional columns do not correspond to any known versions of mortuary literature (see further below) and so have not been allocated spell numbers; I therefore refer to them as 'Unnumbered text' in this article.

PT 407

The section in Ibi begins with *PT* 407, 713a–b in the first column and a half (Fig. 2.1, cols. 1–2). Nothing survives from the preceding columns, but one may expect that they bore the earlier parts of *PT* 407. The text mentions the purification of the king, his being given a place in the sky, his identification with Re in his solar bark, and his being rowed across the *Akhet*. There follows the completion of the opening of the mouth, nose, and ears, enabling the king to live in the afterlife. This section of *PT* 407 is lost from Ibi's version; only the end of the spell is preserved in cols. 1–2, a passage mentioning the purification and protection of the king by Re: 'Qakare governs [for the one who is older than he. The Sun cleans Ibi,[4] the Sun defends] Ibi from that which might be done badly against him'.

PT 268

Following *PT* 407, *PT* 268 (Fig. 2.1, cols. 2–13) presents the various stages preceding the coronation of the king at the Great Compound (*ḥwt ꜥ3t*) as well as his accession to the next world. The spell begins with the cleansing of the king: '[This Ibi washes himself as the Sun appears] and the Great Ennead [shines]'. Then, after he has purified himself, the spell mentions the king seizing the *wrrt*-crown and being nurtured by Isis and Nephthys: 'Should the Ombite become elevated to the fore [of the shrine, Ibi will take away] the elite (*p3t*) as a limb of Ibi. Qakare will seize the crown [from the

[1] See Leclant *et al.* 2001, 6–9 for the conventions of the Mission archéologique française de Saqqâra (MafS), where 'sarcophagus' (abbreviated 'S') replaces 'funéraire' (F).

[2] I am grateful to John Baines for discussion and comments during the completion of this article and to Marie-Noëlle Fraisse (MafS) for providing me with her hieroglyphs font (in progress).

[3] The translation is based on Allen 2015.

[4] The cartouche does not systematically alternate between Ibi and Qakare; for the readers convenience I have restored the name in the translation consistently as 'Ibi' when the cartouche is in lacuna.

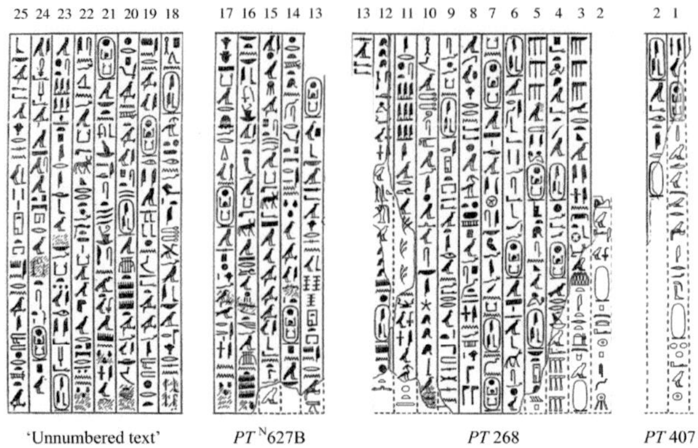

Fig. 2.1: Ibi/S/S V. © Christelle Alvarez, adapted from Jéquier 1935, pl. 12, cols. 613–37. From right to left: PT *407,* PT *268,* PT *N627B, and 'Unnumbered text' (on the spell division between* PT *268 and* PT *N627B see text). Outlined hieroglyphs are added in the lacunas on the basis of Kurt Sethe's edition (1908–1922).*

Dual] Ennead. Isis nurtures Qakare and Nephthys suckles Ibi'. His ka is then purged by Horus in the Jackal Lake and the Duat Lake before being brought to his body, which is at the Great Compound:

> Horus receives Ibi at his two fingers, cleanses Qakare in the Jackal Lake, and releases the ka of Qakare from the Duat Lake. He purges the flesh of the ka of Ibi and of the body of Qakare with that which is on the Sun's shoulders in the Akhet, which he receives, when the Two Lands shine and he opens the gods' faces. He conducts the ka of Ibi at the Great Compound.[5]

There he will be crowned with the *wrrt*-crown, navigate across to the Field of Rushes, and reach the next world as an *akh*: 'The portals act for him. The (Red Crown's) coil is tied on for him, and he leads the Imperishable Stars. He crosses to the Fields of Reeds with those in the Akhet rowing him and those in the Cool Waters sailing him'. The last sentence of *PT* 268 is omitted, and the text in Ibi ends with the clause: 'Ibi is truly effective, and the arms of Qakare [do not] resist (him)' (on the spell division, see below).

PT N627B

PT N627B begins in col. 13 with the identification of the king as a great falcon that is on the battlements of an undisclosed compound: *Jmn-rn* 'Hidden-of-Name'. The spell then compares parts of his body to deities:

> (the one) who takes Atum's property to him who sweeps the sky away from the earth and Nu. The eyes of this Qakare are now those of the Lord of Sunlight, his lips those of the

[5] Allen (2015, 351) proposes that this refers to the solar temple in Heliopolis.

bull of divine images; his neck is that of the mistress of flame; his claws are those of the bull of the evening; his wings are those of Thighs Forward inside his shrine. Authoritative utterance (*ḥw*) has been given to Qakare as He Whose Face Suffered, the great one beside him who is in Nu.

'Unnumbered text'

'Unnumbered text' is closely related, but not identical to, *PT* ^{N}627B, *CT* 682, and *CT* 990 (Allen 1950, 95 [627B]). *CT* 682 (B1BO 450–65) occurs on the outer coffin of the set belonging to the nomarch Djehutynakht (Boston MFA 20.1822) found at Deir el-Bersha and *CT* 990 is attested in Papyrus Gardiner II 51–61 (London BM EA 10676) and Papyrus Gardiner III 436–42 (Chicago P. OIM 14059). Papyrus Gardiner II and III are fragmentary, but the scattered words that are preserved suggest that their versions were similar or identical in content: the beginnings and the ends of the spells, as well as the same grouping of elements can be identified. The two passages in each Gardiner papyrus and the one on the coffin of Djehutynakht seem to follow a similar pattern: identifying the king with a great falcon and parts of his body with deities; giving authoritative utterance to the king; giving various indications of his access to the beyond; and establishing him in the sky in the bark of Re on the closing day of the year. The 'Unnumbered text' section in Ibi (cols. 18–25) also identifies parts of the king's body with deities and mentions that the king has reached the *Akhet* and is at the prow of the solar bark; he will 'lead the Sun in his two Maat-boats on the day of closing out the year.' It presents most of the themes found in the Coffin Texts 682 and 990, but in a shorter formulation and a very different order. All these texts – *PT* ^{N}627B, 1178a–85c, *CT* 682, 199e–201d, *CT* 990, 310k–12g, and 'Unnumbered text' (Ibi, cols. 18–25) – could therefore be different versions of a ritual utterance with essentially the same content.

Discussion

The four spells of the section Ibi/S/S V 1–25 - *PT* 407, *PT* 268, *PT* ^{N}627B, and 'Unnumbered text' - mention elements related to the cleansing and purification of the king, his receiving the ruling function, and ascent to the sky. These common themes give a sense of homogeneity, continuity, and semantic cohesion. The recurrence of the reference to compounds, *ḥwt ꜥꜣt* (col. 9) and *ḥwt Jmn-rn* (cols. 13, 18–19, 25), also strengthens the relationship between the spells. In spell *PT* 268, Horus washes the king in different lakes and brings him to the Great Compound, where the main part of the ritual will take place. Cols. 10–13 state that, once Ibi is in the Great Compound, the Red Crown's coil will be tied for him before he joins the next world. In *PT* ^{N}627B, the king is identified as a great falcon on the battlements of a hidden compound, where he is given authoritative utterance. Finally, 'Unnumbered text' indicates that the king has now flown above the enclosure and has reached the sky. Thus, the content of the section Ibi/S/S V 1–25 is thematically coherent. The four spells seem to develop a chronological succession of episodes starting with the purification of the king in different lakes, then a ritual at the compound, and finally his flight to the sky. This possible sequence may also be supported by the tenses used: it starts with prospective and ends with perfective forms. The latter occur only in 'Unnumbered text' where they indicate, for instance, that the king has already reached the *Akhet*: *pḥ.n jbj ꜣḫt* (col. 18).

The evidence mentioned so far suggests that the organisation of the spells in this section is intentional. This ordering is justified thematically, despite not being attested in the earlier pyramids of kings (Hays 2012, 680, 683–4, 686–7) and queens (Ankhesenpepy II; Behenu;[6] Neit (Jéquier 1933, 20 [7]); Iput and Wedjebetni are fragmentary (Jéquier 1928; 1933; Allen 1986)). The absence of spell dividers in Ibi is also significant. A spell divider usually has the form of a line or a *ḥwt* sign (Gardiner O6) at the end of a spell, followed by the group *ḏd-mdw* 'recitation', which introduces the next spell. In Ibi's pyramid, however, spells are inscribed one after another without any indication as to where they begin or end. It is thus a matter of interpretation whether or not the transition from one spell to another is intentional.

The end of the version of *PT* 268, 375a in Wenis' and Pepy II's texts reads *n zꜣ ꜥwy=f* 'his arms do not resist (him)', while in Neit's there is a cartouche after *ꜥwy* instead of the suffix pronoun, reading 'the arms of (Neit) do not resist (her)' (Jéquier 1933, pl. 7, col. 36). In Ibi's version, however, *PT* 268 stops before the end of the spell, within paragraph 375a, omitting the suffix pronoun and continuing directly with *PT* ^{N}627B, 1778a which begins with a cartouche. Given the Neit version of *PT* 268, where her cartouche is used in place of the suffix pronoun *=f*, one could argue that the end of this spell in Ibi's pyramid is not missing, but was simply replaced with the cartouche in col. 13 which forms the start of *PT* ^{N}627B. The text in cols. 12–13 would therefore read: *[n] zꜣ ꜥwy=f (Ḳꜣ-kꜣ-Rꜥ)*, 'the arms of (Qakare) [do not] resist (him)'. *PT* 268, 375a would then be inscribed in full, with the cartouche as a direct genitive in place of the pronoun suffix of the Wenis and Pepy II versions. The issue will then be where to demarcate the beginning and the end of the two spells, that is, whether to consider the end of *PT* 268 as coming after the cartouche or before it, since *PT* ^{N}627B, 1778a also starts with a cartouche (*Ḳꜣ-kꜣ-Rꜥ*) *pw bjk ꜥꜣ* 'This (Qakare) is a great falcon'. In order to read *PT* 268, 375a and *PT* ^{N}627B, 1778a appropriately, the cartouche would need to act as both the direct genitive of the word preceding it and the subject of the following sentence.

Two explanations can be offered for the possible omission of the end of *PT* 268. One option is that the copyist might have overlooked some words, having perhaps been confused by seeing two cartouches in close proximity, and continued after the second instead of the first, thus omitting one sentence (375b). Another option is that the editor might have chosen to shorten the spell and to fuse it with the beginning of the next spell, writing the cartouche once instead of twice for aesthetic reasons. A deliberate omission would fit with the assumption of an active editing of the text: as the three spells are exact parallels of earlier versions, the editor

[6] Information kindly provided by Bernard Mathieu (Ankhesenpepy II) and Marie-Noëlle Fraisse (Behenu).

would have selected and combined smaller sections of different spells. Spells are usually inscribed as discrete units whether or not they are arranged in meaningful sequences. For instance, the east wall of the pyramid of queen Behenu exhibits an otherwise unattested sequence of spells, each of which seems to follow the other in a 'narrative progression' (Berger-el Naggar and Fraisse 2015, 47). The spells are inscribed in full and remain distinct units within *ḥwt*-frames, even when they form part of a larger composition. The section in Ibi's pyramid, in contrast, consists of parts of different texts directly juxtaposed one to another, or perhaps even bound together. This combination, together with the absence of spell-dividers, would support the assumption of a deliberate combination.

The transition between *PT* ᴺ627B and 'Unnumbered text' is unclear as well. As explained above, *PT* ᴺ627B and 'Unnumbered text' seem to belong to a similar ritual utterance, but their content is formulated differently. Thus, the last eight columns of 'Unnumbered text' could just as well be given the number *PT* ᴺ627B, although they belong to a different source. *PT* ᴺ627B, otherwise identical to the parallels in older versions, is interrupted by 'Unnumbered text' on col. 18. Given that some clauses are not found in their expected order, cols. 18–25 are likely to have been miscopied. The mention of the two-Maat boats in col. 19, for example, usually follow the mention of the day of completing the year (*hrw [ḥts] rnpt*), but here appears later, in col. 24 (see e.g. *PT* ᴺ627B, 1785b; *CT* 990, 310o). More evidence for the miscopying of this spell is the presence of the same text in a different order in fragment G of the pyramid (Jéquier 1935, pl. 15).[7]

The omission of words and the disorder of the text are likely to have been the result of some inadvertence on the part of the copyist. The omission of groups of words is frequent in the copying of texts, as optical similarities in the original can lead to the eyes skipping forwards or backwards. As regards disorder in texts, Gustave Jéquier mentioned (1935, 5–6) that these mistakes might be produced by distracted copyists or illiterate carvers, or could be due to the lack of time caused by the short reign of Ibi. However, it is clear that the usual procedure to carve texts in pyramids was used: traces of sketches of the texts in red and black paint are visible around the carved inscription (verified *in situ*). These traces document the different operations undertaken before the carving stage and suggest that the inscriptions were checked against an original before being carved.

One might therefore expect the copyist to have noticed any miscopying in the second stage. Since he seems not to have done so, one could argue that he did not know how to read a papyrus source. However, similar instances occur in later periods in the decoration of coffins (see e.g. Allen 1977), temple scenes (Assmann 1970), royal tombs in the Valley of the Kings, and in papyrus manuscripts (Sadek 1985; Lüscher 1998; Mauric-Barberio 2003). In all cases, the disorder resulted from copying an original that was written retrograde. Indeed, it seems that copyists preferred to

[7] The direction of writing in fragment G shows that it belongs to the north or east wall of the burial chamber.

copy a text from right to left, even when it was written from left to right (that is, in retrograde order), and thus started from the end and worked backwards towards the beginning of the text. This method of copying would not have been problematic if the copyist respected the exact arrangement of the original; if he happened to have more space at the bottom of a column and added text from the top of the next one, he would be garbling the text. According to Florence Mauric-Barberio (2003, 187), this order of copying seems to have been very common, but it can only be detected for certain through mistakes.

Disorder and miscopying in Ibi

As mentioned by Thomas George Allen (1950), the lines of the source texts were copied in the wrong order in several sections of the pyramid of Ibi; those texts are therefore unintelligible as they stand. This mistake could only have been made if the source was originally written in columns, which implies that the copyist did not respect the column divisions of the manuscript, thus garbling the texts in the copy. For instance, the direction of writing on the south wall shows that the texts would normally read from right to left, with the signs facing right. Instead, Isabelle Pierre-Croisiau (2004, 264, figs. 4–5) has demonstrated that *PT* 1002[8] (Jéquier 1935, pl. 11, cols. 523–30), which occurs one register above the section studied here, is to be read from left to right with overlaps between one column and another. This mistake can be understood if one attempts to recreate a hypothetical original (Fig. 2.3).

Figure 2.2 shows *PT* 1002 as found in the pyramid of Ibi. The spell, best paralleled in *CT* 517, is expected to begin with *jt=k sm3 wr mwt=k sm3t wrt*: 'your father is the Great Wild Bull; your mother is the Great Wild Cow' (*CT* VI 105e). However, this passage occurs towards the end of the text, inscribed in cols. 7–8 of Ibi, while the end of the spell reading ⟨*n ẖnn*⟩ *Ḏḥwty j.jr.t-n=f n=k*: 'Thoth ⟨will not upset⟩ what he has done for you' (*CT* VI 107c) occurs in col. 1, omitting the verb *n ẖnn*, which occurs isolated in the middle of col. 3. The hypothetical model in Figure 2.3, which is written retrograde, proposes an original layout of *PT* 1002 and accounts for the order in Ibi's version (Fig. 2.2). Indeed, the assumption that the hypothetical model was read in the wrong direction, that is, from right to left instead of left to right, would account for the appearance of the verb *n ẖnn* in col. 3 of the actual text in Ibi's pyramid (Fig. 2.2), despite its position at the bottom of col. 6 of the hypothetical model (Fig. 2.3). The correct reading of the retrograde model (Fig. 2.3) is from cols. 1 to 7. Col. 6, ending with §107 a–c with the last word being *n ẖnn*, would therefore be read before moving on to the next column (col. 7) with the continuation of this clause: *Ḏḥwty j.jr.t-n=f n=k*. However, if read incorrectly in the normal, non-retrograde, direction from right to left, the reader would start with col. 7, continuing with cols. 6, 5, and so on. The reading of col. 6 before col. 5 explains how *n ẖnn* ended up isolated from the rest of its sentence in col. 7.

[8] See also Mathieu and Pierre-Croisiau 2015, 77–95, for a synoptic and commented edition of the spell.

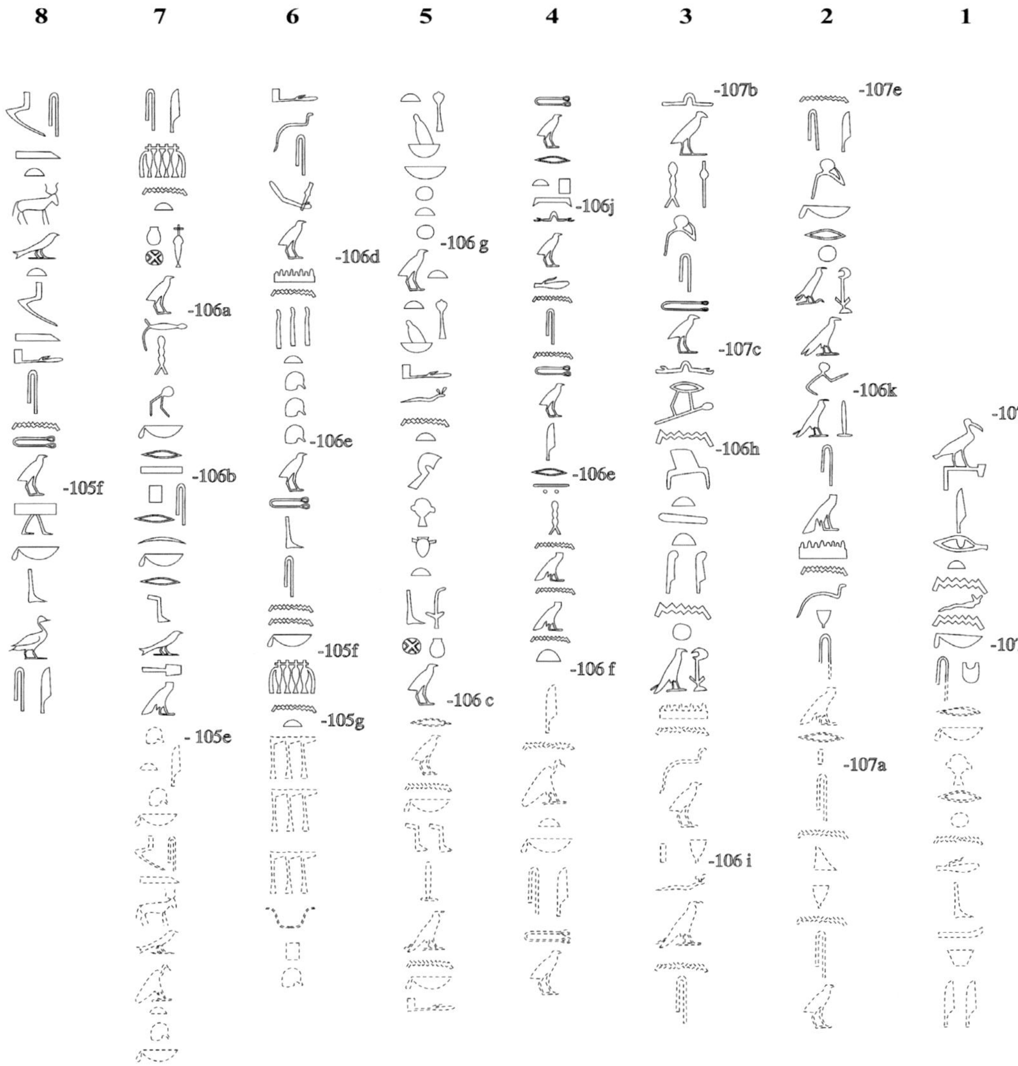

Fig. 2.2: PT *1002 as found inscribed in Ibi. © C. Alvarez.*

A backward copy of an original in retrograde accounts for the garbling of the text in *PT* 1002. However, texts were not intended to be copied in retrograde in Ibi, whereas that was the case in later instances in the Valley of the Kings. In the latter, texts were related to the iconography of the Amduat, having different constraints related to the direction of the vignettes, especially the course of the sun running from left to right. There, the text was meant to be copied so that it would be read in retrograde on the wall. The garbling results from the copyist's preference for starting the inscription from the right, that is, the end. The walls of the pyramids bear no pictorial scenes, but the texts are inscribed from left to right or right to left,

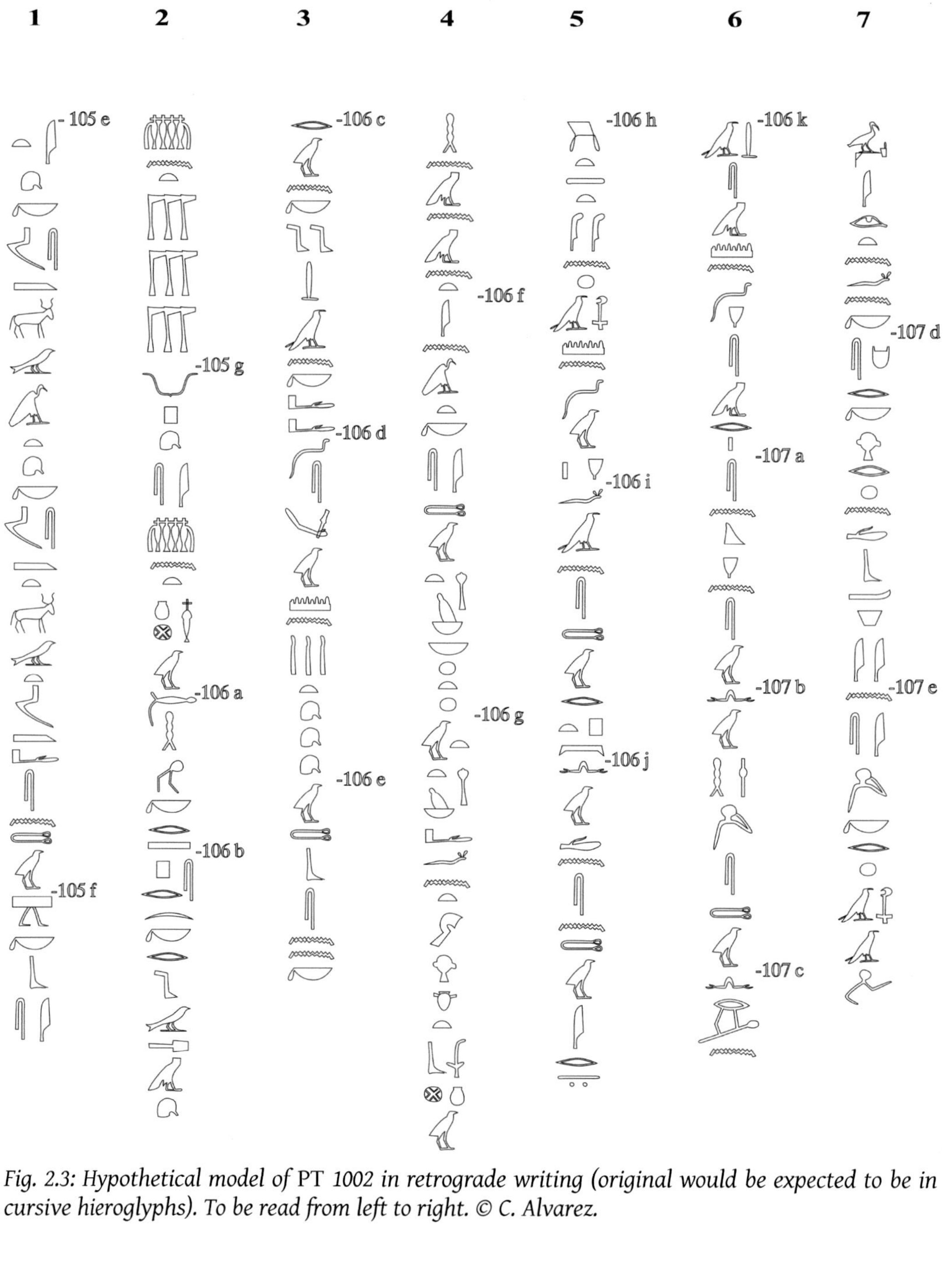

Fig. 2.3: Hypothetical model of PT 1002 in retrograde writing (original would be expected to be in cursive hieroglyphs). To be read from left to right. © C. Alvarez.

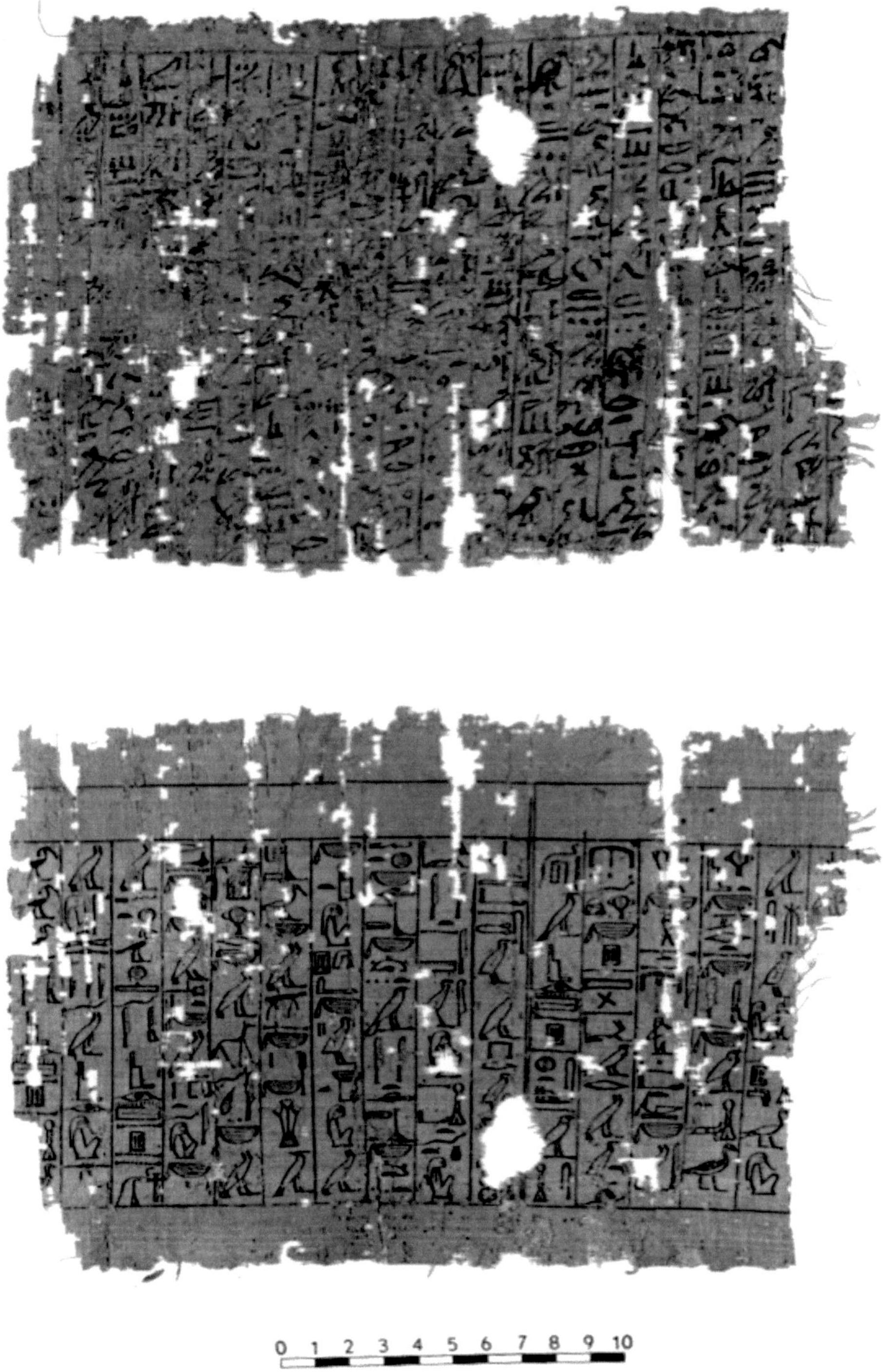

Fig. 2.4: Papyrus T 2147, face A (above) and face B (below). Berger el-Naggar 2004, 90, figs. 1–2.

dependent on the walls on which they were carved. Retrograde writing occurs only in few instances, such as in a section of text on the north wall of the antechamber of Wenis (Hays 2012, 113) and on the east wall of the burial chamber of Wedjebteni and Behenu (Berger-el Naggar and Fraisse 2015, 47).

In the case of Ibi, *PT* 1002 is inscribed in a garbled retrograde among other texts inscribed from right to left on the wall. This suggests that the source was written in retrograde, but that the copyist transcribed it as a text that was to be read from right to left. Several sections of text in Ibi exhibit the same outcome. These mistakes might result from the existence of source manuscripts that were written in both directions; the two practices could have coexisted. Papyrus T 2147 (Fig. 2.4), found in a late Middle Kingdom archive at Saqqara in the funerary temple of Pepy I (Berger el-Naggar 2004, figs. 1–2; see also Parkinson 2009, 148, n. 25) is relevant here, as it shows on its face A spell 217 inscribed from right to left, while on its face B spell 690 is in retrograde writing. Although the two sides are not of the same date – face B being a later papyrus pasted on the verso of face A – this co-occurrence gives an insight into the possible layout of funerary literature on the papyri that were used as sources. Face A corresponds more to the type of material used in the tomb, as the text is in cursive writing. The layout of the text is very similar to one register in the pyramid of Ibi, with the amount of signs per column in the papyrus slightly higher. If a copyist were to use this model, he would have to adapt the text to the amount of space available on the wall that is, by adding more signs to the following column. This, normally, would not be an issue, as the direction of reading is the same. A text similarly displayed but in retrograde, however, might mislead the copyist, leading him to mechanically copy the text from right to left, altering the layout of the columns, and thus garbling the text.

These observations suggest that those who inscribed the text on the wall had to work with material written in different directions and adapt it for the planned context. Manuscripts written from right to left were easily copied on the south wall, where the texts were intended to be inscribed in the same direction. However, an original in retrograde would cause more trouble, as it had to be transposed to right-to-left. This could further suggest that spells were inscribed on source papyri in a way that could confuse the copyist, that is, perhaps without spell dividers, spell titles, or closing statements (see Baines 2004, 26–30). John Baines (2004, 30) suggests that 'manuscripts of ritual texts were not very long, and that when a copy of a composition or sequence of compositions was needed, it was assembled and modified *ad hoc*'. Later evidence shows that some papyri, such as the Papyrus of Ani (London P. BM EA 10470) and the Papyrus of Nestanebtasheru (London, Pap. Greenfield, P. BM EA 10554), consist of individual decorated papyrus sheets of variable lengths that were only later selected and joined together in order to form a papyrus roll (Leach and Parkinson 2010, 46–7; see also Sadek 1994). The possible use of shorter papyrus sheets in the pyramid would support the assumption of the miscopying of material inscribed in different directions. Such heterogeneous material for the decoration of the tomb might have been confusing; it would have been difficult to distinguish at a glance where a spell began or ended and whether it was retrograde or in normal writing.

Conclusion

In this article, I treated different sections of texts in the pyramid of Ibi. The analysis of Ibi Ibi/S/S V 1–25 proposes that a sequence of spells for which no parallel is known is a deliberate compilation, demonstrating that the editor intervened actively and assembled the content coherently. It is thus untenable to assume that the arrangement of spells in Ibi's pyramid is random here. According to Harold Hays's typology of the Pyramid Texts, fixed sets of texts both recur and diverge from one pyramid to another, with the addition of new spells, omission of others, or location on different walls (Hays 2006, 305). The disposition of the texts in Ibi is comparable with some features in the pyramids – especially in the selection of the spells on the north wall – but the sequences of spells on the south wall differ significantly.

Later evidence, however, shows a less linear development of sequences of spells. Compilations of mortuary literature then became a matter not only of addition and omission of spells in sequences, but also of both new combinations of existing material, as on the First Intermediate Period or early Middle Kingdom coffin of Anu from Saqqara (Mathieu 2009, 302–3; Russo 2012, 91–2), and combinations of new material, as on the early Middle Kingdom coffin of Neha from el-Qatta (Allen 2013; see also Morales 2013). The omission or inversion of short sections of text, passages, or a whole spell from a sequence, as well as the addition of a different text, is also found on First Intermediate Period coffins from Middle Egypt (Bène and Guilhou 2004, 66–7). Élise Bène and Nadine Guilhou (2004, 82) have inferred that a new corpus may have been produced in Middle Egypt, with texts from various origins being combined in a new strategy. The existence of a similar process in Ibi's pyramid might suggest that a comparable tendency to compile texts existed already in the late Old Kingdom. Mortuary texts occurred in non-royal contexts as well, but a considerable lack of textual evidence between the end of the 6th dynasty and the appearance of the Coffin Texts hinders our understanding of their transmission. Further investigation of the texts of Ibi as well as of the Pyramid Texts of queens in the complex of Pepy I currently under study by the Mission archéologique française de Saqqâra may shed further light on its development.

The analysis of the order of *PT* 1002 on the south wall of Ibi shows that the original model used for the decoration of the tomb was correct, but miscopied. The error of the copyist would have been due to sources arranged in different ways, in retrograde and in normal right-to-left writing. This observation might also be applicable to the sequence I term 'Unnumbered text' and to other sections of Ibi's texts, an assumption I intend to test against other texts in the future. Reconstructing hypothetical models and thus going further back in the material process of textual transmission might help us to approach the programme intended to be inscribed in the pyramid of Ibi and to further understand the process of copying texts into pyramids.

References

Allen, J. P. 1976. 'The funerary texts of king Wahkare Akhtoy on a Middle Kingdom coffin'. In J. H. Johnson and E. F. Wente (eds.) *Studies in honor of George R. Hughes, January 12, 1977*, Studies in Ancient Oriental Civilization 39: 1–29. Chicago: The Oriental Institute.

Allen, J. P. 1986. 'The Pyramid Texts of queens *Jpwt* and *Wḏbt-n.(j)*'. *Journal of the American Research Center in Egypt* 23: 1–25.

Allen, J. P. 2013. 'A neglected funerary text'. *Journal of Egyptian Archaeology* 99: 300–7.

Allen, J. P. 2015. *The ancient Egyptian Pyramid Texts*, Writings from the Ancient World 38. Atlanta: Society of Biblical Literature Press.

Allen, T. G. 1950. *Occurrences of Pyramid Texts, with cross indexes of these and other Egyptian mortuary texts*, Studies in Ancient Oriental Civilization 27. Chicago: The University of Chicago Press.

Assmann, J. 1970. *Der König als Sonnenpriester. Ein kosmographischer Begleittext zur kultischen Sonnenhymnik in thebanischen Tempeln und Gräbern*, Abhandlungen des Deutschen Archäologischen Instituts Kairo, Ägyptologische Reihe 7. Glückstadt: J. J. Augustin.

Baines, J. 2004. 'Modelling sources, processes and locations of early mortuary texts'. In S. Bickel and B. Mathieu (eds.) *D'un monde à l'autre. Textes des Pyramides et Textes des Sarcophages. Actes de la table ronde internationale 'Textes des Pyramides* versus *Textes des Sarcophages', Ifao, 24–26 septembre 2001*, Bibliothèque d'Étude 139: 15–41, 2nd ed. Cairo: Institut Français d'Archéologie Orientale.

Bène, E. and Guilhou, N. 2004. 'Le "Grand Départ" et la "Suite A" dans les Textes des Sarcophages'. In S. Bickel and B. Mathieu (eds.) *D'un monde à l'autre. Textes des Pyramides et Textes des Sarcophages. Actes de la table ronde internationale 'Textes des Pyramides* versus *Textes des Sarcophages', Ifao, 24–26 septembre 2001*, Bibliothèque d'Étude 139: 57–83, 2nd ed. Cairo: Institut Français d'Archéologie Orientale.

Berger el-Naggar, C. 2004. 'Des Textes des Pyramides sur papyrus dans les archives du temple funéraire de Pépy Ier'. In S. Bickel and B. Mathieu (eds.) *D'un monde à l'autre. Textes des Pyramides et Textes des Sarcophages. Actes de la table ronde internationale 'Textes des Pyramides* versus *Textes des Sarcophages', Ifao, 24–26 septembre 2001*, Bibliothèque d'Étude 139: 85–90, 2nd ed. Cairo: Institut Français d'Archéologie Orientale.

Berger-el Naggar, C. and Fraisse, M.-N. 2015. 'La paroi est de la chambre funéraire de Béhénou: le dernier voyage de la reine'. In R. Legros (ed.) *50 ans d'éternité. Jubilé de la Mission archéologique française de Saqqâra (1963–2013)*, Bibliothèque d'Étude 162: 41–52. Cairo: Institut Français d'Archéologie Orientale.

Hays, H. M. 2006. *The typological structure of the Pyramid Texts and its continuities with Middle Kingdom mortuary literature*. Ann Arbor: University of Michigan.

Hays, H. M. 2012. *The organization of the Pyramid Texts. Typology and disposition*. Leiden: Brill.

Jéquier, G. 1928. *Fouilles à Saqqarah. La pyramide d'Oudjebten*. Cairo: Institut Français d'Archéologie Orientale.

Jéquier, G. 1933. *Fouilles à Saqqarah. Les pyramides des reines Neit et Apouit*. Cairo: Institut Français d'Archéologie Orientale.

Jéquier, G. 1935. *Fouilles à Saqqarah. La pyramide d'Aba*. Cairo: Institut Français d'Archéologie Orientale.

Leach, B. and Parkinson, R. B. 2010. 'Creating borders: new insights into making the Papyrus of Ani'. *British Museum Studies in Ancient Egypt and Sudan* 15: 35–62. [online] ⟨http://www.britishmuseum.org/PDF/LeachParkinson.pdf⟩, accessed 11 February 2015.

Leclant, J., Berger el-Naggar, C., Mathieu, B., and Pierre-Croisiau, I. 2001. *Les textes de la pyramide de Pépy Ier I. Description et analyse*. Mémoire de l'Institut français d'archéologie orientale 118/1. Cairo: Institut Français d'Archéologie Orientale.

Lüscher, B. 1998. *Untersuchungen zu Totenbuch Spruch 151*, Studien zum Altägyptischen Totenbuch 2. Wiesbaden: Harrassowitz.

Mathieu, B. 2004. 'La distinction entre Textes des Pyramides et Textes des Sacrophages est-elle légitime ?'. In S. Bickel and B. Mathieu (eds.) *D'un monde à l'autre. Textes des Pyramides et Textes des*

Sarcophages. Actes de la table ronde internationale 'Textes des Pyramides versus *Textes des Sarcophages', Ifao, 24-26 septembre 2001,* Bibliothèque d'Étude 139: 247–62, 2nd ed. Cairo: Institut Français d'Archéologie Orientale.

Mathieu, B. 2009. 'Le "Livre de Nout" du chancelier Ânou. "Nouvelles" versions de Textes des Pyramides'. In I. Régen and F. Servajean (eds). *Verba manent. Recueil d'études dédiées à Dimitri Meeks par ses collègues et amis,* Cahiers 'Égypte Nilotique et Méditerranéenne' 2: 295–305. Montpellier: Université Paul Valéry - Montpellier III.

Mathieu, B. and Pierre-Croisiau, I. 2015. 'Une nouvelle formule des Textes des Pyramides: *TP* 1002. Edition synoptique et traduction commentée'. In R. Legros (ed.) *50 ans d'éternité. Jubilé de la Mission archéologique française de Saqqâra (1963-2013),* Bibliothèque d'Étude 162: 77–95. Cairo: Institut Français d'Archéologie Orientale.

Mauric-Barberio, F. 2003. 'Copie de textes à l'envers dans les tombes royales'. In G. Andreu (dir.) *Deir el-Médineh et la Vallée des Rois: la vie en Égypte au temps des pharaons du Nouvel Empire. Actes du colloque organisé par le Musée du Louvre, 3-4 mai 2002*: 173–94. Paris: Éditions Khéops.

Morales, A. J. 2013. *The transmission of the Pyramid Texts into the Middle Kingdom: philological aspects of a continuous tradition in Egyptian mortuary literature.* Unpublished PhD thesis, University of Pennsylvania. [online] ⟨http://repository.upenn.edu/dissertations/AAI3565179⟩, accessed 12 September 2014.

Parkinson, R. B. 2009. *Reading ancient Egyptian poetry. Among other histories.* Chichester: Wiley-Blackwell.

Pierre-Croisiau, I. 2004. 'Nouvelles identifications de Textes des Sarcophages parmi les "nouveaux" Textes des Pyramides de Pépy Ier et de Mérenrê'. In S. Bickel and B. Mathieu (eds.) *D'un monde à l'autre. Textes des Pyramides et Textes des Sarcophages. Actes de la table ronde internationale 'Textes des Pyramides* versus *Textes des Sarcophages', Ifao, 24-26 septembre 2001,* Bibliothèque d'Étude 139: 263–78, 2nd ed. Cairo: Institut Français d'Archéologie Orientale.

Russo, B. 2012. 'Funerary spells at Saqqara South: some considerations about the inscriptions of Anu's coffin (Sq20X) and their date'. *Zeitschrift für Ägyptische Sprache und Altertumskunde* 139: 80–92.

Sadek, A. A. F. 1985. *Contribution à l'étude de l'Amdouat. Les variantes tardives du Livre de l'Amdouat dans les papyrus du Musée du Caire,* Orbis Biblicus et Orientalis 65. Fribourg and Göttingen: Academic Press Fribourg; Vandenhoeck & Ruprecht.

Sadek, A. A. F. 1994. 'Le papyrus Louvre N 3071'. In C. Berger, G. Clerc, N. Grimal (eds.) *Hommages à Jean Leclant. Varia,* Bibliothèque d'Étude 106/4: 323–35. Cairo: Institut Français d'Archéologie Orientale.

Sethe, K. 1908–1922. *Die altägyptischen Pyramidentexte nach den Papierabdrücken und Photographien des Berliner Museums.* Leipzig: J. C. Hinrichs.

Theis, C. 2010. 'Die Pyramiden der Ersten Zwischenzeit nach philologischen und archäologischen Quellen'. *Studien zur Altägyptischen Kultur* 39: 321–39.

Chapter 3

Provisioning an Egyptian quarry workforce

Sarah K. Doherty[1]
Gebel el Silsila Survey Project

Introduction

Known to the ancient Egyptians as *Khenu* or *Kheny*, 'the place of rowing', the site of Gebel el Silsila is located *c.*65 km north of Aswan, between the sandstone temples of Kom Ombo and Edfu (grid reference: Gebel el Silsila West Bank 24° 39.1' N., 32° 55.6' E.; East Bank 24° 39.4' N., 32° 55.9' E. (Klemm and Klemm 2008, 180) and features ancient Egypt's largest sandstone quarries extending for *c.*2.5 km on both sides of the Nile (Harrell 2013; Nilsson 2014; Nilsson and Almásy 2015). In ancient times, it was considered to be one of the sources of the Nile and was sacred to Hapi, as well as to Sobek, Amun, and Ptah. The high quality sandstone of Gebel el Silsila was selected as the building resource for the temples dedicated to these and other gods throughout Upper Egypt – including Karnak, Luxor, the Ramesseum, Dendara, Edfu, and Kom Ombo. Gebel el Silsila particularly came to prominence from the reign of Queen Hatshepsut onwards, when the use of limestone for constructing temples was replaced with sandstone. However, there is evidence of activity at Gebel el Silsila from prehistoric times to the present day (Nilsson 2014).

Quarry working at Gebel el Silsila was almost certainly state controlled (Bloxam 2010), but it is likely that quarrying only occurred on an 'as needed' basis, i.e. when statuary was made or temples and other significant buildings were constructed. Papyri and rock stelae, such as the stelae of Ramesses IV at Wadi Hammamat, describe

[1] Acknowledgements go to the Permanent Committee of the SCA for giving the team permission to work at Gebel el Silsila, and to the inspectorates of Kom Ombo with their director, A. Moniem Said, and equally to the general directors of Aswan at the time, Nasr Salama, A. Hakim Haddad, and F. Abuzied. The Gebel el Sislila Survey Project work was made possible by the generous financial support of the following institutions: Lund University, the Swedish Royal Academy of Sciences (Enboms stiftelse), Helge Axson Johsons Stiftelse, Magnus Bergvalls Stiftelse, Stiftelsen Lars Hiertas Minne, Birgit and Gad Rausings Stiftelse, and the Swedish Scientific Council (VR). Sincere thanks to Dr. Maria Nilsson, director of the project, and the wider Gebel el Silsila team for their support and for making this work possible.

hundreds of persons coming to work at quarries, but only on a temporary basis (Couyat and Montet 1912; Goyon 1957). It is probable that the quarry workers were not locals, but specialists brought in to work at quarries such as those at Gebel el Silsila.

Since 2012, the work undertaken at Gebel el Silsila, as part of *The Gebel el Silsila Survey Project* directed by Maria Nilsson (Lund University), has revealed a series of small dry-stone walled encampments above the quarry faces along both banks of the Nile. Scattered in and around these huts are a variety of Ramesside (1292–1069 BCE) and Early Roman era (30 BCE–117 CE) pottery. As the pottery remains from Gebel el Silsila have been entirely ignored by previous scholars, the Gebel el Silsila team has, for the first time, begun to establish a typology and to unpick the eating, cooking, and storage habits of the inhabitants of Gebel el Silsila over the millennia. The sherds analysed so far seem to suggest diverse functions for the camps with, perhaps, storage facility, a 'wine bar', and overnight campsites occurring in different places. By focusing on the archaeological remains and the ceramics evidence, it will be possible to conjecture the places where the quarry workers were living, perhaps temporarily, as well as the functions and activities going on within the site. This article aims to provide preliminary analyses of some ceramic material collected from the campsite remains during the 2014 and 2015 seasons and to make inferences on the ceramic picture at Gebel el Silsila.

Previous work at Gebel el Silsila

Gebel el Silsila is known from the chapels of Seti I and Ramesses II, the speos of Horemheb, its numerous New Kingdom stelae, and over thirty funerary rock-cut offering chapels; these were identified by the work of scholars such as Ricardo Caminos (1952; 1955; 1987a; 1987b), Georges Legrain (1903a; 1903b; 1903c; 1903d) and, more recently, Rosemarie Klemm and Dietrich D. Klemm (2008) and James A. Harrell (1989; 2013) with the *Quarry Scapes Project*. These quarries preserve not only evidence of stone extraction methods and techniques (Nilsson and Almásy 2015), but also a great variety of graffiti, including Epipalaeolithic petroglyphs and Predynastic pictographs, figurative representations that span the entire Pharaonic Period, and inscriptions in hieroglyphs, hieratic, demotic, Greek and Latin (Caminos and James 1963; Kucharek 1998; Thiem 2000; Martinez 2009; Nilsson 2013; 2014).

Whilst the epigraphy and the religious monuments of the site have been well studied by a variety of scholars (e.g. Caminos 1955; Caminos and James 1963; Thiem 2000; Bommas 2003), the archaeological remains and, in particular, the pottery and material culture of the site have proven less popular. Apart from minor excavations conducted in the late 19th and early 20th centuries by Archibald Sayce (1907), Legrain (1903a; 1903b; 1903c; 1903d), and Francis Llewellyn Griffith, who mentioned 'a great deal of pottery' (1889, 233) somewhere to the north, the site has not been explored archaeologically. As a result, the pottery has been entirely ignored at Gebel el Silsila and the current team has had the rare chance of commencing the study of an almost untouched site.

Written evidence for quarry workers

The written evidence for quarry workers and personnel is quite scanty. Inscriptions at Wadi Hammamat suggest that the personnel required for some of the great state-led quarrying expeditions were very large, but these numbers could have been exaggerated for propagandistic purposes. The Great Rock stela of Ramesses IV at Wadi Hammamat records that the largest expedition, in year three, third month of *shemu*, day 27 of his reign, consisted of 8,368 men – including 5,000 soldiers, 2,000 personnel of the Amun temples, 800 *apiru*-people, and 130 stonemasons and quarrymen – under the personal command of the high priest of Amun, Ramessesnakht (Kitchen 2012, 12–14). It is noteworthy that only 130 individuals out of this 8,368 strong expedition are actually assigned to the task of quarrying. Perhaps the soldiery acted as support staff and basket carriers for the quarrymen. The use of such expeditionary style forces indicates that the quarry personnel were not likely to be locals, but rather specialists brought to the area by the pharaoh for a specified amount of time in order to undertake the task of quarrying a given amount of stone for the creation of building works planned by the king. Presumably, the quarry workers would have then returned to their homes until requested again by the king. The Turin papyrus (Harrell 1992; 2013; Harrell and Brown 1992) detailed the work forces that migrated from quarry to quarry; an indication that, perhaps, they were contracted workers. Hélène Cuvigny (1996, 144) suggested that Roman quarry workers at Mons Claudianus may have been paid monthly, and were perhaps contracted for six months to a year. This would suggest quite long-term occupation of some quarry sites.

Most of the published inscriptional evidence relating to quarrying at Gebel el Silsila concerns the digging out of obelisks, and the extraction and transportation of stone for temples, rather than the quarry workers themselves. The stela of Akhenaten on the East Bank depicts the king worshipping Amun while quarrying sandstone for his new temple of Aten at Karnak (Forbes 2004, 68). There is also a stela of his father, Amenhotep III, quarrying stone to construct a temple for Ptah, as well as a scene from the reign of Ramesses II depicting the transportation of obelisks on sledges and boats (Martinez 2009). In addition, quarry expeditions are described in Gebel el Silsila textual material from, at least, the 11th dynasty, and a wide variety of boat graffiti exists throughout the site (Nilsson 2013; Ward and Nilsson 2015).

Evidence in the quarry landscape

Elizabeth Bloxam (2010) suggested a variety of methods that could be employed to reconstruct the activities of workers within a quarry scape, notably studying evidence for transportation of blocks, extraction sites, settlements, tools, spoil heap locations, ceramics, and material culture. At Gebel el Silsila, the large size and spectacular nature of the 104 quarries (Q34 alone measures 280 × 160 m, Nilsson and Ward, forthcoming) as well as their huge spoil heaps testify to the sheer amount of quarrying that must have been undertaken at the site. This would have entailed a wide variety of personnel including stonemasons, supervisors, basket carriers, transportation managers, and other support staff. However, the location of the settlement for such a large amount of quarry staff is still uncertain.

Evidence from other quarry sites suggests relatively low-level quarrying with minimal traces of settlements or campsites, perhaps for only a few hundred individuals. In quarries outside of the Nile valley such as Gebel el Asr ('Khephren's quarry'), Widan el Faras, and Umm el Sawan (see Fig. 3.1), settlement is suggested by the presence of small ephemeral encampments with dry-stone walls and the use of natural rock overhangs (Caton-Thompson and Gardner 1934, 117–20; Shaw 1994; Shaw and Bloxam 1999; Shaw *et al.* 2001; Bloxam and Storemyr 2002, 33–4; Bloxam 2003; Bloxam and Heldal 2007, 315–16). Ceramics are also minimal in these quarry sites, as well as in quarries in general; hence the numbers of people involved in these activities cannot be ascertained which, in turn, explains the historical reliance on textual sources. However, recent findings at these quarries – even taking into account poor preservation – cannot attest to labour forces being over a maximum of 200 individuals. For example, the site of the Old Kingdom quarry at Gebel el Asr was found to contain only two small camp dwellings, suggesting perhaps 25 people living there (Bloxam 2003; 2010). This largely contradicts the Wadi Hammamat quarry inscriptions, which list expeditions into the tens of thousands (Couyat and Montet 1912; Goyon 1957).

It is unclear whether there was any kind of royal monopoly on quarrying, but the vast amount of quarrying that was undertaken at Gebel el Silsila, or at other sites, would have required a great deal of organisation. Few individuals would have had the financial resources to sponsor such endeavours. Ian Shaw (1994, 111) suggests that there was evidence for intermittent private exploitation at the quarries of Hatnub (calcite) and Gebel el Zeit (lead sulphite) based on the size of the structures and their haphazard organisation. At Hatnub, the Old Kingdom structures were large, multi-roomed, and likely housed organised gangs, whereas the New Kingdom structures were more humble one-roomed affairs that had been loosely constructed with limestone slabs and boulders (Shaw 1987). According to Shaw (1994, 113), this indicates small temporary groups without bureaucratic organisation. The Gebel el Zeit galena mines – located on the gulf of Suez, 50 km south of Ras Gharib – date to the Middle to New Kingdoms with settlements occurring in two different areas. Site 1 contained 30 gallery mines with associated dry-stone wall encampments spread over the hillside of the Wadi Kabrit and a small sanctuary. Site 2 covered a larger area in the southern part of Wadi Kabrit, with hundreds of mine shafts with associated dry-stone encampments and votive areas (Castel and Soukiassian 1989). Finally, the Old Kingdom gypsum quarries at Umm el Sawan contained some 250 small huts similar to those at Hatnub, together with evidence for local production of flint to work the gypsum into vases (Caton-Thompson and Gardner 1934). In contrast, the quarry workers of the Middle Kingdom site of Wadi el Hudi, near

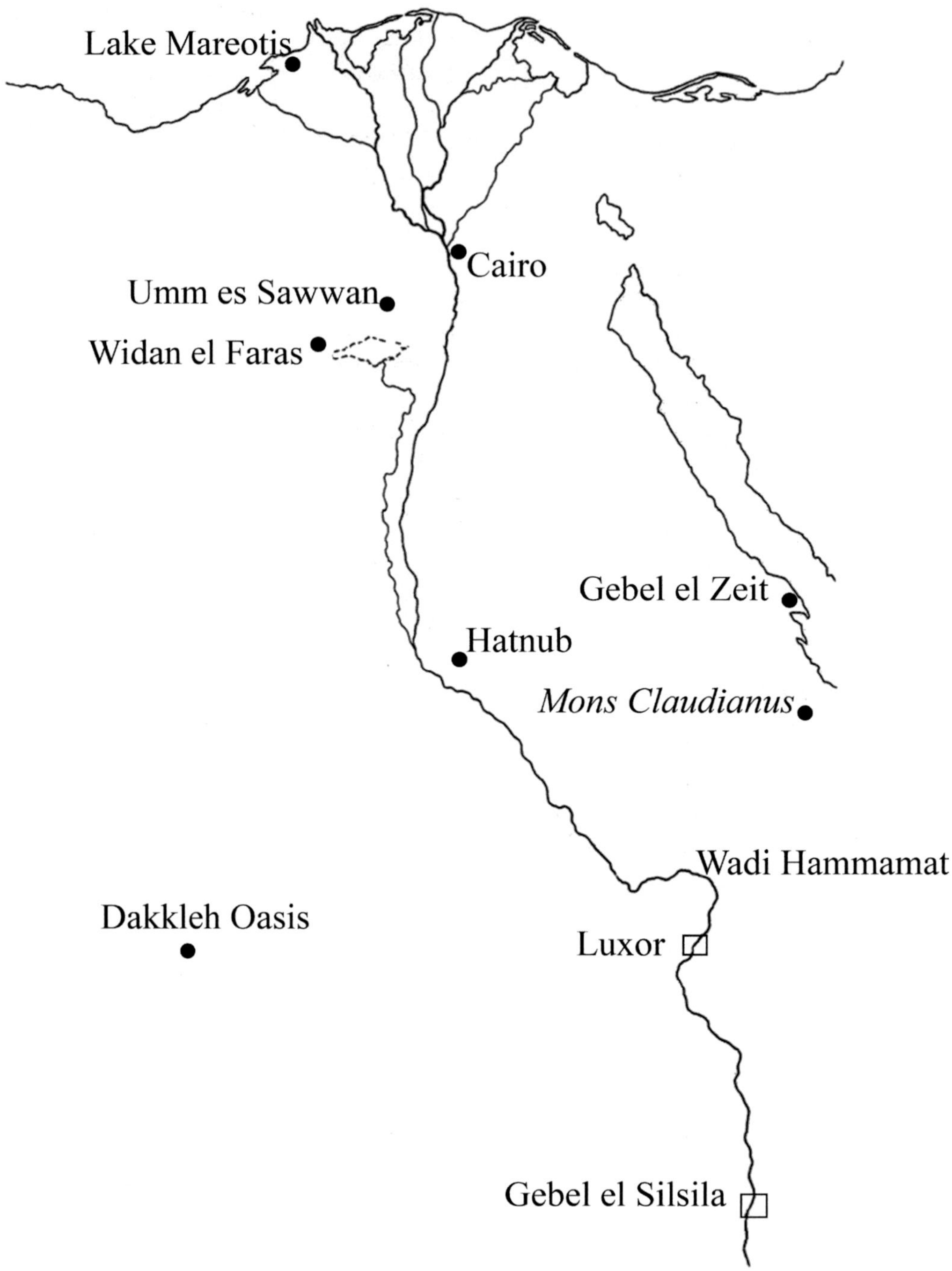

Fig. 3.1: Location of Gebel el Silsila and other quarry sites. Doherty 2015.

the first cataract of the Nile, built their settlement behind walls within a military-style encampment (Fakhry 1952; Sadek 1980–1985; Shaw and Jameson 1993), in a similar fashion to later Roman quarry sites such as Mons Claudianus (Peacock and Maxfield 1997).

Archaeological evidence for campsites at Gebel el Silsila

To date, approximately ten settlement areas containing dry-stone walled camps have been identified at Gebel el Silsila, although this number is certain to increase as the team expands its survey of the site. This paper focuses on the material culture remains from six of these settlement areas on the West Bank and two on the East Bank.[2] The encampments are in the main quarry located above the working faces, though some have been built upon earlier sandstone spoil heaps. At Gebel el Silsila West, the following areas were selected for study: Pottery Hill, Pottery Hill 2, Wadi Tean, Mo's Tavern, S Camp, and Black Camp (Fig. 3.2). At Gebel el Silsila East, Corridor A Upper Huts, and Southern Hill sherds were processed. Different functions can be identified at these camps based on the analysis of the ceramic remains at these sub-sites.

Ceramic methodology and analysis

As Gebel el Silsila has been studied little in terms of pottery, a new typology was developed to enable comparison with sister sites around Egypt. In order to achieve this, an entire collection of diagnostic surface sherds was undertaken; these were then fully processed and studied. The method employed was as follows: 1) Individual subsites were identified from field surveys and were ascribed an area number; 2) Sherds were gathered into *maktafs* (baskets) at the subsite; 3) The sherds were separated into diagnostics (i.e. bases, handles, rims, and sherds that have distinguishing features such as spouts, lids, paint, decoration, or pot marks) and body sherds (indeterminable shapes). The body sherds were further separated out into their different clay types based on the Vienna system of classification (Bourriau and Nordström 1993: marl clay, silt, roman, aswan, islamic, and modern), then counted and weighed. As this was a preliminary survey undertaken to establish a typology at some sites where there was a large amount of sherds, e.g. Pottery Hill (PH), only the diagnostics were sampled; 4) The diagnostic sherds were washed, dried, sorted into categories based on their defining characteristics, and sub-divided by shape, form, and other features. If there was more than one per type, all were counted, made a note of in the bulk recording form and pottery field notebook, and the best example was set aside to be registered for the ceramics database; 5) The selected sherds were given an identifying ceramic number for the database, and all the details were recorded into a ceramic record form. Measurements were taken of the height, width, length, and thickness; characteristics such as colour, clay type, and manufacturing marks were recorded.

[2] M. Nilsson and J. Ward (forthcoming) have already described some of the examples on the East Bank, above Q34.

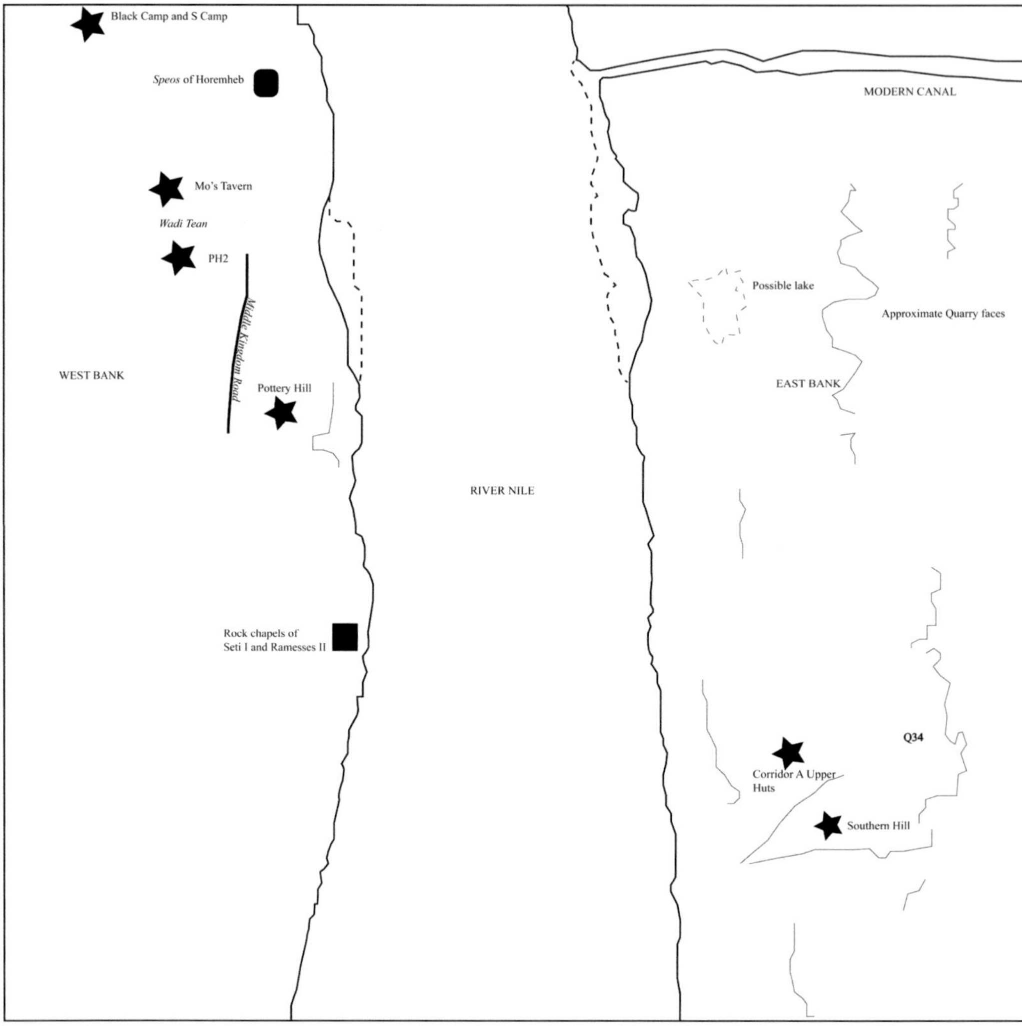

Fig. 3.2: Locations of selected campsites of Gebel el Silsila. © S. Doherty.

Each sherd was then labelled, using a fine-nibbed pen, with the site code, the year, the subsite, and the ceramic number e.g. GES14/PH/C24; 6) The sherd's profile was then drawn on permatrace using a 7H pencil, contour gauge, ruler, and callipers following the estimated diameter and defining characteristics of the shape the complete vessel likely had; 7) The sherd was photographed using either a Digital SLR Canon EOS 550 D camera or a Sony SLT A35 with an EF 60 mm macro lens, and then bagged to be stored or returned to the site; 8) The drawings were later transferred into Adobe Photoshop and Illustrator. The ceramic forms, bulk recording forms, and photographs were all entered into a Filemaker database.

Gebel el Silsila West

Pottery Hill, Pottery Hill 2, Wadi Tean, and Mo's Tavern are located within close proximity of each other and are likely to be contemporary sites (Fig. 3.2). They are positioned to the north of the speos of Horemheb, in the escarpment above Klemm and Klemm's section three (2008, 182, fig. 275) where they identified, within a Ptolemaic/ Roman Period quarry, a large harbour with a loading ramp and an ancient stairway.

Pottery Hill

Pottery Hill is adjacent to an ancient sandstone roadway containing Middle Kingdom inscriptions. It consists of a *c.*400 sq. m mound containing *c.*25 dry-stone walled circular huts. There are relatively few pottery sherds within the huts themselves, but there are vast quantities of sherds, chunks of semi-complete vessels, and complete profiles all around the area, in some cases cascading down in a rough fan shape from the hut entrances. As there was so much ceramic material at Pottery Hill, it was decided, as a preliminary investigation, to select diagnostic pieces from the area to get a sense of the typology of the site. More thorough analyses will be undertaken later.

The results of preliminary analyses suggest that Pottery Hill contains one of the largest ceramic repertoires of the entire site, although it spans just over

Fig. 3.3: Pottery Hill as viewed from the north. Doherty 2015.

400 sq. m. Out of 1,879 diagnostic sherds collected (Figs. 3.4 and 3.5), 97 new types were identified; most dated to Early Roman times (mid-1st century CE). Interestingly, the data gathered so far suggests that Pottery Hill, where mostly amphorae and jars rather than cooking vessels were discovered, may have been used for storage. Out of the 703 jar rims, 462 (25%) were those of amphorae, and only 44 (6%) belonged to Roman cooking/serving dishes. Ceramic finds of note include Early Roman barbotine sherds (these examples of fine ware vessels were found to contain 'drops' of kaolinate clay derived from Aswan; see Fig. 3.4), miniature vessels, two small complete bowls, 34 painted body sherds, a skillet handle, and nine sherds containing pot marks made after firing.

Pottery Hill 2, Wadi Tean, and Mo's Tavern

Located across the Middle Kingdom road, to the north-west of Pottery Hill, the area comprises two *koms* (Pottery Hill 2 and Mo's Tavern) with a dry wadi bed known as Wadi Tean in between. These three sites appear to have been used during the Early Roman Period, perhaps as a lookout point over the road, but this has yet to be determined. They all contained some of the most well-preserved and complete ceramic examples found so far at Gebel el Silsila. On its northern side Pottery Hill 2

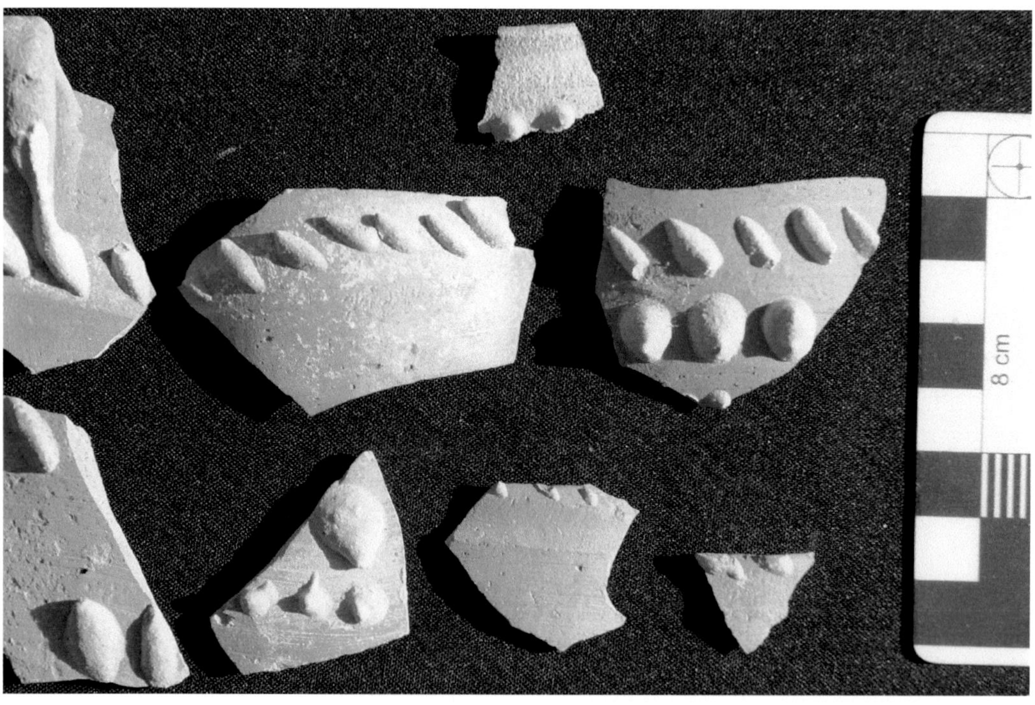

Fig. 3.4: Examples of barbotine sherds from Pottery Hill. Doherty 2014, Gebel el Silsila Project.

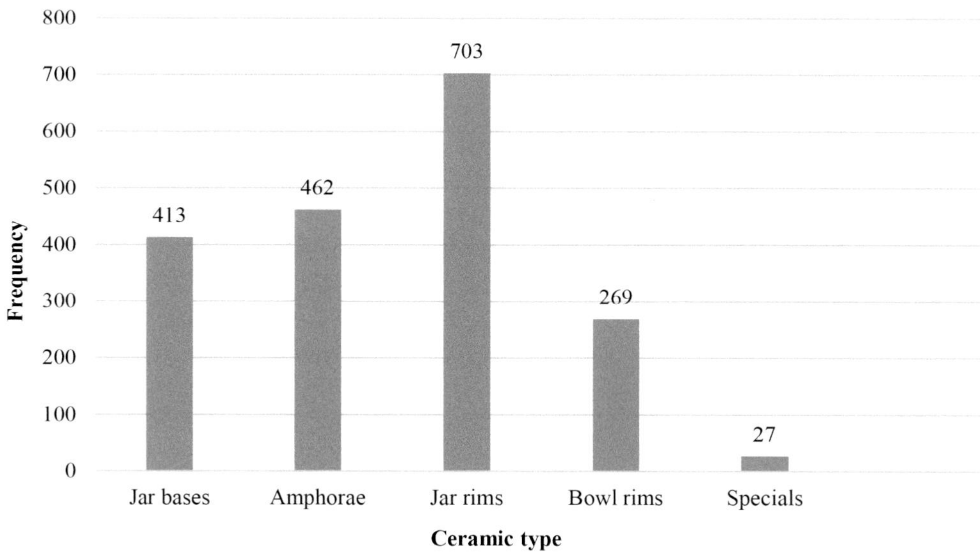

Fig. 3.5: Frequency of the different ceramic types from Pottery Hill. Doherty 2014, Gebel el Silsila Project.

presents the remains of a ramp-like structure and, within the hill, a small crevice which appears to have been used as a temporary shelter contains the remains of plaster work. The *kom* yielded four complete vessels (or with complete profiles, at least): two bowls, one jar, and one dish. At Mo's Tavern, a complete collection of all sherds was undertaken, which returned 754 body sherds (6.84 kg) and 57 diagnostics, of which 18 were new types. Notable finds included a 48 cm diameter coil-made lid with handle (in 23 pieces; Fig. 3.6), as well as a complete profile of a jar (in 12 pieces), and a wine strainer, both with an early 1st century CE date. A complete collection of the ceramics was also undertaken at Wadi Tean; it recovered 1,022 body sherds (17.9 kg) and 129 diagnostics (5.7 kg), of which five were new types and two were complete profiles.

Black and S Camps

Black Camp is located close to the modern road on Gebel el Silsila West, to the north west of the speos of Horemheb, close to the area labelled 'large tower' by Klemm and Klemm (2008, 182, fig. 275, 187, fig. 283). It comprises an unusually shaped building, with a curved 'bay window' wall, made of black dry sandstone, which gives its name to the place. Only a preliminary analysis of the available surface sherds was undertaken there. It consists of a mixture of New Kingdom (18th dynasty) and Early Roman sherds. Some 46 diagnostics were collected, including 18th dynasty Marl D amphora handles and bases, string impressed bowls, and a ceramic counter.

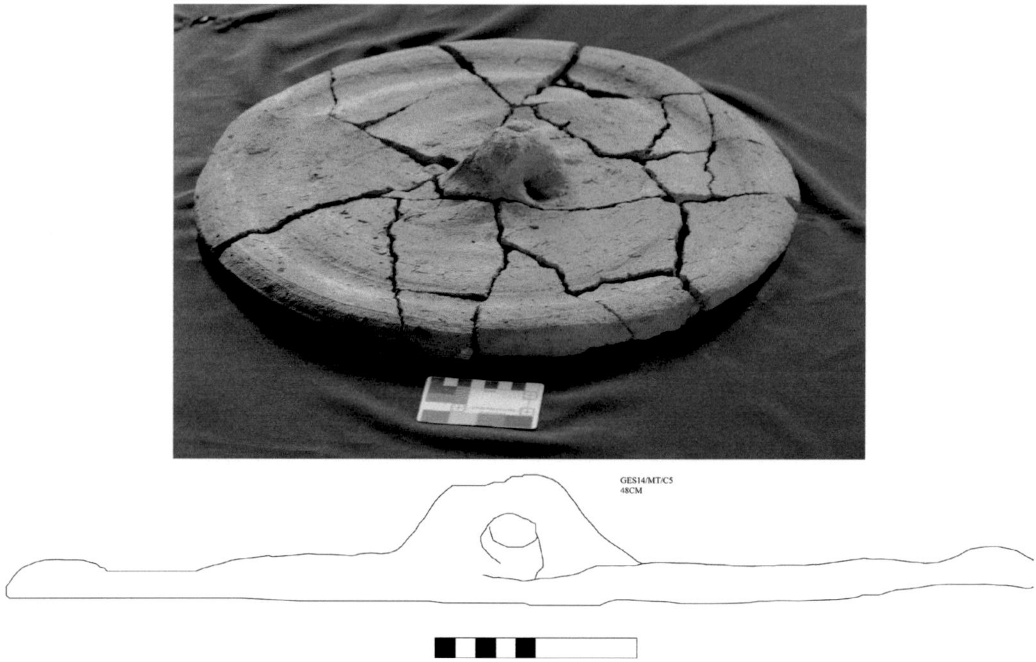

Fig. 3.6: GES14/MT/C5. A complete lid made of Nile C coils of clay and white wash. Early Roman Period, 48 cm in diameter. Type 11.3. Scale is 8 cm in the photograph, 15 cm in the profile. Doherty 2014, Gebel el Silsila Project.

Considering its localisation, it is likely that the campsite was related to the New Kingdom quarries nearby. S Camp is positioned a little to the north of Black Camp and includes the remains of five to six dry-stone walled huts. To date, it has only been subject to a brief examination and no diagnostic sherds have been found.

Gebel el Silsila East

Corridor A Upper Huts

Corridor A Upper Huts refers to the escarpment immediately above the corridor cut into the sandstone of the 'main quarry' Q34 (see Fig. 3.2), where dry-stone walled huts have been located. Five distinct sectors of ancient ruins (three located on top of the heaps and two on the plateau) were recorded with a total of 54 clearly defined stacked stone huts measuring between 2.5 × 2.5 m and 4 × 5 m (see Nilsson and Ward, forthcoming, for further discussion). Around these huts, 29 new ceramic types were identified (22 rims (1.36 kg), three bases (1.15 kg), and four handles (0.2 kg)), and a further 7.8 kg of diagnostic material and 52.84 kg of body sherds were processed. The dating of these new sherds is mixed: 21% Early Roman, 17% Ptolemaic, and 10% New Kingdom (18th–20th dynasties). Additionally, 0.2 kg of slag were also found there, as well as a Nile silt sherd with a V-shaped hole drilled into it.

Southern Hill

Southern Hill is situated in the plateaux to the south of Corridor A Upper Huts (see Fig. 3.2). Five to six discrete dry-stone walled huts, of similar dimensions to those located above Corridor A, were found. Some 3,931 body sherds – with 426 diagnostic rims, 92 bases, and 28 handles – were gathered from this area. However, more work is required in this area, as the sherds were gathered towards the end of the March 2014 season, and there was insufficient time for complete analyses. Nonetheless, ten new types were recognized, as well as nine rims and one complete profile of a shallow dish (Fig. 3.7). The types included bowls, casserole dishes, a costrel, and water jars, suggesting Early Roman eating vessels.

Discussion

As yet, most of the processed pottery appears to date to the Early Roman Period. Roman pottery usually fires to a deep crimson red and is hard to break. The clays also have lots of additions such as pebbles, ground up ceramic pieces, or limestone. Often the rims are quite elaborate – folded over, elongated, or modelled – and the jars have one or two small handles. The Early Roman dating (1st century CE up to the

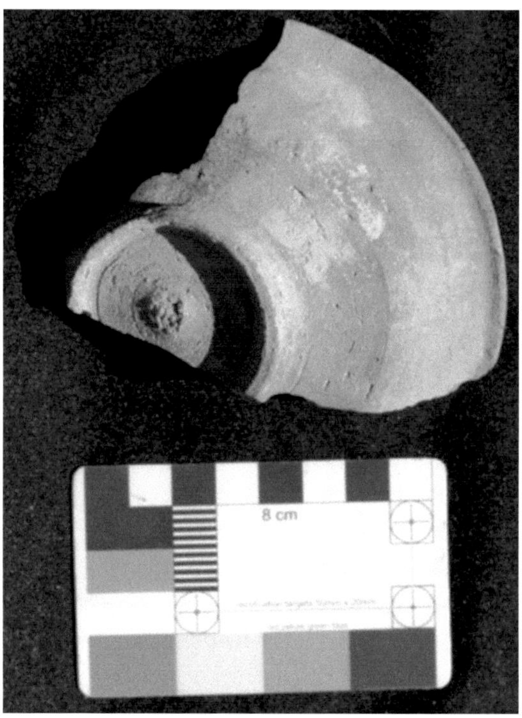

Fig. 3.7: Shallow dish with carinated, outer rolled rim and ring base, which was underfired in the kiln GES14/Q34/S2. Early Roman Period, 12 cm diameter. Type 9.16.1. © S. Doherty.

reign of Emperor Trajan (98–117 CE)) fits rather well with the texts and epigraphic material that have been analysed so far by Maria Nilsson and Adrienn Almásy (2015), with the latest written evidence being from the reign of Emperor Claudius (41–54 CE). The presence of Roman ceramics also correlates with the earliest material from the granite quarry of Mons Claudianus (Tomber 2006) and overlaps with the great period of sandstone temple building, when many of the Upper Egyptian Ptolemaic temples were being expanded by the Romans.

However, in and around the huts in Corridor A Upper Huts, a real mixture of datable ceramics were uncovered, suggesting a long duration of activity. This would correlate with the extremely large size of the Q34 quarry, the biggest at Gebel el Silsila, where Corridor A Upper Huts is to be found. The quarries may have been inhabited only for short amounts of time during the dynastic periods, as the Turin papyrus and the stela of Ramesses IV suggest. Roman quarrying, on the other hand, may have been of longer duration at Gebel el Silsila. This is evidenced by the fact Roman ceramics make up the bulk of the ceramics analysed during the 2014 and 2015 seasons, and suggested by the considerable temple building undertaken in Upper Egypt by Roman emperors. As further examination of the subsites of Gebel el Silsila is undertaken, more New Kingdom ceramics will certainly be discovered; in some cases in the main quarry, up to 10% of the ceramics at the campsites have been New Kingdom material. Given that Klemm and Klemm (2008, 180–3) considered that much of the northern west bank of Gebel el Silsila contained Middle Kingdom quarries, as the quarry chisel marks suggest, it is possible that some ceramics from that period may also be uncovered. However, as yet, no Middle Kingdom (or earlier) sherds have been discovered in the locality. One would also expect more Ptolemaic pottery to have survived. As the analyses, thus far, were made upon surface collected pottery, future excavations may reveal the lower Ptolemaic levels.

Unlike contemporary Roman sites, very few imported ceramics have been unearthed at Gebel el Silsila. Some examples may have derived from Eastern Mediterranean sources (similar to type 63 in Tomber 2006, 172) and Asia Minor (Tomber 2006, 84, 86, type 57-419; 168, cilician fabric 2), while the hitherto farthest afield sherd detected is from Tunisia. Indeed, some tableware includes African red slip wares usually found in the form of bowls, which may be obtained from Tunisia (Tomber 2006, 102–3, type 19; Wodzińska 2010, 140). Most of the ceramics at Gebel el Silsila, in contrast, derive from quite local sources. Many of the amphorae can be sourced from Lake Mareotis (the modern Lake Mariut) near Alexandria (Tomber 2006, 148–9, type 12-861), while other jars are from Dakhleh and the neighbouring oases; all would likely have contained wine. The fine wares are mostly vessels with barbotine decoration, 'poor man's glass' or drinking cups with 'drips or blobs' of kaolinite white clays that can be sourced in the Aswan region (Tomber 2006, 31–2, type 16; Wodzińska 2010, 86). Other examples include more local Nile silt wares, such as straight necked Aswani amphorae with long rounded handles (Majcherek 1993; Tomber 2006, 157–8, type 36-926).

Conclusion

Through this evidence, Gebel el Silsila appears to be the exception to the rule that quarry sites do not contain much pottery material. Overall, the ceramics picture at Gebel el Silsila is not as cosmopolitan as in other contemporary Roman sites (Marchand and Marangou 2007) with the vast majority of the ceramics coming from the Nile Valley. This could be an indicator of the status of the quarry workers and personnel, suggesting either their relatively modest status or that they were, perhaps, native to the area and brought their own local pottery. The 'provincial' nature of the ceramic types could confirm that the quarry workers at Gebel el Silsila were of a relatively low status when compared to contemporary Roman sites in Egypt. The pottery assemblages of the campsites indicate that the shelters were mostly utilised for the storage of foodstuffs, wine, and water and it is likely that the huts, being so small, were only used for brief overnight stays.

Much more work needs to be undertaken to understand the related functions of these various subsites within Gebel el Silsila. Thus far, only one of the 104 quarries, and eight of the ten campsites, have had ceramic analysis. On the west bank, Pottery Hill has surprised us with the sheer quantity of material located within a relatively small area, while other sites, such as Black Camp, are offering some indications of earlier phases at Gebel el Silsila through the discovery of small quantities of New Kingdom pottery, perhaps linked to the speos of Horemheb and rock cut chapels in the area. It is hoped that further analyses will provide the Gebel el Silsila team with some insight into the pre-Roman occupation of the site as well as some understanding of where the storage facilities were located and where the quarry workers were eating and (perhaps) living while they were working on site.

References

Bloxam, E. 2003. *The organisation, transportation and logistics of hard stone quarrying in the Egyptian Old Kingdom: a comparative study*. Unpublished PhD thesis, University College London.

Bloxam, E. 2010. 'Quarrying and mining (stone)'. In W. Wendrich (ed.) *UCLA Encyclopedia of Egyptology*. Los Angeles. [online] ⟨http://digital2.library.ucla.edu/viewItem.do?ark=21198/zz0026jkd5⟩, accessed 4 March 2015.

Bloxam, E. and Heldal, T. 2007. 'The industrial landscape of the Northern Faiyum Desert as a World Heritage Site: modelling the "outstanding universal value" of third millennium BC stone quarrying in Egypt'. *World Archaeology* 39 (3): 305–23.

Bloxam, E. and Storemyr, P. 2002. 'Old Kingdom basalt quarrying activities at Widan el-Faras, Northern Faiyum Desert'. *Journal of Egyptian Archaeology* 88: 23–36.

Bommas, M. 2003. 'Gebel es-Silsilah im Neuen Reich'. In H. Guksch, E. Hofmann, and M. Bommas (eds.) *Grab und Totenkult im Alten Ägypten*: 88–103. Munich: Beck.

Bourriau, J. and Nordström, H.-A. 1993. 'Ceramic technology: clays and fabrics'. In D. Arnold and J. Bourriau (eds.) *An introduction to ancient Egyptian pottery*: 149–90. Mainz: Zabern.

Caminos, R. 1952. 'Gebel es-Silsilah No. 100'. *Journal of Egyptian Archaeology* 38: 46–61.

Caminos, R. 1955. 'Surveying Gebel es-Silsilah'. *Journal of Egyptian Archaeology* 41: 51–5.

Caminos, R. 1977. 'Gebel es-Silsile'. In W. Helck, E. Otto, and W. Westendorf (eds.) *Lexikon der Ägyptologie* II: 441–7. Wiesbaden: Harrassowitz.

Caminos, R. 1987a. 'Amenophis III's vizier Amenhotep at Silsilah East.' *Journal of Egyptian Archaeology* 73: 207–10.

Caminos, R. 1987b. 'Epigraphy in the field'. In J. Assmann, G. Burkard, and V. Davies (eds.) *Problems and priorities in Egyptian archaeology*: 57–67. London: Kegan Paul International.

Caminos, R. and James, T. G. H. 1963. *Gebel es-Silsilah* I. *The shrines*, Archaeological Survey of Egypt 31. London: Egypt Exploration Society.

Castel, G. and Soukiassian, G. 1989. *Gebel el-Zeit* I. *Les mines de galène (Egypte, IIe millénaire av. J.-C.)*, Fouilles de l'Institut Français d'Archéologie Orientale 35. Cairo: Institut Français d'Archéologie Orientale.

Caton-Thompson, G. and Gardner, E. 1934. *The desert Fayum*. London: Royal Anthropological Institute of Great Britain and Ireland.

Couyat, J. and Montet, P. 1912. *Les inscriptions hiéroglyphiques et hiératiques du Ouâdi Hammâmât*, Mémoires publiés par les membres de l'Institut Français d'Archéologie Orientale 34. Cairo: Imprimerie de l'Institut Français d'Archéologie Orientale.

Cuvigny, H. 1996. 'The amount of wages paid to the quarry-workers at Mons Claudianus'. *Journal of Roman Studies* 86: 139–45.

Doherty, S. 2014. 'Pottery report 2014'. In M. Nilsson (ed.) *Gebel el Silsila survey project season 2014*. Unpublished archaeological survey report for the SCA/MSA.

Doherty, S. 2015. 'Gebel el Silsila temple east, March 2015. Preliminary pottery report'. In M. Nilsson (ed.) *Gebel el Silsila survey project season 2015*. Unpublished archaeological survey report for the SCA/MSA.

Fakhry, A. 1952. *The Egyptian deserts. The inscriptions of the amethyst quarries at Wadi el Hudi*. Cairo: Government Press.

Forbes, D. 2004. 'Where tourists seldom venture. The sandstone quarries and rock-cut chapels of Gebel el Silsila in Upper Egypt'. *KMT* 15 (3): 64–75.

Griffith, F. L. 1889. 'Notes on a tour in Upper Egypt'. *Proceedings of the Society of Biblical Archaeology* 11: 228–34.

Goyon, G. 1957. *Nouvelles inscriptions rupestres du Wadi Hammamat*. Paris: Imprimerie Nationale, Librairie d'Amérique et d'Orient Adrien-Maisonneuve.

Harrell, J. A. 1989. 'An inventory of ancient Egyptian quarries'. *Newsletter of the American Research Center in Egypt* 146: 1–7.

Harrell, J. A. 1992. 'Ancient Egyptian limestone quarries: a petrological survey'. *Archaeometry* 34 (2): 195–211.

Harrell, J. A. 2013. 'Gebel el-Silsila'. In R. S. Bagnall, K. Brodersen, C. B. Champion, A. Erskine, and S. R. Huebner (eds.) *The encyclopedia of ancient history*: 2865. Oxford: Wiley-Blackwell.

Harrell, J. A. and Brown, V. M. 1992. 'The world's oldest surviving geological map: the 1150 B.C. Turin papyrus from Egypt'. *Journal of Geology* 100 (1): 3–18.

Kitchen, K. 2012. *Ramesside inscriptions* VI. *Ramesses IV to XI, and contemporaries*. Oxford: Wiley-Blackwell.

Klemm, R. and Klemm, D. D. 2008. *Stones and quarries in ancient Egypt*. London: The British Museum Press.

Kucharek, A. 1998. *Die Felskapellen der 18. Dynastie in Gebel es-Silsilah*. Unpublished MA dissertation, University of Heidelberg.

Legrain, G. 1903a. 'Notes d'inspection III. La chapelle de Senmaout à Gebel Silsileh'. *Annales du Service des Antiquités de l'Égypte* 4: 193–7.

Legrain, G. 1903b. 'Notes d'inspection IV. Sur l'architecte Aménôthès qui vécut sous Aménôthès III.' *Annales du Service des Antiquités de l'Égypte* 4: 197–212.

Legrain, G. 1903c. 'Notes d'inspection V. Sur Maïa qui vécut sous la règne d'Harmhabi'. *Annales du Service des Antiquités de l'Égypte* 4: 213–18.

Legrain, G. 1903d. 'Notes d'inspection VI. La nécropole archaïque du Gebel Silsileh'. *Annales du Service d'Antiquités de l'Égypte* 4: 218–20.

Majcherek, G. 1993. 'Roman amphorae from Marina el-Alamein'. *Mitteilungen des Deutchen Archäologischen Instituts, Abteilung Kairo* 49: 215–21. Mainz: Zabern.

Marchand, S. and Marangou, A. (eds.) 2007. *Amphores d'Égypte de la Basse Époque à l'époque arabe*, Cahiers de la Céramique Égyptienne 8. Cairo: Institut Français d'Archéologie Orientale.

Martinez, P. 2009. 'Une commande royale pour le Ramesseum: une stèle inédite de Ramsès II au Gebel es-Silsileh'. *Memnonia* 20: 133–72.

Nilsson, M. 2013. *Preliminary report. Gebel el Silsila survey project spring season 2013*. Unpublished archaeological survey report for the SCA/MSA.

Nilsson, M. 2014. 'Pseudo script in Gebel el Silsila: preliminary results of the 2012 epigraphic survey'. In K. Accetta, R. Fellinger, P. Lourenço Gonçalves, S. Musselwhite, and W. P. van Pelt (eds.) *Current Research in Egyptology 2013. Proceedings of the fourteenth annual symposium, University of Cambridge, March 19-22, 2013*: 122–41. Oxford: Oxbow Books.

Nilsson, M. and Almásy, A. 2015. 'Quarrying for Claudius, protected by Min: a small quarry in Gebel el-Silsila East'. *British Museum Studies in Ancient Egypt and Sudan* 22: 87–110. [online] ⟨http://www.britishmuseum.org/research/publications/online_journals/bmsaes/issue_22/nilsson_and_almasy.aspx⟩, accessed 4 March 2015.

Nilsson, M. and Ward, J. (forthcoming). 'Gebel el Silsila: field report from the main quarry'. *Journal of Near Eastern Studies*.

Peacock, D. P. S. and Maxfield, V. A. 1997. *Mons Claudianus. Survey and excavation 1987-1993* I. *Topography and quarries*, Fouilles de l'Institut Français d'Archéologie Orientale 37. Cairo: Institut Français d'Archéologie Orientale.

Sadek, A. I. 1980–1985. *The amethyst mining inscriptions of Wadi el-Hudi*. Warminster: Aris & Phillips.

Sayce, A. 1907. 'Excavations at Gebel Silsila'. *Annales du Service des Antiquités de l'Égypte* 8: 97–105.

Shaw, I. 1987. 'The 1986 survey of Hatnub'. In B. J. Kemp (ed.). *Amarna Reports* IV: 160–7. London: Egypt Exploration Society.

Shaw, I. 1994. 'Pharaonic quarrying and mining: settlement and procurement in Egypt's marginal regions'. *Antiquity* 68 (258): 108–19.

Shaw, I. and Bloxam, E. 1999. 'Survey and excavation at the ancient pharaonic gneiss quarrying site of Gebel el-Asr, Lower Nubia'. *Sudan and Nubia Bulletin* 3: 13–20.

Shaw, I. and Jameson, R. 1993. 'Amethyst mining in the Eastern Desert: a preliminary survey at Wadi el-Hudi'. *Journal of Egyptian Archaeology* 79: 81–97.

Shaw, I., Bloxam, E., Graham, A., Bunbury, J., Lee, R., and Darnell, D. 2001. 'Survey and excavation at the Gebel el-Asr gneiss and quartz quarries in Lower Nubia (1997–2000)'. *Antiquity* 75 (287): 33–4.

Thiem, A.-C. 2000. *Speos von Gebel es-Silsileh: Analyse der architektonischen und ikonographischen Konzeption im Rahmen des politischen und legitimatorischen Programmes der Nachamarnazeit*, Ägypten und Altes Testament 47. Wiesbaden: Harrassowitz.

Tomber, R. 2006. 'The pottery'. In D. P. S. Peacock and V. A. Maxfield (eds.) *Mons Claudianus. Survey and excavation 1987-1993* III. *Ceramic vessels and related objects*: 3–236, Fouilles de l'Institut Français d'Archéologie Orientale 54. Cairo: Institut Français d'Archéologie Orientale.

Ward, J. and Nilsson, M. 2015. 'Mallets, chisels, sledges and boats: the art of quarrying at Gebel el Silsila'. In J. Lundock, M. S. Pinarello, C. Walsh, J. Yoo (eds.) *Current Research in Egyptology 2014. Proceedings of the fifteenth annual symposium, University College London and King's College London, April 9-12, 2014*: 59–72. Oxford: Oxbow Books.

Wodzińska, A. 2010. *A manual of Egyptian pottery* IV: *Ptolemaic Period-Modern*, AERA Field Manual Series 1. Boston: Ancient Egypt Research Associates.

Chapter 4

'That his perfect name may be remembered': added inscriptions in the tomb of vizier Kagemni at Saqqara

Julia Clare Francis Hamilton
University of Auckland, New Zealand

Introduction

The ancient Egyptian tomb is a nexus of numerous forms of travel that occur in an Egyptian funerary landscape, which include the funerary procession to the tomb, the otherworldly journey of the deceased to the afterlife, and the ongoing travel of kin, dependents, and other visitors, to and from the cemetery. This movement of living people within a necropolis leaves mere traces in a built environment that reveals much to us about the deceased – whose bodies are interred in the cemetery and whose memories are preserved in funerary monuments – yet very little about the living populations that facilitated its continual use. Added inscriptions and graffiti left upon tomb walls in the cemetery offer a glimpse of a living community moving and operating within a funerary landscape. Such evidence can be considered more broadly as belonging to ancient Egyptian cultural memory, and linked to performative activities that brought visitors to cemeteries, such as feast-day processions and offering rituals. This paper explores the possibility that added inscriptions within the late Old Kingdom tomb of vizier Kagemni Memi, in the Teti pyramid cemetery at Saqqara, contribute to a body of evidence for ancient visitors travelling to the cemetery and moving within the tomb itself. I suggest that one possible outcome of adding inscriptions to the walls was that their authors could receive the benefits of being associated with the tomb-owner by making their own names indelible, while indirectly honouring Kagemni's desire to be remembered in posterity.[1]

[1] This paper is drawn from a wider examination by the author of the *Veneration of Vizier Kagemni at Saqqara during the late Old Kingdom and First Intermediate Period*, completed as a Master's dissertation at the University of Auckland in 2014 and supervised by Professor Anthony Spalinger. Thanks are due to

Vizier Kagemni Memi at Saqqara

Vizier Kagemni Memi (*K3(=ỉ)-gm.n(=ỉ) rn=f nfr Mmỉ*) is well known to Egyptologists as the vizier of King Teti in the earlier part of his reign in the 6th dynasty (*c.*2347–2337 BCE). He is also recognisable for his appearance as a character in the 12th dynasty *Teaching for Kagemni*, fragments of which are preserved on Papyrus Prisse. Kagemni was a judicial *ꜥḏ-mr* official during the reign of Unas and was presumably appointed vizier during Teti's reign (Edel 1953, 223). The circumstances in which the vizierate was attained during the late Old Kingdom are unknown and, in fact, the only evidence of a vizier being appointed to their role comes from the *Teaching for Kagemni* (Strudwick 1985, 319, n. 1). Kagemni held the title *ỉmy-r3 šmꜥw (T3)-mḥw* 'overseer of Upper and Lower Egypt', which clearly expressed his authority over the whole country (Brovarski 2013, 92). Furthermore, Kagemni's wife was Nebtynebkhet Seshseshet, one of Teti's daughters (Harpur and Scremin 2006, 155 [243]). It can be surmised from this data that Kagemni was the high-ranking Memphite official *par excellence.*

Kagemni, as the highest-ranking official in the funerary institution of Teti, also possessed titles that linked him closely with the Saqqara necropolis. He was *sḥḏ Ḏd-swt-Ttỉ* 'inspector of the Pyramid of Teti', and *sḥḏ ḥmw-nṯr Ḏd-swt-Ttỉ* 'inspector of the priests of the Pyramid of Teti'. Furthermore, his position as *ỉmy-r3 nỉwt Ḏd-swt-Ttỉ* 'overseer of the pyramid town of the Pyramid of Teti', which was not shared by his successors Mereruka and Ihy, likely afforded him significant status in the pyramid town of *Ḏd-swt-Ttỉ*, 'Enduring are the places of Teti' – a thriving residential centre in the late Old Kingdom and First Intermediate Period (as attested in the *Teaching of Merikare*: Parkinson 1997, 224, n. 39; Malek 1997, 94–5, fig. 1). The community of this town was buried in the cemetery, either in the large tombs of the high officials or in the 'streets' surrounding them.

Kagemni's tomb was erected close to Teti's pyramid and placed near its northern face. As one of the largest tombs in the cemetery – a surface of 1024 sq. m and sides 32 m long (Firth and Gunn 1926, 20) – it would have been a visible monument in the funerary landscape, even in the shadow of Teti's pyramid. The tomb has an entrance in its eastern façade leading to the interior storerooms and chapels. These contain stunning scenes of offerings and daily activities described as representing 'a peak in artistic achievement' of the Old Kingdom (Kanawati 1999, 283).

While the tomb reliefs themselves have been a popular object of study (Badawy 1979; 1981; Kanawati 1999; Harpur and Scremin 2006; Jones 2012), the corpus of added inscriptions and graffiti in Kagemni's tomb, which resemble aspects of the graffiti and visitors' inscriptions found in later Egyptian cemeteries, has been overlooked. These inscriptions consist of rough, shallow hieroglyphs or semi-hieratic etchings on the tomb's interior reliefs, usually located next to figures of offering bearers. Yvonne

Professor Spalinger and Doctor Jennifer Hellum for comments on this work during the completion of the dissertation, and to Chris de L'isle and the anonymous reviewers of this paper for editorial comments.

Harpur and Paolo Scremin's (2006) publication of the scene details of Kagemni's tomb is an excellent record of the reliefs; however, the volume does not provide photographic images of the scenes in their entirety. It is difficult, admittedly, to detect added inscriptions when line drawings do not always distinguish between the original inscriptions in the tomb and what may be later additions. It has been possible, nonetheless, to identify a corpus of added inscriptions to the formal reliefs in Kagemni's tomb. It is clear that an opportunity exists for a further study of Kagemni's tomb, and those of others in the cemetery, to identify and document such inscriptions.

Ancient Egyptian graffiti and visitors' inscriptions

Graffiti, both ancient and modern, are found everywhere throughout Egypt, acting as a real map of human presence in the Egyptian landscape; quarries, mines, desert roads and their stops, temples and cemeteries, all bear ancient graffiti (Navrátilová 2007, 16; a survey is provided in Peden 2001; see also the response to Peden in Darnell 2002). In epigraphy, a distinction is usually made between an inscription that is scratched (*graffito*) or painted (*dipinto*), but in Egyptology, both categories tend to be termed 'graffiti' (Navrátilová 2010, 306–13). Egyptian graffiti vary in content and execution: some are lengthy *dipinti* (e.g. Den Doncker 2012; Ragazzoli 2013), while others are short scratchings noting a name and a date, and sometimes just a name. Surely, such inscriptions were not always planned and composed beforehand; their assumed or possible spontaneity is a characteristic that distinguishes graffiti from formal texts and painted or figurative reliefs. In spaces that were frequently accessed and reused, such as cemeteries, there is a conspicuous sub-group of ancient Egyptian graffiti, usually called visitors' inscriptions (Helck 1952; Wildung 1975). In the New Kingdom, these are particularly well attested in Thebes and Memphis, where added inscriptions and painted *dipinti* were left by scribes on the public parts of funerary monuments to record their visit, prefaced by a formula *ỉwt pw ỉr(t) ỉn sš N* 'this is the visit made by the scribe N' (Ragazzoli 2013, 270; for Memphite examples: Navrátilová 2007, 16–17; Starring 2011, 147–8).

The added inscriptions which are discussed in this paper occupy an uncertain space in the wider corpus of ancient Egyptian graffiti, and what follows is a preliminary discussion of the potential interest of such Old Kingdom examples to researchers. The inscriptions can be distinguished from the formal relief programme found in the tomb based on the rough quality of the hieroglyphic graffiti and can thus not be mistaken for an original part of the primary tomb reliefs. Additionally, they seem to capture a moment in time in which a visit to the tomb was made either before or after the interment of its owner, including during construction. In contrast, however, they lack the length, authorial intent, and clear historical context of New Kingdom graffiti. Nonetheless, this corpus of added inscriptions offers glimpses of people visiting the tomb, using graffiti as a medium to integrate themselves into the social world of the tomb-owner and memorialise their own name.

Added inscriptions in the tomb of Kagemni

The added inscriptions found in Kagemni's tomb are largely found at standing height or crouching level and consist, in most cases, only of a name, and occasionally a title as well. They congregate mostly in rooms three and six, and are located next to figures of offering bearers, or otherwise nameless figures in the tomb reliefs. Excellent examples of this variety occur on the west wall in room three of Kagemni's tomb (Figs. 4.1 and 4.2). This scene, which is pastoral in nature, features numerous activities on the upper register, including cows being milked, mats being brushed, and boys feeding a puppy. In the lower register, two wading herdsmen direct cattle fording a stream, while five more men are found in papyrus skiffs further on. One of them, perched on a stern, facing the herd, attracts a mother with a calf which he holds by its forelegs in one hand, and with a rope around its neck in the other. Above the heads of the two herdsmen in the lower register, the names *Ṯss* (Tjeses) and *Ḫnm-nfr* (Khnumnefer) have been incised in rough hieroglyphs (see Fig. 4.1).

Fig. 4.1: Detail from the pastoral and cattle fording scene from the west wall in room three of Kagemni's tomb. The added names of Tjeses and Khnumnefer are found next to the faces of the two men herding cattle. Adapted from 'Mastaba of Kagemni' © Manna Nader, Gabana Studios Cairo. Used with permission.

The title *ḥm-k3* '*k3*-servant' and, once again, the name Tjeses appear above the head of the man in the skiff holding the calf; the name *Ḫr-ỉb* (Kherib) occurs above the head of the man immediately to his right (see Fig. 4.2). Finally, on the far right of this register, the name Khnumnefer appears again in a large scrawl, possibly by a different hand from that on the far left. That their names are inscribed twice raises the possibility that Tjeses and Khnumnefer had a particular affinity with this scene. Harpur (2006, 379) notes that Tjeses' name occurs next to two men with calves; did he wish to be recognised as 'the man with the calf'? More generally, one also wonders whether added inscriptions aimed at directly identifying oneself with the people represented in the reliefs.

Further attestations from other rooms within the tomb neatly demonstrate the variety in the execution of these inscriptions by numerous different hands. For example, a more proficient hieroglyphic inscription for the *ỉmy-r3 pr sš Mḫw* 'steward

Fig. 4.2: Detail from the pastoral and cattle scene from room three, to the right of Fig. 4.1 and towards the centre of the full scene. Two men in a skiff: the title ḥm-k3 and, once again, the name Tjeses appear above the man on the left; the name Kherib is inscribed above the man on the right. Adapted from 'Mastaba of Kagemni' © Manna Nader, Gabana Studios Cairo. Used with permission. For a line drawing of the full scene, see Harpur and Scremin (2006, 493, fig. 7).

and scribe, Mekhu' is found in room six, which is adjacent to the hall containing the interior false-door. Assuming that the person who made this inscription was indeed the scribe Mekhu, its quality compared to the much rougher inscriptions in room three would then be unsurprising (on the difficulty of mastering scripts see Baines 1984, 693–8). Another difference is that this inscription occurs in a much higher register of the relief, out of reach. Harpur and Scremin (2006, 448) suggest that the person responsible for this particular addition 'must have found a way to reach this particular spot from the ground level, or added the inscription whilst standing on sand banked up in the room below the level of the row of figures'.

The most substantial inscription, which can also be assigned a more secure date, has been recorded by Battiscombe Gunn (Firth and Gunn 1926, 116) for the *smr wꜥtỉ ꜣIdw* 'sole companion, Idu' and *sꜣ=f mry=f Gmn(ỉ)* 'his beloved son, Gemni'. Gunn described it as being a scratched graffito in 'rough, semi-hieratic signs 3–4 cm high... on the centre of the east wall of the large undecorated room leading to a staircase' (Firth and Gunn 1926, 116). Regrettably, being in an undecorated room, this inscription was not captured in Harpur and Scremin's study of the tomb scenes details and it is not possible to comment further on the style of the composition. A striking feature of this inscription is that, according to Gunn, it appears to have been completed in two parts: the initial recording of Idu and his son Gemni, and a subsequent addition of *smr wꜥtỉ* above the name of the latter, which Gunn suggested was by a different hand, perhaps that of the son (Firth and Gunn 1926, 116).

The interest in this inscription is twofold. First, if Gunn's assessment is correct, it is an undisputable case of individuals – a father and a son – entering Kagemni's tomb and marking their names on the surface of the tomb wall, but, unlike other inscriptions described in this paper, in a manner which did not integrate their names with the primary material in the decorated halls. No definitive reason can be offered for Idu and Gemni's choice of this undecorated space, and one can only speculate their relationship to Kagemni. It is appealing to consider that they had some distant professional connection to Kagemni or, as minor officials, at least desired such a relationship. Second, the occurrence of a shortened form of Kagemni's name, *Gmn(ỉ)* (Ranke 1935, 351 [12]) – which is most likely a hypocoristic (Vernus 1986, 127), or *kurz* (Scheele-Schweitzer 2014, 77, 80) version of the full name – provides a tentative date for the inscription. Only nine instances of the name *Gmn(ỉ)* are known, all in the Teti pyramid cemetery on late Old Kingdom and First Intermediate Period monuments. This is a strong evidence that these hypocoristic names (33 instances appear in the cemetery) were made in reference to the vizier and that their use was limited to the period between the late Old Kingdom (6th dynasty onwards) and the First Intermediate Period.[2]

[2] From chapter four of the author's unpublished MA dissertation, *Veneration of Vizier Kagemni during the late Old Kingdom and First Intermediate Period* (University of Auckland, 2014).

Dating and interpretation

One concern in this analysis is the dating. Unlike more substantial graffiti from the New Kingdom in Memphis and Thebes, which can be dated based on style and intertextual references (Navrátilová 2011a; Ragazzoli 2013), there is little evidence which can provide a firm date in most of the inscriptions found in Kagemni's tomb. However, as the concentration of use in the cemetery dates to the late Old Kingdom through to the early Middle Kingdom (Firth and Gunn 1926; Piątek 2001), it seems likely that the inscriptions belong to this period. Many of the names attested in this cemetery seem typical of the Old Kingdom (Ranke 1935; Scheele-Schweitzer 2014), but this remains an unsecure means of dating. Burials are attested in the cemetery up to the Late Period and, with few other available criteria with which to date these names beyond reasonable doubt, the possibility of a later date for these inscriptions cannot be wholly excluded.

Indirect evidence does exist for the dating of these inscriptions, however. Although not recorded *in situ*, three of the names found in added inscriptions – Idu (Firth and Gunn 1926, 219 [5–7]), Khui (Firth and Gunn 1926, 221 [26–7]; Quibell and Hayter 1927, 16), and Seshemnefer (Firth and Gunn 1926, 225 [55], pl. 11 [10]) – are also attested on late Old Kingdom and First Intermediate Period style offering-tables and false-doors excavated from the two 'streets' of minor burials adjacent to Kagemni's tomb. The connection between the named individuals in the tomb and the funerary objects for similarly named persons is tenuous, but the possibility remains that these individuals, who asserted a role in Kagemni's funerary cult with a graffito, were also buried in the vicinity of his tomb.

Offering an interpretation of this material presents a challenge. In fact, one can only presume connections between these inscriptions and the activities and funerary duties that brought the visitors to the tombs. As Hana Navrátilová (2007, 17) questions: are these records the results of antiquarian or religious interest in the cemetery or its occupants, or could they be the remnants of scribes and craftsmen working in the necropolis? The two need not be mutually exclusive. Alternatively, Dietrich Wildung (1975) and Wolfgang Helck (1952) have argued that such inscriptions could be viewed as a source for confirming the religious sense of the Egyptians and their pious visits and pilgrimages to temples and cemeteries. Indeed, Pascal Vernus (1998, 159) has commented that Kagemni's tomb was 'very alluring and likely would have been a promising destination for the pious'. I hypothesise that some of these inscribed names found within Kagemni's tomb can, indeed, be attributed to visitors to his tomb who may have had, or desired, a professional connection to Kagemni and a personal involvement in his posthumous funerary cult.

Another clue lies in the professed titles of the visitors, particularly those attested as *ḥm-kꜣ*, given that these priests were involved in the funerary rituals that accompanied burial – elaborately illustrated in Kagemni's tomb (Badawy 1981, 85–93) – and tasked with providing offerings. Examples include Hemakhti (Harpur and Scremin 2006, 236

[373], 449–50) and the previously mentioned Tjeses, who may therefore have been engaged in the ongoing service of Kagemni's funerary cult as well as those of Teti's other high officials buried in the same cemetery. *Kꜣ*-servants might have only seldom carried out in full the performance of making offerings for the deceased at the tomb, but this would at least have included the pouring of water – a role which was inherited by the descendants of these priests (see Assmann 2005, 330–48 on provisioning the dead). These added inscriptions may thus be an informal by-product of the *kꜣ*-servants performing their duties in the tomb.

The added inscriptions, however, do not exclusively refer to *kꜣ*-servants and further titles are attested such as those given by Khui (Harpur and Scremin 2006, 275 [428], 315 [491]) and Hefgegu (Harpur and Scremin 2006, 216 [339], 443). Both claimed to be scribes of the *phyle*, and were thus associated with the construction and maintenance of Teti's pyramid and funerary cult. Mekhu and Senbebuwek (Harpur and Scremin 2006, 43 [65], 371), however, were only referred to as scribes, which suggests a more distant professional association with Kagemni not necessarily connected to his personal funerary cult. By adding their inscriptions to the primary reliefs, the authors integrated themselves into Kagemni's social world, and perhaps even into his extended household.

Furthermore, for people bearing a shortened version of Kagemni's name, such as Idu's son Gemni, the placing of their names on a visit to his tomb may have carried a distinct meaning. It was thought that the memory of a deceased person lived on when their name was uttered, and inscriptions placed in accessible and open areas of a funerary monument invited visitors to keep the memory of the deceased alive (Vernus 1995, 50–3). The given name *Gmn(ỉ)* and the choice to make this inscription within Kagemni's tomb may, together, suggest a desired relationship between the family of Gemni and Kagemni as a local patron in Saqqara (see a comparable New Kingdom case study from Dra' Abu el-Naga in Rummel 2003). There appears to be a reciprocal benefit here: the perceived prestige of such a relationship profited Gemni's family in both this life and the hereafter, while simultaneously honouring the memory of the vizier.

The number and variety of added inscriptions within Kagemni's tomb beg the question: to what extent was Kagemni's tomb accessible to visitors? In the inscriptions on the outer tomb entrance, Kagemni speaks:

> ... With regard to any man who shall enter this, my tomb, not having purified himself, I shall seize his neck like a bird's so that the living see (it) and are fearful of an excellent and equipped *akh* who knows the rites. (Strudwick 2005, 285–7)

It is uncertain how visitors to the cemetery might have accessed the tomb and moved through the tomb space. Presumably visitors were, in the first instance, family members of the deceased and professional cult-servants who may have been assigned to more than one tomb. A noteworthy addition to Kagemni's tomb are the external false-door and offering table, which were set into the outer east wall on the same axis as the much larger interior false-door and offering table (Firth and Gunn 1926, pl. 5D). Kagemni was thus provisioned with multiple sites for offerings, and one interpretation for this architectural feature is that it allowed those who were not permitted to enter the tomb to make offerings to the deceased vizier. Could this indicate that, at one point, there has been a clear demarcation between sacred and non-sacred areas of the tomb? Or that the access was restricted for those who were not purified (on account of Kagemni's external inscriptions)? The presence of added inscriptions inside Kagemni's tomb may indicate that such restrictions, if they ever really existed, broke down over time.

It remains possible that these inscribed names and titles are attributable to later visitors who did not have a connection to the vizier. It was first suggested by Gunn (Firth and Gunn 1926, 114) that graffiti found in the cemetery were 'probably by persons who are not represented by the figures in question, but who, for playful or serious motives have chosen to immortalise themselves in this way'. Gunn, like Alan Gardiner (see Navrátilová 2011b), was largely dismissive of the potential for graffiti to offer anything but onomastic data to the researcher. Yet, whether or not these later visitors had 'playful or serious motives', their inscriptions are trace evidence of their travel to the cemetery, and became, perhaps unintentionally, a part of the continuum of the funerary cult of the deceased.

Kagemni was an official of supreme eminence in his lifetime and, in addition, had a distinct standing in the community buried in the Teti pyramid cemetery. In death, he may have been considered an ideal figure for the local community to appeal to for intercession in its everyday life; he was undoubtedly a popular figure in the area according to the number of names constructed with his own. While the inscriptions discussed here do not directly invoke the vizier in the same fashion as a funerary formula, their presence on Kagemni's tomb wall was, perhaps, enough. By incising their names and titles within his tomb, these visitors could receive the benefits of their association with the tomb-owner.

As argued by Navrátilová (2007, 311) and Ute Rummel (2003) with regard to New Kingdom visitors' graffiti, such inscriptions made within tombs can be envisaged as part of the visitors' cult – the social communication with which Egyptians wished to be associated after death (Baines and Lacovara 2002) – and ancient Egyptian cultural memory. They provided a response to the implicit and, if an 'appeal to the living' was present, explicit wishes of the tomb-owner that to be remembered by the living (see Baines 1987; Assmann 2005, 377–9; Moreno García 2010). Furthermore, once carved into relief, these inscriptions were integrated into the formal visual language of display in the tomb, in which texts, pictorial elements (both painted and carved), as well as the monument itself, played a role (Baines 2007, 1–30). By integrating their names and titles into the primary tomb reliefs, these individuals became members of the extended household of Kagemni. Additionally, Chloé Ragazzoli (2013, 290) has argued that graffiti in the form of simple signatures, like the inscription of a name, memorialised the presence of a person in a certain area. The preservation of the name, in this way, permitted permanence beyond the threshold of death for the person named – a characteristically Egyptian concern.

Conclusion

The immense appeal of these inscriptions is that they offer a glimpse into the lives of ancient Egyptians – temple priests, cult servants, or scribes – who may have lived in the town of *Ḏd-swt-Ttỉ*, beyond the more prominent figures of high officials buried in the cemetery. We need not look further than Kagemni's tomb scenes to envisage this community: the priest reciting transfiguration spells from papyrus; the three priests kneeling before him in the *hnw*-gesture; the attendants in procession; the men employed in cattle-herding. Additional studies of added inscriptions and graffiti in the Teti pyramid cemetery will further our understanding of the community interred in the cemetery, as well as of the one documented in the material remnants of its visits to it. In this way, we might access the traces of the living community of *Ḏd-swt-Ttỉ*, whose annual feast day processions (Spalinger 1996) and offering rituals – now muted and only accessible through funerary texts and reliefs – would have filled the cemetery and its environs with noise, movement, and smells. The tombs of the Teti pyramid cemetery require greater attention outside of the artistic achievements of their reliefs; this paper demonstrates one of the possibilities for such future research.

References

Assmann, J. 2005. *Death and salvation in ancient Egypt*, trans. D. Lorton. Ithaca: Cornell University Press.

Badawy, A. 1979. 'L'art au tombeau de Kagemni, au beau nom de Memi'. *Gazette des Beaux-Arts* 94: 193–202.

Badawy, A. 1981. 'The spiritualization of Kagemni'. *Zeitschrift für Ägyptische Sprache und Altertumskunde* 108: 85–93.

Baines, J. 1984. 'Schreiben'. In W. Helck, E. Otto, and W. Westendorf (eds.) *Lexikon der Ägyptologie* V: 693–8. Wiesbaden: Harrassowitz.

Baines, J. 1987. 'Practical religion and piety'. *Journal of Egyptian Archaeology* 73: 79–98.

Baines, J. 2007. *Visual and written culture in ancient Egypt*. Oxford: Oxford University Press.

Baines, J. and Lacovara, P. 2002. 'Burial and the dead in ancient Egyptian society. Respect, formalism, neglect'. *Journal of Social Archaeology* 2 (1): 5–36.

Brovarski, E. 2013. 'Overseers of Upper Egypt in the Old to Middle Kingdoms'. *Zeitschrift für Ägyptische Sprache und Altertumskunde* 140: 91–111.

Darnell, J. 2002. 'Review of Peden, A. J. 2001. The graffiti of Pharaonic Egypt.' *Journal of the American Oriental Society* 122 (4): 885–6.

Den Doncker, A. 2012. 'Theban tomb graffiti during the New Kingdom. Research on the reception of ancient Egyptian images by ancient Egyptians'. In K. Kóthay (ed.) *Art and society. Ancient and modern contexts of Egyptian art. Proceedings of the international conference held at the Museum of Fine Arts, Budapest, 13–15 May 2010*: 23–34. Budapest: Museum of Fine Arts.

Edel, E. 1953. 'Inschriften des Alten Reiches II. Die Biographie des *K3j-gmjnj* (Kagemni)'. *Mitteilungen des Instituts für Orientforschung* 1: 210–26.

Firth, C. M. and Gunn, B. 1926. *Excavations at Saqqara. Teti pyramid cemetery*. Cairo: Imprimerie de l'Institut Français d'Archéologie Orientale.

Harpur, Y. and Scremin, P. 2006. *The chapel of Kagemni: scene details*. Reading: Oxford Expedition to Egypt.

Helck, W. 1952. 'Die Bedeutung der ägyptischen Besucherinschriften'. *Zeitschrift der Deutschen Morgenländischen Gesellschaft* 102: 39–46.

Jones, P. 2012. 'A new interpretation for a Kagemni wall scene'. *Göttinger Miszellen* 235: 31–44.

Kanawati, N. 1999. 'Some iconographic peculiarities in the Teti cemetery'. In C. Ziegler (ed.) *L'art de l'Ancien Empire égyptien. Actes du colloque organisé au Musée du Louvre par le service culturel les 3 et 4 avril 1998*: 281–310. Paris: La documentation française.

Malek, J. 1997. 'The temples at Memphis. Problems highlighted by the EES survey'. In S. Quirke (ed.) *The temple in ancient Egypt. New discoveries and recent research*: 90–101. London: The British Museum Press.

Moreno García, J. 2010. 'Oracles, ancestor cults and letters to the dead: the involvement of the dead in the public and family affairs in pharaonic Egypt'. In A. Storch (ed.) *Perception of the invisible. Religion, historical semantics and the role of perceptive verbs*: 133–53. Cologne: Rüdiger Köppe.

Navrátilová, H. 2007. *The visitor's graffiti of dynasties XVIII and XIX in Abusir and Northern Saqqara*. Prague: Czech Institute of Egyptology.

Navrátilová, H. 2010. 'Graffiti spaces'. In L. Bareš, F. Coppens, and K. Smoláriková (eds.) *Egypt in transition. Social and religious development of Egypt in the first millennium BCE. Proceedings of an international conference, Prague, September 1-4, 2009*: 305–32. Prague: Univerzita Karlova.

Navrátilová, H. 2011a. 'Intertextuality in ancient Egyptian visitors' graffiti?'. In F. Hagen (ed.) *Narratives of Egypt and the ancient Near East. Literary and linguistic approaches*, Orientalia Lovaniensia Analecta 189: 257–67. Leuven: Peeters.

Navrátilová, H. 2011b. 'Gardiner and graffiti'. *Egyptian and Egyptological Documents, Archives, and Libraries* 2: 171–86.

Parkinson, R. 1997. *The tale of Sinuhe and other ancient Egyptian poems*. Oxford: Oxford University Press.

Peden, A. 2001. *The graffiti of pharaonic Egypt. Scope and roles of informal writings (c.3100–332 BC)*. Leiden: Brill.

Piątek, B. 2001. 'The development of the Teti pyramid necropolis (3rd–12th dynasty). Perspectives of the research'. In J. Popielska-Grzybowska (ed.) *Proceedings of the first central european conference of young egyptologists. Egypt 1999: perspectives of research, Warsaw, 7–9 June 1999*, Warsaw Egyptological Studies 3: 105–13. Warsaw: Institute of Archaeology.

Quibell, J. and Hayter, A. 1927. *Excavations at Saqqara. Teti pyramid north side*. Cairo: Imprimerie de l'Institut Français d'Archéologie Orientale.

Ragazzoli, C. 2013. 'The social creation of a scribal place: the visitors' inscriptions in the tomb attributed to Antefiqer (TT 60) (With newly recorded graffiti)'. *Studien zur Altägyptischen Kultur* 42: 269–323.

Ranke, H. 1935. *Die ägyptischen Personennamen I. Verzeichnis der Namen*. Hamburg: Augustin.

Rummel, U. 2003. '"Ramsesnacht-dauer" – Die Beziehung zwischen Namenspatron und Namensträger am Beispiel einer Besucherinschrift aus Dra'Abu el-Naga'. In N. Kloth, K. Martin, and E. Pardey (eds.) *Es werde niedergelegt als Schriftstück. Festschrift für Hartwig Altenmüller zum 65. Geburtstag*, Studien zur Altägyptischen Kultur, Beihefte 9: 367–77. Hamburg: Buske.

Scheele-Schweitzer, K. 2014. *Personennamen des Alten Reiches. Altägyptische Onomastik unter lexikographischen und sozio-kulturellen Aspekten*. Wiesbaden: Harrassowitz.

Spalinger, A. 1996. *The private feast lists of ancient Egypt*. Wiesbaden: Harrassowitz.

Starring, N. 2011. 'Interpreting figural graffiti: case-studies from a funerary context'. In M. Horn, J. Kramer, D. Soliman, N. Staring, C. van den Hoven, and L. Weiss (eds.) *Current Research in Egyptology 2010. Proceedings of the eleventh annual symposium, Leiden University, January 2010*: 145–56. Oxford: Oxbow Books.

Strudwick, N. 1985. *The administration of Egypt in the Old Kingdom. The highest titles and their holders*. London: Kegan Paul International.

Strudwick, N. 2005. *Texts from the Pyramid Age*, Writings from the Ancient World 16. Atlanta: Society of Biblical Literature.

Vernus, P. 1986. *Le surnom au Moyen Empire. Répertoire, procédés d'expression et structures de la double identité du début de la XIIe dynastie à la fin de la XVIIe dynastie*. Rome: Biblical Institute Press.

Vernus, P. 1995. *Essai sur la conscience de l'histoire dans l'Egypte pharaonique*. Paris: H. Champion.

Vernus, P. 1998. *The gods of ancient Egypt*. London: Tauris Parke Books.

Wildung, D. 1975. 'Besucherinschriften'. In W. Helck, E. Otto, and W. Westendorf (eds.) *Lexikon der Aügyptologie* I: 766–7. Wiesbaden: Harrassowitz.

Chapter 5

Did the ancient Egyptian traveller consider Ha, god of the Western Desert, while traversing his domain?

Kata Jasper
Eötvös Loránd University, Hungary

Introduction

The question posed in the title of this article may seem trivial at first sight; yet, bearing the data at our disposal in mind, the unequivocal answer is Ha was not considered during desert travel. Furthermore, we have very few indications concerning the relationship between the Western Desert as a physical entity and Ha, Lord of the West, even though, according to many Egyptologists (Gardiner 1917, 792; Wildung 1977a; Kees 1980, 26; Aufrère 1991, 4; Yoyotte 1991–1992, 628; 1993–1994, 670; Darnell *et al.* 2013, 3), he was the personification of the territory. Considering that the connection is more evident between the Eastern Desert and Sopdu, Lord of the East (Schumacher 1988), who quite often appears beside Ha (Yoyotte 1993–1994), the question is even more puzzling. It is therefore difficult to explain why the Egyptians did not pray to Ha. In the following, I investigate this seemingly trivial issue in order to point to the complex and diverse nature of Egyptian personifications (Gardiner 1917; Bonnet 1952, 386–8; Guglielmi 1982; Baines 1985).

To this end, this investigation provides insight into the ancient Egyptians' attitude towards travel, especially through the desert, the potential dangers involved, and the role that Egyptian gods played in this activity. It also highlights the absence of a cult or priesthood related to Ha before the 26th dynasty, which leads to further questions: why did a deity, personifying such an extensive territory as the Western Desert, not have a cult in Egypt? How did the ancient Egyptians perceive the world around them? How did the perception of nature manifest in the various layers of the Egyptian religion? In this paper, I can only scrape the surface of this very complex topic, but I would like to approach the problem by investigating the character of Ha and the deities who were somehow in association with extended geographical areas.

Travelling in the desert

Travel was an integral part of Egyptian everyday life according to written and archaeological sources. On the one hand, written sources pertaining to travel in the desert (for an overview, see Riemer and Förster 2013, 39–42) include expedition reports (for example the inscriptions of Harkhuf: Lichtheim 1973, 23–7; Fecht 1979, 113–14, 120–5), private letters (especially the correspondence between Dhutmose and Butehamun: Černý 1939; Wente 1967), literary texts (for *Reiseliteratur* as literary genre, see Blumenthal 1982, 53–65; Moers 1999; Loprieno 2003; Galán 2005; Winand 2011), and rock graffiti (see Darnell *et al.* 2002; Diego Espinel 2012; Darnell 2013; Lazaridis 2015). On the other hand, the archaeological evidence (e.g. Förster and Riemer 2013) includes edifices of both sacred and profane character, used as shelters and sanctuaries at the same time (Diego Espinel 2012, 94).

Desert travel was undertaken for economic, professional, or religious reasons, and it involved the entirety of Egyptian society (Köpp 2013, 118–21; Köpp-Junk 2013, 2–5). It is also known that, although the fluvial route was 'the natural highway' (Kuhlmann 2002, 126) of transportation, locomotion was not confined to shipping on the Nile. Considering the fact that riverine travel was not always the better option (Darnell *et al.* 2002, 1–2; Kuhlmann 2002, 126), journeys through the desert formed an integral part of long distance travel from the earliest periods onwards (Kuhlmann 2002, 135; 2005, 287; Köpp-Junk 2013, 2; Lazaridis 2015, 51–2). Numerous desert roads, such as the Farshut Road and the Alamat Tal Road to bypass the Qena Bend (Darnell 2002, 140–2; Darnell *et al.* 2002, 36–7, 45–6), were therefore used as shortcuts (Riemer and Förster 2013, 48–9).

The ancient Egyptians had ten different words for the desert: *ḫꜣs.t* 'desert savanna, bushy savanna, gebel'; *ḫꜣf.t* 'desert edge, desert border'; *ḏꜥ* 'desert, area of meteorological phenomena'; *nw.t* 'hunting reservation'; *smn.t* 'desert as a territory of exploration'; *dšr.t* 'desert, Arabian Desert'; *jmꜣ(.w)-wr* 'desert, a large area covered by *jmꜣ*-tree'; *tꜣ-fk* 'bald region, desert'; *ḫrb* 'devastated, dry place, desert'; *jꜣb.tt, jmn.tt* 'the Eastern Desert, the Western Desert'. They also had four other expressions for the various types of transitional zones between desert and cultivated areas: *ꜥḏw* 'limit of the cultivated area'; *zmj.t* 'desert edge, desert border'; *spꜣ.t* 'desert district'; *mrw/mr.t* 'desert strip' (Aufrère 1991, 7–18). The richness of vocabulary reflects the relative importance of the territory and gives insight into the Egyptian' perception of desert areas.

Even though hunting was considered the only leisurely activity which could have been undertaken there (Kuhlmann 2005, 287–8), the desert was not an altogether negative place: it was a territory which was not just a bare, dry, and empty zone, but also bore the source of life in itself; it had underground water, vegetation, wild life, mineral potential, and sometimes even rain. It represented the marginal region where the sun rose and set. Furthermore, it had various mortuary connotations, as it was also the location of most of the necropoleis. Above all, the desert was the domain of the Egyptian gods (Aufrère 1991, 7–18).

In addition to the use of shortcuts, long-distance trade and the exploitation of raw materials acted as significant incentives for desert travel (for the significance of the Eastern and Western Deserts in general, see Kemp 1983, 119–24; Riemer and Förster 2013, 46–9). The Eastern Desert proved to be a rich source of building materials and minerals such as gold, precious and semi-precious stones, copper, and galena. Additionally, the routes running towards the states of Western Asia are an indicator of its strategic importance (Kemp 1983, 123–4; Aufrère 1991, 8–9; Kuhlmann 2002, 128; 2005, 287). Despite the agricultural significance of its oases, Klaus Kuhlmann considers that it is the draw of trade with the Libyans, and especially with the Nubians, that increased the importance of the Western Desert in the eyes of the Egyptian state (2002, 126–7, 131, 139; 2005, 288). Perhaps due to the higher value attributed to the Eastern Desert, a less ambiguous relationship might have developed between the Eastern Desert and its god Sopdu, Lord of the East, than the one between Ha and the Western Desert.

The Egyptians had to familiarise themselves with the desert before they could exploit its trading and mining potential (Aufrère 1991, 34; Darnell *et al.* 2002, 3; Riemer and Förster 2013, 32–3, 42–4). The traveller would have faced many challenges there including not only aridity, heat, storms, diseases, and animals, but also robbers and the danger of getting lost (Aufrère 1991, 8, 33–8; Köpp 2013, 123–4; Köpp-Junk 2013, 10). Despite its risks, the desert simultaneously was a well-known and prevalent venue, and travelling in it might not have been more dangerous than navigating on the Nile, where crocodiles and snakes were potential dangers (Moers 2001, 191–210, 219–32).

Popular piety

The ancient Egyptians used amulets and prayers to protect themselves in their everyday lives as well as during travel. Rock inscriptions in the desert attest to the importance of divine protection for the safe return and well-being of travellers. One such inscription, for example, is devoted to the avoidance of dehydration (Aufrère 1991, 34). The Egyptians tended to pray to their local god who, in the form of a statue, resided in a shrine or a temple. They could experience 'divine presence' and connect with it in the temple, at home or, in cases where the divine image was being transported, even en route (Assmann 2001, 1–52). This is supported by the correspondence between two scribes from Deir el-Medineh, Dhutmose and Butehamun. The gods related to the areas in which Dhutmose was travelling, such as Horus of Kuban or Horus of Abiba, are mentioned in his letters (e.g. pLeiden I 369, 3–4: Černý 1939, 1, l. 5; pLeiden I 370, 3: Černý 1939, 9, l. 5), suggesting that the protection of travellers was handed over to the gods of the territories through which their journeys led them (pPhillipps vs. 4–5: Černý 1939, 30, l. 6–8; pTurin 1971, 9–10: Černý 1939, 31, l. 14–16; pBM 10284, 5–6: Černý 1939, 48, l. 13–14).

But to whom did desert travellers actually pray? It was the domain of Horus and Hathor in particular (Kemp 1983, 129–30, 141; Darnell *et al.* 2002), but other deities were associated with it as well, such as Thoth, Sopdu, Montu, Min and, in later periods, Amun[1] and Anubis (Aufrère 1991, 9–11). Most of them were major divinities, but they did not have specific or exclusive ties to these territories. Similarly, a large number of desert graffiti are mere copies or reduplications of the Nile Valley ideas (Diego Espinel 2012, 93) as, for example, the repetition of the deities listed in *The Story of Sinuhe* (B 205–12: Yoyotte 1964) at the Wadi el-Hôl (Darnell *et al.* 2002, 99–101). The texts of other rock inscriptions are more in tune with the actual landscape of which they form a part (Diego Espinel 2012, 93), as the mention of the purpose of travel and the formulae for safe return attest (Baines 2007, 15; Köpp-Junk 2013, 10).

Ha, god of the Western Desert

Although Ha is known as the god of the Western Desert, we do not possess any written or pictorial evidence of prayers to Ha in association with travels in the Western Desert. A simple explanation for this phenomenon is that Ha was not worshipped before the 26th dynasty, when his priests appear in the historical record and his shared cult with Ptah and Sekhmet in Saqqara is first attested (see the statue of Ahmose, Memphis (Berlin, 14765): Wildung 1977b, 33–5 §13; further references to the *ḥm-nṯr Ḥꜣ*: the Apis stela, Serapeum (Louvre, IM 4018): Chassinat 1900, 178; Vercoutter 1962, 5, 66–9, pl. 9); the statue of Amenirdis son of Khuherishef, Karnak Cachette (Cairo, CG 48632): Josephson and Eldamaty 1999, 74–5). Jean Yoyotte furthermore assumed that Ha was worshipped in Heracleopolis at that time (1991–1992, 627). It is also in the 26th dynasty that Ha first appeared in the oases (see the tomb of Baeniutiu, Bahariya oasis: Fakhry 1942, pl. 34B; the chapels of ʻAin el-Muftella, Bahariya oasis: Fakhry 1942, pl. 51A; the temple of Hibis, Kharga oasis: Davies 1953, pls. 5, 18).

In order to adequately interpret the absence of cultic veneration for such a long time, the references in which Ha appears in association with the west or the desert should be investigated further. Henry George Fischer drew attention to four deities associated with extensive territories like the oases, the Western Desert, or the Delta region: Ha, Lord of the Western Desert; Igai, Lord of the oases; Iaqes, Lord of the mouth of the Nile; and Hepui, Lord of the Delta marshes (1957, 223), but without elaboration, however. Nevertheless, a thorough study of their written and pictorial attestations may reveal that these figures formed a specific group which may have already been in existence from the late Old Kingdom onwards. As it is beyond the scope of this paper to give a complete overview of the sources which mention these divinities, only the most informative data is presented here. In the case of Ha, particular emphasis

[1] It is remarkable that, at Darb Ain Amur, Amun is represented with a specific epithet: *nb p.t* 'lord of the sky'. This might refer to his sovereignty over cosmic elements that affect meteorological conditions and the motion of the stars, and thus, the success of the journey (Lazaridis 2015, 51).

will be put on the Pyramid and Coffin texts, as the ideas formulated in them seem to appear again in later sources.[2]

The existence of a relationship between these four gods cannot be supported on the sole basis of the Pyramid Texts, as they contain references only to Ha and Igai. The latter (Leitz 2002, I, 570c–1a) is mentioned in a spell against the *ḥpjw*-snake (*PT* 377, 662a–e) and in a passage in association with resurrection (*PT* *732 = P/B/Se B 95–7[3]). As for Ha (Leitz 2002, V, 10b–11c), he appears as a deity who takes away the hunger of the dead (*PT* 204, 118c–19b). Two further spells state that the dead king shall be glorified as various deities, such as Ha (*PT* 483, 1013a–d; *PT* 610, 1712a–c). Iaqes (Leitz 2002, I, 112c–13b) and Hepui (Leitz 2002, V, 123b–4a), on the other hand, are not mentioned in the Pyramid Texts. Their priests are, however, attested in Old Kingdom sources (*ḥm-nṯr Jꜣqs*: tomb of Wash-Ptah Izi, North Saqqara, Nr. 24 (D 38): Mariette and Maspero 1889, 271; Strudwick 1985, 79–80; Fischer 1996, pl. 1; statue of Babaef, Giza (G 5230): Strudwick 1985, 82–3; *ḥm-nṯr Ḥpwy*: lintel of *Nsj*-[…]: Hassan 1944, 276; statue of Babaef, Giza (G 5230): Strudwick 1985, 82–3), as are Igai's (false door of Hetjes, Saqqara (S 3073): Kahl *et al.* 1995, 186–90; the tomb of Ipi, el-Kom el-Ahmar: Gomaà 1983, 140). At the same time, Ha had 'followers' *ḫt-Ḥꜣ*, who may have been members of the administrative elite (Altenmüller 2013, 2).

These four deities also appear on the *Sed*-festival scene of Osorkon II at Bubastis (Naville 1892, pl. 12) among the gods of the entire land who are present to confirm the legitimate accession of the king (Lange 2009, 215). In this scene, Ha and Igai are standing in the Upper Egyptian naoi, while Iaqes and Hepui appear in the procession of Lower Egyptian domains. Thus, the gods belonging to similar territories are represented next to each other in pairs. This depiction has its origin in Old Kingdom tradition (Langue 2009, 212), and its earliest attestation might be the scene sequences in the mortuary temple of Pepy II in South Saqqara, but in which unfortunately the representations of only Iaqes and Hepui remain (Jéquier 1938, pls. 58, 60), though Ha and Igai may have originally been depicted as well.

Later on, in the Coffin Texts, their common nature became more apparent. In a passage on the repelling of enemies coming from the four cardinal points, Iaqes and Hepui appear together with Ha, among other deities. Each god protects his sphere by driving away potential enemies. Their relationship with the cardinal points is mentioned explicitly:

> *jw-tj=fj r=k m p.t <jw=f n> ꜣ.t wrr.t=k jw-tj=fj r=k m tꜣ jw=f n ꜣ.t šfšf.t=k jw-tj=fj r=k n rsw[.t] […] ḫsf=f sn jn Sṯj.t nb.t Ꜣbw stj=s r=s[n] m šsr.w=s pw mr.w spd.w [n (?)]=sn jw-tj=fj r=k n mḥ.tj j<w>=f n Jꜣqs […] Ḥpwy jw-tj=fj r=k n jꜣb.tjw jw=f n Spdw nb Jꜣb.tt ḫsf{.n}<=f> sn ds=k jm=sn jw-tj=fj r=k n jmn.tjw jw=f n Ḥꜣ nb Jmn.tt ḫsf=f sn n ꜣ.t Jtm m prj.w=f n.w ꜣḫ.t*

[2] The Old Kingdom references cited in this article are the earliest known written attestations of these deities.

[3] Newly numbered spell, according to Allen 2013. For translation, see Allen 2005, 118 [P 286].

> He, who shall come against you from the sky, he belongs to the power of your crown. He, who shall come against you from the earth, he belongs to the power of your dignity. He, who shall come against you from/for the south, [...] he will reject them. It is Satet, Lady of Elephantine, who will shoot towards them with her arrows, which will be painful and sharp for them. He, who shall come against you from/for the north, he belongs to Iaqes [...] Hepui. He, who shall come against you from/for those of the East, he belongs to Sopdu, Lord of the East. He will reject them, (while) your knife is in them. He, who shall come against you from/for those of the West, he is for Ha, Lord of the West. He will repel them by the power of Atum in his coming forth from the horizon. (spell 313, *CT* IV 89j–90f)[4]

As for Igai, he also appears in three Coffin Texts spells (Leitz 2002, I, 571a [1–3]) two of which are associated with Ha and contain various references to the decay of the body. It is noteworthy that the five verbs expressing putrefaction alliterate with the name of the figures:

> *m gwꜣ m rn=k pw n Jgꜣj m ḥwꜣ m rn=k pw n Ḥꜣ m jnp m rn=k pw n Jnpw m sꜣb r tꜣ m rn=k pw n zꜣb*
>
> Do not choke in this your identity of Igai! Do not putrefy in this your identity of Ha! Do not decay in this your identity of Anubis! Do not flow to the ground in this your identity of jackal! (spell 755, *CT* VI 384o–q)
>
> *m ḥwꜣ m rn=k pw n Ḥꜣ m fnṯw m rn=k pw n fnṯ [m g]wꜣ m rn=k pw n Jgꜣj [m] jrpw m rn=k pw n Jnpw m sꜣb ḥwꜣꜣ.t=k jmj.t=sn m rn=k pw [n] zꜣb*
>
> Do not putrefy in this your identity of Ha! Do not rot in this your identity of the *fnṯ*-serpent! Do not choke in this your identity of Igai! Do not decay (*jrp/jnp* see Wb I, 96 [3]) in this your identity of Anubis! Your faeces shall not flow, what is in them, in this your identity of jackal! (spell 756, *CT* VI 386a–e)

Among these four deities, Ha has by far the most Coffin Texts references. He appears in eleven passages of the corpus (Hannig 2006, 3104c [43981]), with further indications of his role as a god designating the western sphere (*CT* II 395c; *CT* VI 259b–c). His name is also cited in some passages which focus on the theme of 'transition' i.e. from this world to the hereafter (*CT* I 139c; *CT* V 125a; *CT* VI 38z–aa). Finally, Ha also appears in a passage where the deceased refers to himself as his child in his western desert:

> *jnk sḏ.tj Ḥꜣ m zmj.t=f jrj.n.t<w> ꜥḥꜥ.w=j r-gs Wsjr mm ntj.w s.t=j zmj.t=f ꜣḫ.t=j pw zmj.t=f jmn.tt*
>
> I am the child of Ha in his desert, and my place was prepared beside Osiris, among those who exist. His desert is my residence. His western desert is my horizon. (spell 695, *CT* VI 329d–f)

Later attestations of these four gods indicate a weaker interrelationship, except for Iaqes and Hepui who continue to occur as a pair (see several similar references in Leitz 2002, I, 113b and V, 124a; see also Kees 1941). Together with Ha, they appear

[4] For late parallels of this passage, see pLouvre 3129 C, 47–52 and pBM 10252, 16,4–16,10: Schott 1929, 31,11–33,17 (transcription and translation: Fiedler 2011, 179–82); pMMA 35.9.21, 30,7–31,12: Goyon 1999; Fiedler 2011, 383–7. Special thanks to Ann-Katrin Gill for calling my attention to these references.

once again as a group among the deities along the outer wall of the sanctuary in Edfu (Rochemonteix and Chassinat 1984, 53 [43–4], [52]). Igai is however not attested later since Ptolemaic references are unknown (Leitz 2002, I, 570c–1a).

In the late parallels of Coffin Texts spell 313 (for reference, see n. 3), Iaqes and Hepui are no longer mentioned among the northern deities that repel enemies. However, their strong relationship with the northern Delta region (Kees 1941; Gardiner 1944, 29–30; Yoyotte 1970, 34) may account for their depiction with the deities accompanying the northern constellations on astronomical ceilings from the New Kingdom onwards (for reference list, see Neugebauer and Parker 1969, 195). The connection between their role as personifications of royal insignia and their territory – the Delta region – requires further investigation.

Ha appears to have a strong relationship both with the western sphere, as well as with the west as a burial place and transitional zone associated with the netherworld. This relationship is emphasised in the two Coffin Texts spells by mentioning him in conjunction with decay (spells 755 and 756). Additionally, we know that Ha was connected with the Western Desert, while from a religious point of view, the jackals and thus Anubis were considered to be animals related to this territory (Assmann 2001, 82). Thus, these passages from the Coffin Texts illustrate how the desert and its regions manifest themselves in deities and sacred beings, and how these layers of manifestations are linked to the concept of the necropolis – situated on the West Bank of the Nile, in the periphery of the cultivated area, and therefore the desert – as a place of decay. Moreover, this desert region was designated with the Egyptian term *zmj.t*, 'desert edge, desert border' (Aufrère 1991, 15), that is the same term used in Coffin Texts spell 695.

Discussion

It is meaningful that these four gods did not share a similar development. Ha, Iaqes, and Hepui were deities belonging to large, expansive realms, and who occasionally represented the cardinal point associated with their territory. They also seem to have lacked any worship in their respective areas. The same, however, cannot be said about Igai. While his first appearance in the Nile Valley is attested in the 3rd dynasty (mastaba of Khabausokaris, Saqqara: Arafa 2005, 12), there is also evidence of his cult within the Dakhla oasis in the 4th dynasty, year 27 of Kheops (Kuhlmann 2002, 136, fig. 10), as well as references from the 12th dynasty to his temple in the oasis (inscription of Sa-Igai, Mut el-Kharab: Hope *et al.* 2008, 56–9, fig. 6).

Thus, a question remains: to what extent was Igai different from the three other gods who, contrary to him, did not have a temple, a priesthood, or a depiction in connection with their domain. Establishing a distinction between 'place' and 'space' may bring us closer to the answer; namely, I differentiate the notion of a concrete, definite locality that I name 'place' from that of a large, more abstract area that I define as 'space'. In this respect, a 'place' might have its own history, past, and god, while a 'space' might not be limited enough to possess such characteristics. Large territories such as the Western Desert or the Delta region can be considered as 'spaces', while an oasis, which has edges and well-defined borders, may be treated as a 'place'. This would account for the fact that the latter had its own deity, Igai, along with a developed cult, whereas a similar phenomenon did not happen in the Western Desert or the Delta region with their own associated deities.[5] Based on this investigation, one may conclude that this group of deities associated with extended territories may have represented elements of a cosmogony that was not formulated.

A further conclusion may be drawn based on the relationship between the Western Desert and Ha or, more appropriately, between the space and the god personifying it. This relationship can be considered concrete evidence of a religious concept. As Jan Assmann has shown, the cosmos (or nature) '*was* the sacred itself' where the gods played, to a greater or lesser extent, an active role which meant that 'essentially every (although perhaps not in each and every case) deity…had a cult place and thus a cultic/local dimension of the unfolding of his or her essence' (2001, 80). This statement conflicts with the example of those gods who do not seem to have had a cult place. According to John Baines, however, the 'instability of the relationship between ritual and mythical actions and events and mythological interpretations of them' is 'a problem usually acute with personifications' (1985, 9). This instability is visible with Ha who, as a personification of the Western Desert, did not have a cult before the 26th dynasty and for whom there is no evidence of prayers in the context of travel in the Western Desert. Amid studying his character, it has been revealed that his link with the Western Desert as a physical space actually shifted to the west in general, in a mortuary and directional sense.

Yet, a final question persists: what understanding did the average ancient Egyptian have of the god Ha before the 26th dynasty? They surely perceived Min, Hathor, or Horus – gods with known cult places from earliest times – as parts of their reality, but this does not appear to have been the case with Ha, whose equivocal character may have been confusing for the ancient actors as well. Thus, what occurred in the 26th dynasty with Ha receiving a priesthood, a cult, and appearing in the western oases might be seen as an answer to this ambivalence. Egyptian intellectuals were particularly keen on studying ancient archives[6] and systematising aspects of Egyptian culture (Assmann 1992, 181–2, 193–4). Thus, the creation of the cult to Ha might be based on his nature in ancient religious texts, and may have stemmed from a desire to systemise the unclear nature of Ha and his relationship with his territory.

---

[5] The distinction between 'place' and 'space' might also explain the appearance of Amun with the epithet *nb p.t* 'lord of the sky' in the desert. It does not refer to any concrete cultic place (Lazaridis 2015, 51), and the mention of his lordship over the sky was probably perceived to have been enough to express the protection of this god over as unlimited a territory as the desert.

[6] In association with the systematising process of the Late Period, I would like to thank my anonymous reviewer for drawing my attention to the educated Late Period actors who might have found references to Ha in ancient sources.

References

Allen, J. P. 2005. *The ancient Egyptian Pyramid Texts*, Writings from the Ancient World 23. Leiden: Brill.

Allen, J. P. 2013. *A new concordance of Pyramid Texts*. Brown University. [online] ⟨https://www.dropbox.com/sh/0xo88uy04urnz0v/o16_ojF8f_⟩, accessed 19 November 2015.

Altenmüller, H. 2013. 'Zu zwei Titeln des Alten Reiches, ein Vorschlag zu ihrer Interpretation. Die Titel des "Priesters der Heqet" und des "Gefolgsmanns des Ha"'. In M. Bárta and H. Küllmer (eds.) *Diachronic trends in ancient Egyptian history. Studies dedicated to the memory of Eva Pardey*: 1–14. Prague: Charles University in Prague, Faculty of Arts.

Arafa, N. 2005. 'Le dieu Igai'. *Discussions in Egyptology* 63: 11–22.

Assmann, J. 1992. *Das kulturelle Gedächtnis. Schrift, Erinnerung und politische Identität in frühen Hochkulturen*. Munich: C. H. Beck.

Assmann, J. 2001. *The search for god in ancient Egypt*, trans. D. Lorton. Ithaca: Cornell University Press.

Aufrère, S. 1991. *L'univers minéral dans la pensée égyptienne* I. *L'influence du désert et des minéraux sur la mentalité des anciens Égyptiens*, Bibliothèque d'Étude 105/1. Cairo: Institut Français d'Archéologie Orientale.

Baines, J. 1985. *Fecundity figures. Egyptian personification and the iconology of a genre*. Warminster: Aris & Phillips.

Baines, J. 2007. 'Travel in third and second millennium Egypt'. In C. Adams and J. Roy (eds.) *Travel, geography and culture in ancient Greece, Egypt and the Near East*: 5–30. Oxford: Oxbow Books.

Blumenthal, E. 1982. *Altägyptische Reiseerzählungen: Die Lebensgeschichte des Sinuhe. Der Reisebereich des Wen-Amun*, Reclams Universal-Bibliothek 928. Leipzig: Reclam.

Bonnet, H. 1952. *Reallexikon der ägyptischen Religionsgeschichte*. Berlin: Walter de Gruyter & Co.

Černý, J. 1939. *Late Ramesside letters*, Bibliotheca Aegyptiaca 9. Brussels: Fondation Égyptologique Reine Élisabeth.

Chassinat, É. 1900. 'Textes provenant du Sérapéum de Memphis (suite)'. *Recueil de travaux relatifs à la philologie et à l'archéologie égyptiennes et assyriennes* 22: 9–26, 163–80.

Darnell, J. C. 2002. 'Opening the narrow doors of the desert: discoveries of the Theban desert road survey'. In R. Friedman (ed.) *Egypt and Nubia. Gifts of the desert*: 132–55. London: The British Museum Press.

Darnell, J. C., Darnell, D., Friedman, R., and Hendrickx, S. 2002. *Theban desert road survey in the Egyptian Western Desert* I. *Gebel Tjauti rock inscriptions 1-45 and Wadi el-Ḥôl rock inscriptions 1-45*, Oriental Institute Publications 119. Chicago: Oriental Institute of the University of Chicago.

Darnell, J. C. 2013. *Theban desert road survey* II. *The rock shrine of Paḥu, Gebel Akhenaton, and other rock inscriptions from the western hinterland of Qamûla*, Yale Egyptological Publications 1. New Haven: Yale Egyptological Institute.

Darnell, J. C., Klotz, D., and Manassa, C. 2013. 'Gods on the road: the pantheon of Thebes at Qasr el-Ghueita'. In C. Thiers (ed.) *Documents de théologies thébaines tardives (D3T 2)*, Cahiers 'Égypte Nilotique et Méditerranéenne' 8: 1–31. Montpellier: Université Paul Valéry – Montpellier III.

Davies, N. de G. 1953. *The temple of Hibis in el Khārgeh oasis* III. *The decoration*, Publications of the Metropolitan Museum of Art Egyptian Expedition 17. New York: Metropolitan Museum of Art.

Diego Espinel, A. 2012. 'Gods in the Red Land: development of cults and religious activities in the Eastern Desert'. In H. Barnard and K. Duistermaat (eds.) *The history of the peoples of the Eastern Desert*, Cotsen Monograph 73: 91–102. Los Angeles: University of California.

Fakhry, A. 1942. *The Egyptian deserts. Baḥria oasis* I. Cairo: Government Press.

Fecht, G. 1979. 'Die Berichte des *Ḥrw=ḫwj.f* über seine drei Reisen nach *J3m*'. In M. Görg and E. Pusch (eds.) *Festschrift Elmar Edel. 12. März 1979*, Ägypten und Altes Testament 1: 105–34. Bamberg: M. Görg.

Fiedler, N. 2011. *Sprüche gegen Seth. Bemerkungen zu drei späten Tempelritualen*. PhD thesis, Universität Heidelberg. [online] ⟨http://www.ub.uni-heidelberg.de/archiv/13643⟩, accessed 8 July 2015.

Fischer, H. G. 1957. 'The god and the general of the oasis on a stela of the late Middle Kingdom'. *Journal of Near Eastern Studies* 16 (4): 223–35.

Fischer, H. G. 1996. *Varia Nova*, Egyptian Studies 3. New York: The Metropolitan Museum of Art.

Förster, F. and Riemer, H. (eds.) 2013. *Desert road archaeology in ancient Egypt and beyond*, Africa Praehistorica 27. Cologne: Heinrich-Barth-Institut.

Galán, H. M. 2005. *Four journeys in ancient Egyptian literature*, Lingua Aegyptia Studia Monographica 5. Göttingen: Seminar für Ägyptologie und Koptologie.

Gardiner, A. H. 1917. 'Personification (Egyptian)'. In J. Hastings (ed.) *Encyclopedia of religion and ethics* IX: 787–92. Edinburgh: T. & T. Clark.

Gardiner, A. H. 1944. 'Horus the Beḥdetite'. *Journal of Egyptian Archaeology* 30: 23–60.

Gomaà, F. 1983. 'Bemerkungen zur Nekropole von el-Kom el-Ahmar Sawaris'. *Die Welt des Orients* 14: 135–46.

Goyon, J.-C. 1999. *Le papyrus d'Imouthès fils de Psintaês au Metropolitan Museum of Art de New York (papyrus MMA 35.9.21)*. New York: The Metropolitan Museum of Art.

Guglielmi, W. 1982. 'Personifikation'. In W. Helck, E. Otto, and W. Westendorf (eds.) *Lexikon der Ägyptologie* IV: 978–87. Wiesbaden: Harrassowitz.

Hannig, R. 2006. *Ägyptisches Wörterbuch* II. *Mittleres Reich und Zweite Zwischenzeit*. Mainz: Zabern.

Hassan, S. 1944. *Excavations at Giza V. 1933-1934. With special chapters on methods of excavation, the false-door, and other archaeological and religious subjects*. Cairo: Service des Antiquités de l'Égypte.

Hope, C. A., Bowen, G. E., Dolling, W., Healy, E., Milner, J., and Kaper, O. E. 2008. 'The excavations at Mut el-Kharab, Dakhleh oasis in 2008'. *The Bulletin of the Australian Centre for Egyptology* 19: 49–71.

Jéquier, G. 1938. *Fouilles à Saqqarah. Le monument funéraire de Pepi II* II. *Le temple*. Cairo: Imprimerie de l'Institut français d'archéologie orientale.

Josephson, J. A. and Eldamaty, M. M. 1999. *Catalogue général of Egyptian antiquities in the Cairo Museum. Nrs. 48601-48649. Statues of the XXVth and XXVIth dynasties*. Cairo: Supreme Council of Antiquities Press.

Kahl, J., Kloth, N., and Zimmermann, U. 1995. *Die Inschriften der 3. Dynastie. Eine Bestandsaufnahme*, Ägyptologische Abhandlungen 56. Wiesbaden: Harrassowitz.

Kees, H. 1941. 'Kulttopographische und mythologische Beiträge'. *Zeitschrift für Ägyptische Sprache und Altertumskunde* 77: 24–7.

Kees, H. 1980. *Totenglauben und Jenseitsvorstellungen der alten Ägypter. Grundlagen und Entwicklung bis zum Ende des Mittleren Reiches*, 4th ed. Berlin: Akademie-Verlag.

Kemp, B. J. 1983. 'Old Kingdom, Middle Kingdom and Second Intermediate Period c.2686–1552 BC'. In B. G. Trigger, B. J. Kemp, D. O'Connor, and A. B. Lloyd (eds.) *Ancient Egypt. A social history*: 71–182. Cambridge: Cambridge University Press.

Köpp, H. 2013. 'Desert travel and transport in ancient Egypt. An overview based on epigraphic, pictorial and archaeological evidence.' In F. Förster and H. Riemer (eds.) *Desert road archaeology in ancient Egypt and beyond*, Africa Praehistorica 27: 107–32. Cologne: Heinrich-Barth-Institut.

Köpp-Junk, H. 2013. 'Travel'. In E. Frood and W. Wendrich (eds.) *UCLA Encyclopedia of Egyptology*: 1–19. Los Angeles. [online] ⟨http://escholarship.org/uc/item/3945t7f7⟩, accessed 25 March 2015.

Kuhlmann, K. P. 2002. 'The "oasis bypath" or the issue of the desert trade in Pharaonic times'. In T. Lenssen-Erz, U. Tegtmeier, and S. Kröpelin (eds.) *Tides of the desert. Contributions to the archaeology and environmental history of Africa in honour of Rudolph Kuper*, Africa Praehistorica 14: 125–70. Köln: Heinrich-Barth-Institut.

Kuhlmann, K. P. 2005. 'Der "Wasserberg des Djedefre" (Chufu 01/1). Ein Lagerplatz mit Expeditionsinschriften der 4. Dynastie im Raum der Oase Dachla'. *Mitteilungen des Deutschen Archäologischen Instituts, Abteilung Kairo* 61: 243–89.

Lange, E. 2009. 'The sed-festival reliefs of Osorkon II at Bubastis. New investigations'. In G. P. F. Broekman, R. J. Demarée, and O. E. Kaper (eds.) *The Libyan Period in Egypt. Historical and cultural studies into the 21st-24th dynasties. Proceedings of a conference at Leiden University, 25–27 October 2007*: 203–18. Leiden: Nederlands Instituut voor het Nabije Oosten.

Lazaridis, N. 2015. 'Amun-Ra, lord of the sky: a deity for travellers of the western desert'. *British Museum Studies in Ancient Egypt and Sudan* 22: 43–60. [online] ⟨https://www.britishmuseum.org/research/publications/online_journals/bmsaes/issue_22/lazaridis.aspx⟩, accessed 26 November 2015.

Leitz, C. (ed.) 2002. *Lexikon der ägyptischen Götter und Götterbezeichnungen* I, Orientalia Lovaniensia Analecta 110. Leuven: Peeters.

Leitz, C. (ed.) 2002. *Lexikon der ägyptischen Götter und Götterbezeichnungen* V, Orientalia Lovaniensia Analecta 114. Leuven: Peeters.

Lichtheim, M. 1973. *Ancient Egyptian literature. A book of readings* I. *The Old and Middle Kingdoms*. Berkeley and Los Angeles: University of California Press.

Loprieno, A. 2003. 'Travel and fiction in Egyptian literature'. In D. O'Connor and S. Quirke (eds.) *Mysterious lands*, Encounters with ancient Egypt: 31–51. London: UCL Press.

Mariette, A. and Maspero, G. 1889. *Les mastabas de l'Ancien Empire. Fragment du dernier ouvrage de A. Mariette publié d'après le manuscrit de l'auteur par G. Maspero*. Paris: F. Vieweg.

Moers, G. 1999. 'Travel as narrative in Egyptian literature'. In G. Moers (ed.) *Definitely: Egyptian literature. Proceedings of the symposion "Ancient Egyptian literature: history and forms", Los Angeles, March 24–26, 1995*, Lingua Aegyptia Studia Monographica 2: 43–61. Göttingen: Seminar für Ägyptologie und Koptologie.

Moers, G. 2001. *Fingierte Welten in der ägyptischen Literatur des 2. Jahrtausends v. Chr. Grenzüberschreitung, Reisemotiv und Fiktionalität*, Probleme der Ägyptologie 19. Leiden: Brill.

Naville, E. 1892. *The festival-hall of Osorkon II in the great temple of Bubastis (1887–1889)*, Memoir of the Egypt Exploration Fund 10. London: Kegan Paul.

Neugebauer, O. and Parker, R. A. 1969. *Egyptian astronomical texts* III. *Decans, planets, constellations and zodiacs*, Brown Egyptological Studies 6. Providence: Brown University Press.

Riemer, H. and Förster, F. 2013. 'Ancient desert roads: towards establishing a new field of archaeological research'. In F. Förster and H. Riemer (eds.) *Desert road archaeology in ancient Egypt and beyond*, Africa Praehistorica 27: 19–58. Cologne: Heinrich-Barth-Institut.

Rochemonteix, M. and Chassinat, É. 1984. *Le temple d'Edfou* I, 1, Mémoires publiés par les membres de la Mission Archéologique Française au Caire 10, 2nd ed. revised and corrected. Cairo: Institut Français d'Archéologie Orientale.

Schott, S. 1929. *Urkunden mythologischen Inhalts. Bücher und Sprüche gegen den Gott Seth*, Urkunden des ägyptischen Altertums 6/1. Leipzig: Hinrichs.

Schumacher, I. W. 1988. *Der Gott Sopdu. Der Herr der Fremdländer*, Orbis Biblicus et Orientalis 79. Fribourg and Göttingen: Academic Press Fribourg; Vandenhoeck & Ruprecht.

Strudwick, N. 1985. *The administration of Egypt in the Old Kingdom. The highest titles and their holders*. London: Kegan Paul International.

Vercoutter, J. 1962. *Textes biographiques du Sérapéum de Memphis. Contribution à l'étude des stèles votives du Sérapéum*, Bibliothèque de l'École des Hautes Études. IVe Section, Sciences historiques et philologiques 316. Paris: Librairie ancienne H. Champion.

Wente, E. F. 1967. *Late Ramesside letters*, Studies in Ancient Oriental Civilization 33. Chicago: The University of Chicago Press.

Wildung, D. 1977a. 'Ha'. In W. Helck, E. Otto, and W. Westendorf (eds.) *Lexikon der Ägyptologie* II: 923. Wiesbaden: Harrassowitz.

Wildung, D. 1977b. *Imhotep und Amenhotep. Gottwerdung im alten Ägypten*, Münchner Ägyptologische Studien 36. Munich: Deutscher Kunstverlag.

Winand, J. 2011. '*The report of Wenamun: a journey in ancient Egyptian literature*'. In M. Collier and S. Snape (eds.) *Ramesside studies in honour of K. A. Kitchen*: 541–59. Bolton: Rutherford.
Yoyotte, J. 1964. 'A propos du panthéon de Sinouhé (B 205–212)'. *Kêmi* 17: 69–73.
Yoyotte, J. 1970. 'Travaux de la mission française des fouilles de Tanis en 1968–1969'. *Comptes rendus des séances de l'Académie des Inscriptions et Belles-Lettres* 114 (1): 32–40.
Yoyotte, J. 1991–1992. 'Égyptologie'. *Annuaire du Collège de France* 92: 628–34.
Yoyotte, J. 1993–1994. 'Égyptologie'. *Annuaire du Collège de France* 94: 667–70.

Chapter 6

Between geographical imaginary and geographical reality: Byblos and the limits of the world in the 18th dynasty

Marwan Kilani
University of Oxford, United Kingdom

Introduction

The aim of this article is to develop in more detail some issues touched on in my doctoral research, which focuses on the interactions and evolution of the city of Byblos in Lebanon during the Late Bronze Age. In that period, Byblos played an active role in the local geopolitical landscape, interacting politically and economically with various micro- and macro-regional actors. Various factors affected these interactions and the city's general development positively or negatively. In this paper I discuss one of these factors, namely an ideological change that may have occurred during the 18th dynasty and could have had a negative influence on Egyptian perceptions of Byblos. It is important to stress that this was most probably not the only factor affecting the fate of the city – the situation was certainly more complex and the product of a combination of different elements. The possible shift in ideology that I examine here, however, has not been discussed in this perspective and thus repays separate treatment. In order to understand this change, I introduce two ideological concepts in the next two sections.

Egyptian ideological narratives about the 'world' before the 18th dynasty

Like almost every society, Egyptians had a clear and well-structured ideological narrative about the geographical world around them. This paradigm, or 'cosmography', becomes fully evident during the Middle Kingdom, although its basic components and structures can be identified already in Old Kingdom sources.

As it is the case for many cultures, Egypt was the centre of the world (Allen 2003, 23; see also Loprieno 2001, 64–74). It could be defined in various ways (*tꜢwy*, *tꜢ-mry*, *kmt,* etc.) and its connotations were naturally positive. All around Egypt, encircling it, there were *ḫ3swt*, 'foreign lands', inhabited by people inherently negative and chaotic, and therefore hostile and inimical. The limits between Egypt and these foreign lands were marked by the *t3š(w)*, 'frontier(s)', of Egypt itself, coinciding with the ideological limits of the beneficial dominion of Pharaoh (Liverani 2001, 32; see Galán 1995, 101–35 for discussion).

The geographical cosmos of the Egyptians did not end there. As John Baines (2007, 14) points out, another term, 'God's Land', 'was used for distant, eastern places from Punt through Sinai to the Lebanese mountains. Despite the Egyptians' stereotyped (not necessarily real) contempt for foreigners and places abroad, remote regions had divine associations, as if they were nearer to the gods, in a conception of a "world" – that is, Egypt – surrounded by hostile areas, beyond which were inaccessible but idealized places at the edge of the larger cosmos'. These various realisations of 'God's Land' thus formed a second belt around Egypt. The distinction between 'foreign lands' and 'God's Land' does not seem to be marked by any defined border.

These 'God's Lands' were sources of rare and precious goods unavailable in Egypt (often referred to as *bj(3)w* or *bj(3)ywt*, 'wonders', 'marvels'), were inhabited by friendly foreigners, and were often associated with the goddess Hathor (see Cooper 2011 for a discussion of the term and critical review of previous scholarship). Appearing for the first time in the sources of the reign of Pepy II, the expression 'God's Land' is well attested in the Middle Kingdom and in later periods (Cooper 2011, 50–1). The concept of *t3 nṯr* seems to be predominantly associated with the 'east'. There are instances, however, where they are explicitly located to the north and to the south of Egypt (Cooper 2011, 52), but never to the west. As Julien Cooper suggests (2011), the *t3 nṯr* could correspond to the whole half of the horizon where the sun rises, thus including the east but also the north-east and the south-east, and could be understood as opposed to the west in the broadest sense, which was associated with sunset, death, and the Netherworld.

Two geographical entities appear to have been the archetypes of these idealised foreign lands: one is Punt, in the south, and the other is Byblos, in the north. As is apparent from many mentions in biographical inscriptions, these two lands were already perceived as geographically complementary in the Old Kingdom. The best example is in the 6th dynasty tomb of Khui at Qubbet el-Hawa (west bank of Aswan), where the names of Byblos and Punt are graphically associated and written as alternates within a single line (Urk. I, 140, l. 17; Newberry 1938; Diego Espinel 2004; Baines 2013, 251–2). The many references to travel to both places in biographical texts confirm the prestige they enjoyed in the Egyptian imaginary, both in the Old Kingdom and later (see for instance Allen 2008 and Marcolin 2010 for other examples of biographical texts of the Old and Middle Kingdoms in which expeditions to Byblos enjoy prominent positions). It is worth noting that, although they were sources of precious goods, Crete and the Aegean regions do not seem to have been considered 'God's Lands'. This is perhaps due to their relatively western location.

Finally, beyond the 'God's Lands' were the edges of the world. These edges were referred to in various ways. Two common terms were *pḥww/pḥwy* 'ends' and *ḏrw* 'ends', 'limits', which could qualify both the *tꜣ* 'land' or the *pt* 'sky' (see below; Galán 1995, 101–35, esp. 128–32: review of scholarship and discussion). At the limits of the world there were the *sẖnwt*, the (four) 'posts' of the sky, which could also indicate the limits of the world itself. The southern limit was also called *wpt tꜣ*, the 'brow/ forehead', while for the northern limit the expression *pḥww (stṯy)*, the 'rear/end (of Syria)', was used. These 'limits' marked the end of this world. As we read in an inscription of Hatshepsut (see below), beyond them is the darkness, a darkness that is more matter for theological speculation than geographical and ideological concern (see Allen 2003 for these mythical parts of the cosmos). The location of these borders, understandably, is not defined; they are just somewhere beyond the 'God's Lands'.

This cosmological structure is summarised graphically in Fig. 6.1. It must be noted that this narrative was an ideological construct and did not necessarily

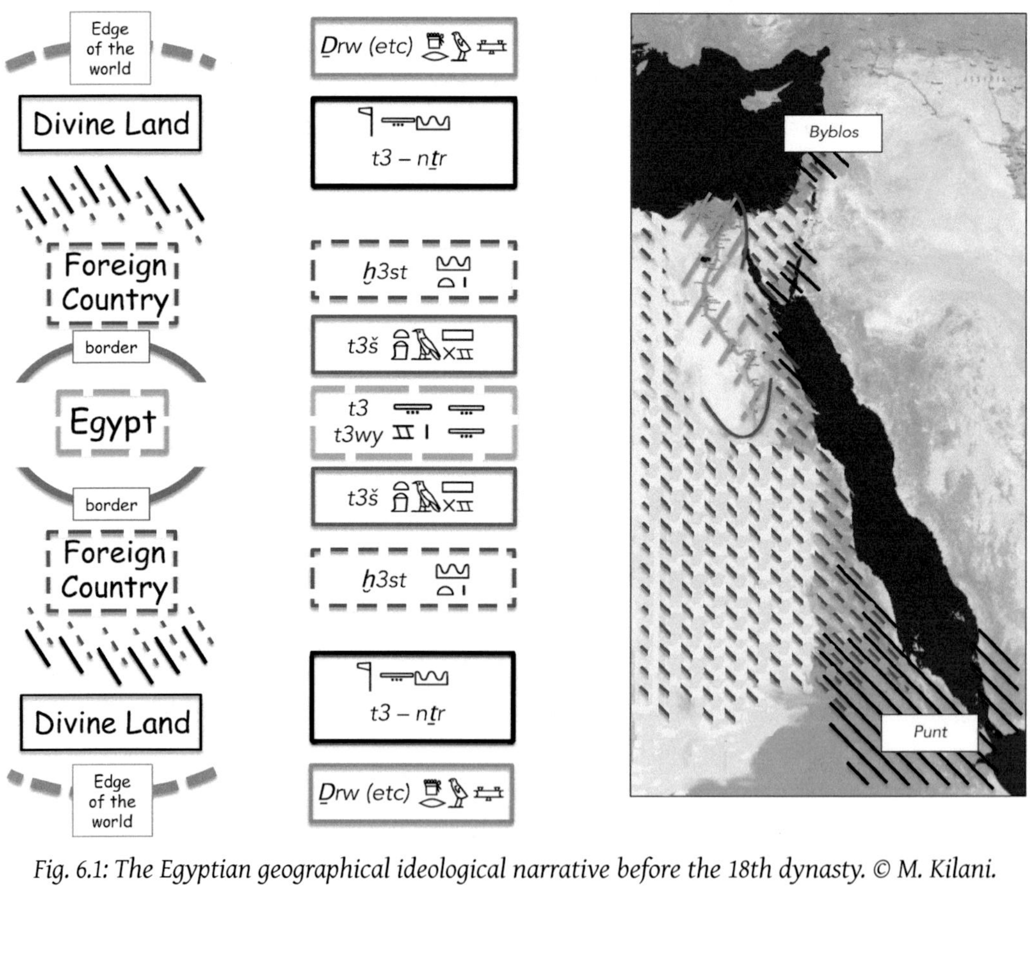

Fig. 6.1: The Egyptian geographical ideological narrative before the 18th dynasty. © M. Kilani.

reflect actual or potential Egyptian geographical knowledge. We cannot exclude that already in the Middle Kingdom, if not even earlier, Egyptians had some awareness or suspicion of the existence of territories located beyond this ideological frame, especially in the north. However, they were probably just too far, both geographically and geopolitically, to require any specific acknowledgement and therefore to affect or to be included into the main cosmographic narrative. Nevertheless, this narrative was ideologically central, and can also be recognised in the fictionalised geographical world of Middle Kingdom literature. There, Egypt, or better the royal residence, is the undisputed centre of the world (Loprieno 2001, 64–74), while highly fictionalised foreign lands characterised by generally positive features lie at its most distant extremes and constitute the limits of the narrative itself. For instance, the mythical island full of every good thing reached by the shipwrecked sailor, or the prosperous land where the good Amunenshi welcomes Sinuhe are perfect examples of such fictionalised and positively connoted lands at the end of the narrative framework.[1]

Finally, it is also worth noting that a very similar pattern emerges in Egyptian conceptions of time as well – and in conceptions of the past in particular. The 'centre' is the present, the domain of the current king, and therefore generally positively connoted. Before that, there was a 'near' past, the domain of the Pharaoh's direct predecessors. This 'near' past often had negative connotations or was at least conceived as worse than the present. Beyond this near past, however, there was an ideal and inherently positive 'remote' past that the current Pharaoh tried to imitate, restore, or even surpass. Neither the 'near' negative past, nor the 'remote' positive past is univocally defined. The first is obviously not fixed, but is continuously redefined in respect to the present itself. It can thus be identified with historical periods generally perceived as 'troubled' (such as the Second Intermediate Period, from the point of view of the early 18th dynasty 'present') or, simply, with the reigns of generic previous pharaohs, whoever they were and whatever they did. As for the 'remote' past, in some cases it is a purely mythical 'time of the god', and in other (especially later) contexts it corresponds to historically real periods that are in some way mythicised and commonly identified as times of success, prosperity, and grandeur. This is exemplified, for instance, by the use and revival of Middle Kingdom artistic elements in the Thutmosid period. This general framework is not spelled out in any source, but its elements and structure can be perceived for all periods of Egyptian history, as has been discussed by Baines (e.g. 1994, 135–8; 2007, 180–3) and Aldo Piccato (1997, 146–9, 152–5). These authors do not, however, describe the ideological framework that I am suggesting here, but they do discuss in detail the elements on which it is based.

[1] See Loprieno 2001, esp. 64–74, for a related discussion on geography in Middle Kingdom literature touching on many of these elements, although he does not spell out the ideological conception of foreign lands being proposed in this paper.

Geographical deeds and duties of the king

From the perspective of royal ideology, a good king was defined and characterised by a series of responsibilities, tasks, and duties. One of them was to *swsḫ tꜣš(w)*, 'to extend the border(s)' of Egypt (Galán 1995, 101–35, esp. 101–3). This concept was central in royal ideology, and it appears already in Middle Kingdom sources (Blumenthal 1970, 187–8). It is, for instance, the first attribute of Senusret III in a hymn from Kahun, where he is said to be the 'protector of the land, who extends his/its frontiers' (Pap. UCL 32157 = Pap. Lahun LV.1, col. 2; Griffith 1898, pl. 1). The same idea appears in Sinuhe: 'He (i.e. the king) is one who extends the frontiers' (Sinuhe B 71: Koch 1990, 38). This concept can also be expressed negatively; in Tutankhamun's Restoration Stela we read that 'the gods ignored this land, (so that) if troops were sent to Djahi to extend the frontiers of Egypt, no success at all would come about for them' (Urk. IV, 2027, l. 12–14). Obviously, from the point of view of Tutankhamun's reign, his predecessors were not good pharaohs and therefore the gods prevented them from extending Egypt's borders (Liverani 2001, 46).

The 18th dynasty: conquering the world

Until the New Kingdom, these two ideological concepts seem to have coexisted on two distinct planes without really interfering with each other. At the beginning of the 18th dynasty, however, they became combined and kings went beyond simply 'extending the borders' to 'extending the borders up to the limits of the world[2]' (Galán 1995, 129).

The earliest attestations of such claims are from the reign of Thutmose I. He was the first Pharaoh to lead military campaigns as far north as the Euphrates (or the Orontes) and as far south as Kurgus. In both places he carved commemorative inscriptions celebrating his conquest of the 'world' (Liverani 2001, 35–6). The one at Kurgus still exists, and it describes Thutmose as someone 'who goes beyond (lit. brings in) the limits of the land upon his area, who treads its two limits (*pḥwy*) with his successful khepesh' (Urk. IV, 85, l. 7–8), while 'his southern frontier is as far as the *Khentyw* of this land, the northern one as far as that inverted river (i.e. the Euphrates or the Orontes)' (Urk. IV, 85, l. 13–4).

It is clear, however, that Thuthmose I's actions in these distant regions did not amount to conquest. They were reached by the Egyptian armies, but were not 'annexed' to the Egyptian kingdom. As observed by Liverani (2001, 25), annexation was not indispensable: in order to claim control of these remote regions, and therefore of the world as a whole, it was enough to show (or claim) to the public in Egypt that the king and his armies could reach them if they so wished. These places retained a semi-mythical aura, perpetuating the idea that, being the farthest one could reach, they were indeed close to the limits of the world.

[2] Defining what this 'world' was is open to discussion and beyond the possibilities of this article. I would tend to think of a world as defined in and by previous narratives, but this side of the question is provisional.

Hatshepsut too committed herself to this ideological duty, but she seems to have chosen a different approach. Rather than sending armies to the north and south, and erecting stelae in remote and exotic locations, she turned her attention towards Punt, which had enjoyed a special status in the Egyptian imaginary at least since the Old Kingdom. A source of rare and precious goods, Punt had a clear economic attraction; Hatshepsut's expedition, however, was not merely a commercial venture. Rather, it was a divinely ordained (and ideologically motivated) mission aiming at extending her authority as far as the 'God's Land' so as to conquer the whole world, as we read in the account of the expedition inscribed in her temple at Deir el-Bahri: 'They (the gods) will put your frontier as far as the breadth of the sky, as far as the limits of total darkness' (Urk. IV, 248, l. 16–17; Naville 1898, 14, pl. 57; Galán 1995, 130; Creasman 2014, esp. 400–2; Taterka in this volume).

As a result of her successful expedition, Hatshepsut felt entitled to claim that 'he (Amun) made my frontier as far as the limits of heaven, so that what the sun-disc encircles labours for me' (Urk. IV, 368, l. 11–12) and that 'my southern frontier is as far as the shores of Punt, [the…being in my f]ist; the eastern frontier is as far as the limits of Asia, the Mentyw of Asia being in my fist' (Urk. IV, 372, l. 5–8). Once again, Hatshepsut's conquest was virtual, not actual; Egypt never annexed Punt. Still, the Egyptian ships could reach that exotic 'God's Land' without opposition, which was enough for her to claim dominion, and to affirm to have extended the borders of Egypt up to the limits of the world.

It was then Thutmose III's turn. To judge from his claims and actions (e.g. in the Annals, Urk. IV, 647, l. 12–14 and elsewhere), he was very aware that a good Pharaoh was expected to extend the borders of Egypt and was clearly determined to equal, and even surpass, his predecessors. He matched Thutmose I's exploits in his campaigns, reaching both the Euphrates (or the Orontes) and Kurgus (Redford 2003, 155, 158, n. 28 and *passim*). There, he set up inscriptions beside those of his grandfather: 'He set up another beside the stele of his father' (Urk. IV, 697, l. 5), and 'he set up his stele in Naharin, extending the frontiers of Egypt' (Urk. IV, 698, l. 15–699, l. 1). The Kurgus inscription still exists (Davies 2003).

Thutmose III also challenged Hatshepsut's exploits, but did so by going in the opposite geographical direction: while she went south, to Punt, he went north, to Byblos. In the Gebel Barkal stela we read: 'Now when My Majesty crossed over to the marshes of Asia, I had many ships constructed of cedar upon the mountains of God's Land, in the vicinity of the Mistress of Byblos' (Urk. IV, 1232, l. 1–3). For Thutmose III, no official account comparable to Hatshepsut's description of her expedition is known. Nonetheless, various royal and non-royal sources from his reign mention an expedition to Byblos, which presents similarities with Hatshepsut's account that can hardly be coincidental. For instance, local forms of Hathor played the role of intermediaries in both expeditions, both of which were also presented as realising the will of Amun. Moreover, Eckhard Eichler (1998, 223–8) observes that Sennefri's description of Thutmose III's expedition has some of the characteristics of a royal tale and is structurally similar to Hatshepsut's account. These similarities could suggest that literary compositions about Byblos analogous to that of Hatshepsut circulated in Thutmose's court. Finally, we know that Thutmose III also commissioned the 'botanical garden'; this room in the temple of Karnak has its lowest register decorated with 'various strange plants and various fine blooms which are in "God's land", br[ought to] His Majesty when His Majesty journeyed to Upper Retenu' (Beaux 1990, 41–2). These reliefs have a clear parallel in the parade of exotic plants and animals depicted in Hatshepsut's Deir el-Bahri temple, and in the real trees from Punt planted at its entrance.

It is thus clear that, as in the case of Hatshepsut's expedition to Punt, Thutmose III's to Byblos was not just a commercial enterprise, but a religious and ideological mission aiming at symbolically extending the dominion of the king up to the 'God's Land' and thus, once again, as far as the limits of the world. In this way, Thutmose III achieved similar feats to Thutmose I and Hatshepsut, which allowed him to make similar claims. He is described as one 'who reaches the limits of the foreign lands that had attacked him' (Urk. IV, 1229, l. 5), while 'his southern boundary stretches to the "Horn of the Earth", south of this land, and his northern one to the Marshes of Asia and the supports of heaven' (Urk. IV, 1230, l. 17–18). Thutmose further affirms: 'what the sun-disc encircles is in my fist' (Urk. IV, 1234, l. 4).

Thutmose III's exploits, however, were different from those of his predecessors. For the first time, the conquests were not just virtual but real. In contrast with Hatshepsut, whose expedition reached Punt and returned, Thutmose's reached Byblos, annexed it to his nascent empire, and went further. He really extended the *tꜣš* of Egypt to the 'God's Land' of Byblos and beyond, bringing its border in contact, not with the end of the world, but rather with other countries and powerful states. These newly reached geographical entities, although probably not completely unknown at the time, were now a concrete and 'close' reality that had to be officially acknowledged and could no longer be vaguely relegated at (or beyond) the limits of the main geographical narrative. As a result, this new geographical reality became increasingly distant from the ideological-geographical paradigm that I have described above.

The world after Thutmose III: a change of paradigm

The emergence and increase in discordance between ideal (and ideological) geographical narratives and geographical knowledge in a period of expansion and exploration is not unique to Thutmose III's Egypt. Rather, it is a phenomenon attested in different societies in various historical periods. Usually, two strategies have been adopted to deal with the resulting contrasts and paradoxes.

The first strategy consists essentially in abandoning the old paradigm after having recognised that it is erroneous, and either replacing it with a new one or moving to a more objective and realistic concept of geography as a whole. A good example of such a shift can be observed in pre-Hellenistic Greece, when the archaic idea of a circular (or shield-like) world, with Delphi at the centre of an island earth encircled by the river Ocean, started to be replaced with more elaborate and realistic geographical concepts (Romm 1992, 12–15). It has been suggested that this change occurred around the 5th century and was, at least in part, influenced by the geographical knowledge acquired through the colonial expansion in the Western Mediterranean and, to a lesser degree, the contacts with the Persian Empire. Traces of this cosmographic debate and shift can be seen for instance in Herodotus, who questioned and dismissed the existence of the river Ocean, thus dismissing the whole old paradigm (Romm 1992, 12–15, 32–6, but see 41–4 for the continuation of the debate in the following centuries).

The second possibility is to adapt the old paradigm to the new geographical knowledge, either by accommodating the new discoveries within it or by extending it beyond the limits of the new geographical reality. Some examples of this phenomenon include the European concept of 'India(s)' before and after Columbus; the myth of Eldorado, always located a little farther beyond the territories explored by the Europeans; and the medieval legend of Prester John's kingdom, a mythical Christian kingdom initially located somewhere beyond Muslim lands, and later found in various other regions including Central Asia, Russia, India, and Ethiopia, partially following the evolution of European geographical knowledge (Grousset 1970, 191; Beckingham and Hamilton 1996; Brooks 2014).

In the Egyptian case, the evidence suggests that both these strategies were adopted, at least at the beginning (Fig. 6.2). When the Egyptians conquered the northern Levant, i.e. one of the traditional regions considered a 'God's Land', regular contacts were established for the first time with other imperial powers such as the Hittite and Mitanni Empires, or Babylonia. The existence of these political entities, or rather the need to acknowledge their presence (as it is possible that Egyptians already had some knowledge of their existence before), undermined the centrality and political uniqueness that characterised Egypt in the old geographical narrative. Egyptians must have realised that this was so and, from the end of the reign of Thutmose III onward, the pharaohs engaged with the international scene in a way that demonstrates that they recognised and adopted a different, polycentric, and more realistic geographical paradigm. This change appears first and foremost from the Egyptian involvement in the diplomatic life of the Near East. It is possible, and even probable, that some form of international diplomatic interactions existed also before the New Kingdom, as could be implied, for instance, in the special regulations for Nubian messengers stated in Senusret III's Semna stela (recto, 4–5; see Obsomer 1989, 181–3). The evidence from the New Kingdom, however, shows a much more developed and complex system, involving elements that would have been hard to reconcile with the old cosmographic narrative. Treaties with new neighbours like the Mitanni or Hatti, attested in the sources for the first time during the reign of Thutmose III or Amenhotep II (Singer 2004), are an example. Such treaties implied Egyptian recognition of an equal status

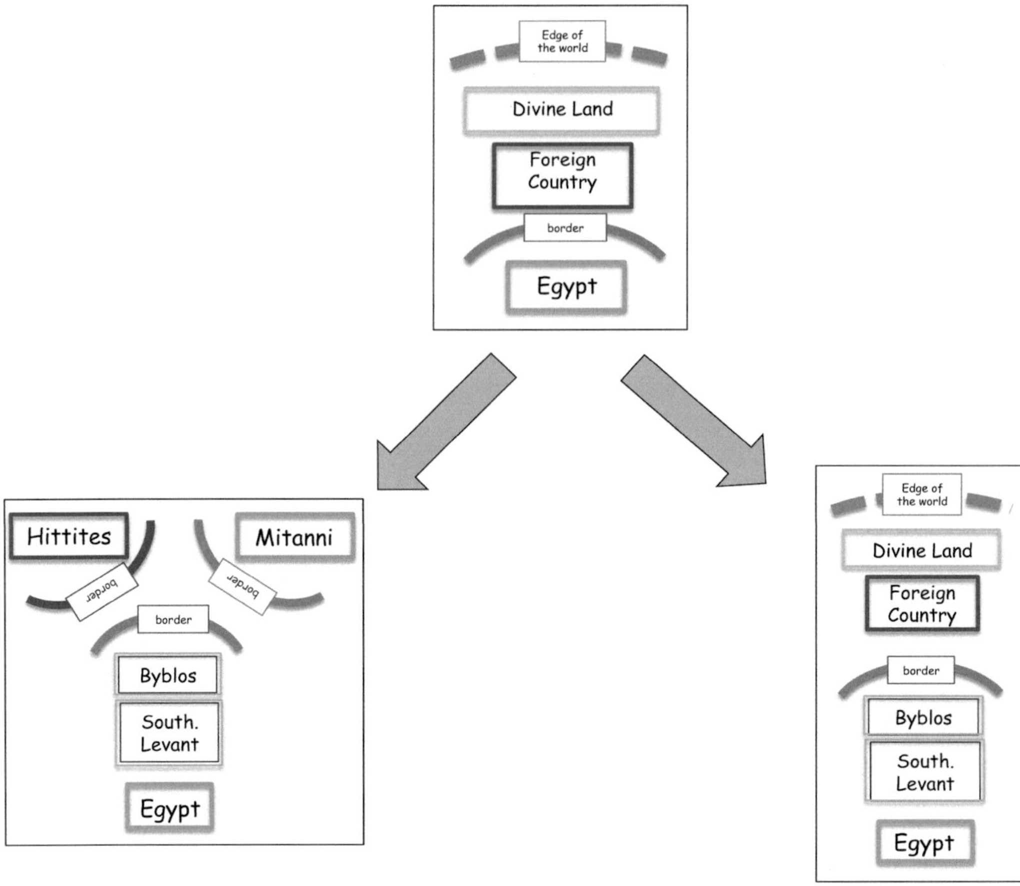

Fig. 6.2: After the 18th dynasty, Egypt adopted two strategies to cope with the new geographical reality; pragmatically abandoning the old paradigm while incorporating other foreign powers (left) and ideologically maintaining and extending it for the purposes of its own internal narrative (right). © M. Kilani.

to foreign countries. The latter, according to the old geographical paradigm and as new direct neighbours of Egypt, were supposed to be inherently and inevitably 'bad', 'chaotic', dangerous, and inferior; or were simply located in areas at, or even beyond, the limits of the old geographical narrative itself.

The increasing acceptance and conscious adoption of foreign cultural elements also hint at such a change. Various aspects of the culture and society were affected. For instance, an increasing number of foreign words was often consciously employed (Hoch 1994; Pap. Anastasi I: Fischer-Elfert 1986; Allen 1997; Schneider 2008), while new foreign cults and gods, sometimes sponsored by kings and states, made their appearance in Egypt, such as the cult of Ba'al and Astarte at Peru-Nefer (Collombert and Coulon 2000, 217–18, 220, 223). Trade was favoured in this new cultural environment, in turn bringing to Egypt more accurate knowledge about the geography of the external world and its organisation. An example of this could perhaps be seen in Amenhotep III's topographical lists at Kom el-Hetan, where we find the earliest attestation of Aegean cities in Egyptian sources (see e.g. Cline and Stannish 2011).

Another relevant topographical list from the reign of Amenhotep III is in the temple of Soleb, in Nubia. In contrast with its predecessors, this list is not simply a sequence of names of real or imaginary conquests. Rather, the geographical names are written on the bases of the columns of the hypostyle hall and are spatially organised according to their geographical position and, at least in part, to their political relevance in relation with Egypt. Thus, the aim of the list was probably not just to enumerate the conquests of the king, but also to represent the whole known world and its geopolitical organisation, both inside and outside the Egyptian sphere of influence (Grimal 2006, 111–13; Grimal 2009, 346). One could go further and suggest that the 'universalistic' nature of the god Aten could also have been influenced by such a paradigm shift, but this aspect of the question would need investigation that is beyond the scope of this article.

All these elements suggest that on economic, administrative, political, and diplomatic levels, the Egyptians were pragmatic enough to be aware of the limits of their traditional Egyptocentric paradigm; having discarded it or at least set it aside, they integrated themselves into a more polycentric and geographically neutral macro-regional frame. This shift was not sudden and immediate, but was a gradual process, and although Thutmose III's campaigns were possibly a catalyst, one should not underestimate the fact that Egypt had contacts with, and some knowledge of, these northern regions in earlier periods. It was, however, only at the time of Thutmose III that these distant territories and their inhabitants became real neighbours. They were not a vague and unimportant feature of a distant land anymore, but became an ordinary reality that had to be acknowledged and dealt with purposefully and politically.

Together with the pragmatic recognition of these connections, however, the older paradigm seems to have survived in royal display and narrative, and the traditional model was adapted to the new geopolitical knowledge and reality. Thus, in official documents, these neighbours and foreign powers beyond the newly extended *tꜣš* of Egypt end up being depicted as the traditional, inherently weak, dangerous and chaotic foreigners encircling Egypt, whether they were in fact enemies or allies. On a couple of occasions this Egyptian rhetoric even led to complaints by their Hittite allies (Brand 2007, 23). This disjuncture between the official royal narrative, which reiterated traditional Egyptocentric views, and the reality of Egyptian international relations, which exhibited a much more pragmatic perception of the world, has already been noted and discussed (e.g. Liverani 2001, 200–2). Here I suggest further that the disjuncture could correlate with, and at least in part reflect, the evolution of the Egyptian cosmographic conceptions discussed above.

Consequences of the change

Whether the Egyptians abandoned their paradigm entirely or adapted it to new geopolitical knowledge, Byblos and its area were surely affected by this shift. Within the old cosmographical frame, Byblos enjoyed the privileged status of 'God's Land' at the edges of the conceptually acknowledged world, a status that evidently played a role in the development of its interactions with Egypt, bringing prestige as well as political and economic advantages.

After Thutmose III's conquest, the city became a vassal state within the borders of Egypt, and consequently its status in the Egyptian imaginary was probably affected accordingly. Until the time of Thutmose III, Byblos was depicted as a distant, exotic but friendly city, renowned for its association with Hathor and for its precious and rare products. Afterwards, however, Byblos seems to have lost its aura of exoticism and remoteness – in contrast with Punt which maintained its mythical aura, perhaps also because it was never actually conquered. Reaching Byblos was not a feat, and although the city probably remained one of the sources for specific goods, it was no longer the only one, possibly not even the main one. The Egyptian commercial network in the Levant had expanded greatly, and Byblos was now one of many coastal cities and political entities – some even farther north – which were either in regular contact with Egypt or even controlled by it. Finally, the Egyptian perception of the Lady of Byblos changed significantly. During the New Kingdom and the early Iron Age, the Lady of Byblos passed from being a form of Hathor to being identified with Isis, who is attested in the city for the first time in the first half of the first millennium BCE, in a development that is difficult to date but that was probably gradual (Hollis 2009). Considering Hathor's association with the 'God's Land', this change is remarkable as it attests a modification in the mythological connections of the city within the Egyptian imaginary. At the same time, considering that a similar shift from Hathor to Isis happened in Egypt too, the development in Byblos could represent an attempt to reinterpret and explain the traditional knowledge that a very ancient Egyptian goddess dwelled in the city in order to fit it into the new cosmographic frame.

The letters of Rib-Addi, the king of Byblos during the Amarna period, are also relevant here (Moran 1992, 137–225). Their numerous references to the city goddess and to a past of friendship and reciprocal support, as well as their many complaints about current (real or perceived) neglect by the pharaohs, show that Rib-Addi was aware of the past prestige of Byblos and that he clearly realised that something had changed. While much in Rib-Addi's letters is rhetorical (Liverani 1974), details show that he had some awareness of the past history of his city (as I discuss in my doctoral thesis) and, to judge by his exasperation, did not seem to understand all the causes of what was happening.

The outcome of this process can be clearly seen in the *Tale of Wenamun*. A detailed discussion of the development of these geographical narratives at the time of Wenamun and in later periods is beyond the scope of this article, but it is worth noting that the Byblos depicted in the tale is very different from that of the time of Thutmose and before. Although the city is still described as a hub for trade in timber in the text, neither Hathor nor a local 'Lady of Byblos' are mentioned anymore, and the Egyptian expedition does not bring offerings for the Lady of Byblos' temple either. The Byblian king remembers and acknowledges its long tradition of interactions with Egypt, but no special prestige is attached to it. Moreover, although Byblos is the destination of Wenamun's expedition, it is not the only Levantine scene of the narrative. It is Wenamun's goal but not the final leg of his odyssey, and certainly not the 'limit' of the world in which the tale takes place; the misadventures of the Egyptian, in fact, continue with his being wrecked on Cyprus. Byblos is not a 'God's Land' at the edge of the world anymore; if anything, judging from the few surviving lines of the Cyprus episode, it is the island, rather than Byblos, that presents features of an exotic, mysterious but positively connoted land. This passage is incomplete, however, and is too short to draw any conclusion from it without a more detailed analysis.

It is possible that Byblos enjoyed short periods of revival, probably connected with some of the other factors mentioned at the beginning of this article; in particular under Ramesses II, perhaps due to its strategic value in the war against the Hittites, and later during the reigns of Shoshenq I and Osorkon I as a commercial partner.[3] However, its ancient prestige and favoured position were gone, and its status within the Egyptian geographical imaginary seems to have changed definitively.

Conclusions

I have suggested how ideological narratives about the structure of the world could have played a role in the definition of Egyptian international interactions, influencing crucial political undertakings. These same acts led to an improvement in Egyptian geographical knowledge, which came to encompass increasingly distant regions, becoming incompatible with those ideological narratives. The evolution of these ideas affected not only Egypt but also the fortunes of foreign regions. It is possible, and even probable, that the special position of 'God's Land' at the edge of the world enjoyed by Byblos in the traditional cosmography favoured the city and its commercial interactions. It perhaps also played some role, together with other factors, in the early 18th dynasty Egyptian expansion in the Levant. It is equally reasonable to propose that the change of paradigm brought to the fore by Thutmose III's conquests also played a role in the decline in Egyptian interest in the city, and hence ultimately in its own decline. The character of Egypt's international interactions cannot have been determined only by these ideological concepts, but it is likely they were a significant factor, one that has been little considered so far.

---

[3] This is further discussed in my doctoral thesis.

References

Allen, J. P. 1997. 'The craft of the scribe (Papyrus Anastasi I)'. In W. W. Hallo and K. Lawson Younger, Jr. (eds.) *The context of scripture* III. *Archival documents from the biblical world*: 9–14. Leiden: Brill.

Allen, J. P. 2003. 'The Egyptian concept of the world'. In D. O'Connor and S. Quirke (eds.) *Mysterious lands*, Encounters with ancient Egypt: 23–30. London: UCL Press.

Allen, J. P. 2008. 'The historical inscription of Khnumhotep at Dahshur: preliminary report'. *Bulletin of the American Schools of Oriental Research* 352: 29–39.

Baines, J. 1994. 'Ancient Egyptian concepts and uses of the past: 3rd to 2nd millennium BC evidence'. In R. Layton (ed.) *Who needs the past? Indigenous values and archaeology*: 138–48. London: Routledge.

Baines, J. 2007. 'Travel in third and second millennium Egypt'. In C. Adams and J. Roy (eds.) *Travel, geography and culture in ancient Greece, Egypt and the Near East*: 5–30. Oxford: Oxbow Books.

Baines, J. 2013. *High culture and experience in ancient Egypt*. Sheffield: Equinox.

Beaux, N. 1990. *Le cabinet de curiosités de Thoutmosis III. Plantes et animaux du 'Jardin botanique' de Karnak*, Orientalia Lovaniensia Analecta 36. Leuven: Peeters.

Beckingham, C. F. and Hamilton, B. 1996. *Prester John, the Mongols and the Ten Lost Tribes*. Aldershot: Ashgate.

Blumenthal, E. 1970 *Untersuchungen zum ägyptischen Königtum des Mittleren Reiches*. Abhandlungen der Sächsischen Akademie der Wissenschaften zu Leipzig, Philologisch-Historische Klasse 61/1. Berlin: Akademie-Verlag.

Brand, P. J. 2007. 'Ideological imperatives: irrational factors in Egyptian-Hittite relations under Ramesses II'. In P. Kousoulis and K. Magliveras (eds.) *Moving across borders. Foreign relations, religion and cultural interactions in the ancient Mediterranean*, Orientalia Lovaniensia Analecta 159: 15–33. Leuven: Peeters.

Brooks, M. E. 2014. 'Visual representations of Prester John and his kingdom'. *Quidditas* 35: 147–76.

Cline, E. H. and Stannish, S. M. 2011. 'Sailing the Great Green Sea? Amenhotep III's "Aegean list" from Kom El-Hetan, once more'. *Journal of Ancient Egyptian Interconnections* 3 (2): 6–16.

Collombert, P. and Coulon, L. 2000. 'Les dieux contre la mer. Le début du "papyrus d'Astarté" (pBN 202)'. *Bulletin de l'Institut Français d'Archéologie Orientale* 100: 193–242.

Cooper, J. 2011. 'The geographic and cosmographic expression *T3-nṯr*'. *Bulletin of the Australian Centre for Egyptology* 22: 47–66.

Creasman, P. P. 2014. 'Hatshepsut and the politics of Punt'. *African Archaeological Review* 31 (3): 395–405.

Davies, W. V. 2003. 'La frontière méridionale de l'Empire: les Égyptiens à Kurgus'. *Bulletin de la Société Française d'Égyptologie* 157: 23–37.

Diego Espinel, A. 2004. 'Minima epigraphica'. *Discussions in Egyptology* 59: 7–20.

Eichler, E. 1998. 'Die Reisen des Sennefri (TT 99)'. *Studien zur Altägyptischen Kultur* 26: 215–28.

Fischer-Elfert, H.-W. 1986. *Die satirische Streitschrift des Papyrus Anastasi I. Übersetzung und Kommentar*, Ägyptologische Abhandlungen 44. Wiesbaden: Harrassowitz.

Galán, J. M. 1995. *Victory and border. Terminology related to Egyptian imperialism in the XVIIIth dynasty*, Hildesheimer Ägyptologische Beiträge 40. Hildesheim: Gerstenberg.

Griffith, F. L. 1898. *The Petrie papyri. Hieratic papyri from Kahun and Gurob (principally of the Middle Kingdom)*. London: Bernard Quaritch.

Grimal, N. 2006. 'Les listes de peuples dans l'Égypte du deuxième millénaire av. J.-C. et la géopolitique du Proche-Orient'. In E. Czerny, I. Hein, H. Hunger, D. Melman, and A. Schwab (eds.) *Timelines. Studies in honour of Manfred Bietak* I, Orientalia Lovaniensia Analecta 149: 107–19. Leuven: Peeters.

Grimal, N. 2009. 'Quelques réflexions sur la géopolitique du Levant au deuxième millénaire av. J.-C.'. *Interconnections in the eastern Mediterranean. Lebanon in the Bronze and Iron Ages. Proceedings of the international symposium, Beirut 2008*, Bulletin d'Archéologie et d'Architecture Libanaises, Hors-Série 6: 339–60.

Grousset, R. 1970. *The Empire of the steppes. A history of Central Asia*, trans. N. Walford. New Brunswick: Rutgers University Press.

Hoch, J. E. 1994. *Semitic words in Egyptian texts of the New Kingdom and Third Intermediate Period*. Princeton: Princeton University Press.

Hollis, S. T. 2009. 'Hathor and Isis in Byblos in the second and first millennia BCE'. *Journal of Ancient Egyptian Interconnections* 1 (2): 1–8.

Koch, R. 1990. *Die Erzählung des Sinuhe*. Brussels: Fondation Égyptologique Reine Élisabeth.

Liverani, M. 1974. 'Rib-Adda, giusto sofferente'. *Altorientalische Forschungen* 1: 175–205.

Liverani, M. 2001. *International relations in the ancient Near East, 1660–1100 BC*. Basingstoke: Palgrave Macmillan.

Liverani, M. 2004. *Myth and politics in ancient Near Eastern historiography*. Ithaca: Cornell University Press.

Loprieno, A. 2001. *La pensée et l'écriture. Pour une analyse sémiotique de la culture égyptienne. Quatre séminaires à l'École Pratique des Hautes Études, Section des sciences religieuses, 15–27 mai 2000*. Paris: Cybele.

Marcolin, M. 2010. 'Una nuova biografia egiziana della VI dinastia con iscrizioni storiche e geografiche'. *Atti della Accademia delle scienze di Torino. Classe di scienze morali, storiche e filologiche* 144: 43–69.

Moran, W. L. 1992. *The Amarna letters*. Baltimore: The Johns Hopkins University Press.

Naville, É. 1898. *The temple of Deir El Bahari* III. *End of northern half and southern half of the middle platform*, Egypt Exploration Fund Memoir 16. London: Egypt Exploration Fund.

Newberry, P. E. 1938. 'Three Old-Kingdom travellers to Byblos and Pwenet'. *Journal of Egyptian Archaeology* 24 (2): 182–4.

Obsomer, C. 1989. *Les campagnes de Sésostris dans Hérodote. Essai d'interprétation du texte grec à la lumière des réalités égyptiennes*. Brussels: Connaissance de l'Égypte ancienne.

Piccato, A. 1997. 'The Berlin leather roll and the Egyptian sense of history'. *Lingua Aegyptia* 5: 137–59.

Redford, D. B. 2003. *The wars in Syria and Palestine of Thutmose III*, Culture and History of the Ancient Near East 16. Leiden: Brill.

Romm, J. S. 1992. *The edges of the earth in ancient thought. Geography, exploration, and fiction*. Princeton: Princeton University Press.

Schneider, T. 2008. 'Fremdwörter in der ägyptischen Militärsprache des Neuen Reiches und ein Bravourstück des Elitesoldaten (Papyrus Anastasi I 23, 2–7)'. *Journal of the Society for the Study of Egyptian Antiquities* 35: 181–205.

Singer, I. 2004. 'The Kuruštama treaty revisited'. In E. O. Forrer, D. Groddek, and S. Rössle (eds) *Šarnikzel. Hethitologische Studien zum Gedenken an Emil Orgetorix Forrer (19.02.1894–10.01.1986)*: 591–607. Dresden: Verlag der Technischen Universität Dresden.

Chapter 7

A journey through burial practices: the protection of the viscera in the 21st dynasty (*c.*1070–945 BCE) in Thebes

Solène Klein[1]
University of Oxford, United Kingdom

Introduction

The protection of the viscera through the mummification process was an essential and characteristic element of ancient Egyptian funerary culture, and implied the use of a specific range of objects directly related to the physical and conceptual protection of the viscera. The first attested elements for viscera protection are the well-known canopic jars and date to the Old Kingdom. In contrast to the consistent use of canopics in earlier periods (Klein 2013), the early first millennium BCE seems to be characterised by a wider range of possibilities for preserving and protecting internal organs: canopic jars, figurines of the Sons of Horus,[2] and viscera chests. While canopic jars and viscera chests physically held and protected the viscera, figurines of the Sons of Horus were placed on (or in) the viscera 'packages', directly inside the abdomen. Although they have been the subject of individual studies, they have never been considered as an ensemble of objects that should be approached as a distinct category, despite the fact that they adopt identical protective functions. Yet, due to their role in the preservation and protection of the body after death, they are key to understanding the transformations in funerary material and beliefs. In order to identify and understand these variations in viscera protection practice, it is essential to conduct a thorough analysis of the material within a wider funerary context that might highlight a rationale behind the transformations.

[1] This paper is drawn from the author's ongoing doctoral research on the protection of the viscera in the early first millennium BCE (21st–26th dynasties, c.1070–525 BCE).

[2] The Sons of Horus (Imset, Hapy, Qebehsenuef, and Duamutef) are appointed to the protection of the corpse of Osiris and are associated with his entrails. Therefore, they become equally involved in the protection of the viscera of the deceased (Servajean 2001, 263–9).

In this paper I explore the protection of the viscera in the 21st dynasty (*c.*1070–945 BCE) in Thebes through the analysis of two burial assemblages from the caches of Deir el-Bahri. In particular, I compare the burial of Nesikhonsu A (*c.*1003–973 BCE), wife of the high priest of Amun Pinedjem II, with that of Taihuty, a chantress of Amun under the pontificate of Pinedjem II (*c.*990–969 BCE). Their well-published contents offer a representative sample of the funerary practices in use in the Royal and the Second caches, to which they belong respectively. To observe how viscera were treated, I focus on selected elements of viscera protection: mummies, canopic jars, and figurines of the Sons of Horus.

The priests of Amun in Deir el-Bahri

In the 21st dynasty, the high priests of Amun assumed rule over Upper Egypt, in parallel with the Tanite kings in the north (e.g. Taylor 2003, 325–9; Jansen-Winkeln 2006). The Theban area thus became a 'state of Amun'. At that time, Deir el-Bahri became a priestly necropolis for the priesthoods of Montu and the Theban triad (Amun, Mut, and Khonsu) – and continued to be so up to the 25th dynasty. Most of the priestly burials were, therefore, located in the vicinity of Hatshepsut's temple, although the Deir el-Medineh cemeteries continued to be used (Aston 2009, 253–8), and few 21st dynasty intrusive burials have been found within New Kingdom tombs in the Assasif (TT 32, room 2: Aston 2009, 164) and Sheikh Abd el-Qurna (TT 55; TT 97: Aston 2009, 234–5). Consequently, the caches of Deir el-Bahri provide most of the Theban prosopographical data for the 21st dynasty.

The beginning of the Third Intermediate Period is characterised by significant changes in burial practices, which, in turn, had an impact on funerary furniture and viscera protection. In Thebes, in particular, there were a number of innovations in the treatment of the body proper; the most significant being an embalming process that tried to produce a less emaciated appearance (Elliot Smith and Dawson 1924, 110–20; Ikram and Dodson 1998, 124–8). For this reason, the four principal internal organs were returned inside the abdomen after having been wrapped separately, instead of being placed in canopic jars (Elliot Smith 1906b, 31–3).

Nesikhonsu A: a case study of the Royal Cache

The history of the discovery of the Royal (or First) Cache on 5th July 1881 by Gaston Maspero and Emile Brugsch in the first valley south of Deir el-Bahri is well known.[3] TT 320 was used as the original family vault of Pinedjem II including his two wives Isetemkheb D and Nesikhonsu A, his daughter Nesitanebashru, and Djedptahiuefankh, who was possibly Nesitanebashru's husband. The analysis of the burial contents (PM I,[2] 658–67; Aston 2009, 220–31, TG 918–22) shows that this family group owned

[3] For a comprehensive recount of the discovery, see Brugsch and Maspero 1881 and Maspero 1889, 511–26; for a modern synthesis, Graefe and Belova 2010, 13–36. For a recent synthesis of the Royal Cache history (i.e. the initial date of the cutting and original ownership of the tomb), for which two scenarios are still considered, see Jansen-Winkeln 2000 and Graefe 2003.

most of the objects found there. At a subsequent date, the tomb was reused as a cache for other members of the high priestly family of the 21st dynasty – Nodjmet, wife of the high priest of Amun Herihor; the high priest of Amun Pinedjem I, his wife Henettawy A, and his daughter, the god's wife Maatkare A; the high priest of Amun Masaharta and his wife(?) Tayuherit – and for the mummies and coffins of a number of pharaohs of the New Kingdom.

Identifying individuals and establishing genealogies is challenging in the Third Intermediate Period in general, and the 21st dynasty in particular, due to the scarcity of sources (e.g. Kitchen 1986, 40–71; Niwiński 1988a, 37–52). However, Nesikhonsu A, whose ancestors were generals and members of the Amun clergy – high priests, (first) chiefs of the musical troupe – is very well known from a number of objects and texts as a wife of Pinedjem II (Kitchen 1986, 65–6 §53; Niwiński 1988b; Naguib 1990, 168–72). Her family tree can be reconstructed from various documents. The property decree of Henettawy C carved on the tenth pylon of the precinct of Amun-Re at Karnak (Maspero 1889, 704–7, 710–11; Gardiner 1962, 57–64), for instance, indicates that the high priest of Amun Nesibanebdjedet II had a daughter named Nesikhonsu, who is generally regarded as Nesikhonsu A. This is supported by Nesikhonsu A's coffin inscriptions in which her father, unfortunately not named, is only referred to as a high priest of Amun. In an oracular amuletic decree from the burial (Cairo CG 58032: Maspero 1889, 594–614, pls. 25–7; Golenischeff 1927, 169–96; Gunn 1955, 83–105), Nesikhonsu A's mother is given as Tahentdjehuty. This decree also gives the names of Nesikhonsu A's children: Tjanefer B, Masaharta C, Itawy A, and Nesitanebetashru A.

The titles attributed to Nesikhonsu A on her funerary equipment acknowledge her high social status as wife of the high priest of Amun (Maspero 1889, 712–15; Gauthier 1914, 280–2; Naguib 1990, 169). She held the titles often granted to her position, for instance: leading lady, *ḥry(.t) wr.t ẖnr.t tp.t n(.t) Jmn-Rᶜ* 'first chief of the musical troupe of Amun-Re', and *ḥry(.t) tj.wt-šps* 'superior of the noblewomen'. Her other titles unexpectedly include *sꜣ-nsw n Kš* 'viceroy of Kush' and *(j)m(y)-r(ꜣ) ḫꜣs.wt rsy.wt* 'overseer of the foreign countries of the South'. Ordinarily held by men, both titles are attested for a woman for the first time. According to Naguib (1990, 169), these were probably honorary titles indicating that she received tax fees on Nubian trade, rather than evidence for an administrative function as such. To these titles were associated the southern priesthoods of Khnum and Nebet-Hetepet: *ḥm.t-nṯr n H̱nm nb Ḳbḥw* 'prophetess of Khnum lord of the cataract' and *ḥm.t-nṯr n Nbt-Ḥtpt n(.t) Sr(w)d* 'prophetess of Nebet-Hetepet of Serud'. Nesikhonsu's priestly titles offer some indications as to the extent of the influence of the administration of the temple of Amun up to the cataract, and provide an example of a broadly attested practice. The high priests of Amun and their family enriched their Theban titles with real or honorary priesthoods which entitled them to receive the related taxes (Naguib 1990, 185).

Nesikhonsu A's burial ensemble: features of content

Nesikhonsu's burial equipment (PM I^2, 664–6; Aston 2009, 227–9) was found in the crudely cut and undecorated burial chamber G (Reeves 1990, 185–6; Graefe and Belova 2010, pl. Plan02), alongside the funerary ensembles of the high priestly families. It included objects that had been either usurped or prepared specially for her – such as her canopic jars, shabtis, and *Book of the Dead* papyrus. However, as the cache was emptied by Brugsch in only two days without any archaeological documentation (Graefe 2003, 74; Graefe and Belova 2010, 77), the following corpus may not be complete and additional elements may have composed her funerary set.

Nesikhonsu's equipment consisted of wooden anthropoid outer- and inner-coffins with a mummy board (Cairo CG 61030), usurped from Isetemkheb D. Her wrapped mummy (Cairo CG 61095) was covered with an Osiris shroud (Cairo JE 26266), floral garlands, and leather ornaments. In the process of unwrapping the mummy, a wax embalmer's plaque, stone eyes, and a heart scarab (London BM EA 25584) were found. Four unused travertine canopic jars (London BM EA 59197–200) without canopic chest were included in her burial equipment. The funerary set also consisted of an Osiris figure containing a *Book of the Dead* papyrus (Cairo JE 26230), an oracular amuletic decree on papyrus, also called 'Amun decree' (Cairo CG 58032), a wooden stela (London UC 14226), three wooden writing boards (Cairo JE 46891; London 'McCullum Board' BM EA 16672; Paris Louvre 'Rogers Board' E 6858), a basket of 70 blue faience goblets, and blue glaze shabtis – without the two shabti boxes that formed the usual quota per person in the 21st dynasty (Aston 1994, 43).

Nesikhonsu's mummy (CG 61095) was partially unwrapped by Maspero on 27th June 1886 (1889, 578–9) and the process was completed by Grafton Elliot Smith 20 years later (1912, 107–9, pls. 82–4). It can be considered a typical example of the distinctive embalming technique of the 21st and 22nd dynasties. The body and limbs were stuffed with packing material introduced under the skin through specific localised entries. However, the distortion and exaggerated packing that marked earlier attempts (e.g. Maatkare A (CG 61088), Henettawy A (CG 61090): Elliot Smith 1912, 99–104, pls. 72–6) is not visible here, indicating that it dates to the late 21st–22nd dynasties. As observed by Elliot Smith (1912, 108) 'the body cavity is packed with sawdust' and the embalming wound indicates that the viscera were, at some point, extracted in order to be mummified separately. According to his report, neither viscera 'packages' nor wax figurines of the Sons of Horus were found during his examination. However, at the beginning of the 20th century, the observation of mummies was constrained by the limited use of non-invasive technologies such as X-rays.

Although it presents similar limitations, the assessment of mummification practices in the Royal Cache provides some insight into the treatment of the viscera. Excluding Nesikhonsu A, out of the ten other bodies of high priests of Amun and their family members, seven[4] were examined by Elliot Smith: Nodjmet (CG 61087), Maatkare A

[4] The mummy of the high priest of Amun Pinedjem I was apparently 'too dilapidated for exhibition' (Edwards 1882), there is no mummy for Tayuherit, and that of Isetemkheb D (CG 61093) was not unwrapped.

(CG 61088), Henettawy A (CG 61090), Masaharta (CG 61092), Pinedjem II (CG 61094), Nesitanebashru (CG 61096), and Djedptahiuefankh (CG 61097). From that group, only three actually contained wrapped bundles of viscera: Henettawy A, Pinedjem II, and Djedptahiuefankh. The others, while having undergone the packing procedures customary of the time, were packed with sawdust with no traces of viscera.

A set of four unused travertine canopic jars (BM EA 59197–200: Edwards 1883, 80–1; Maspero 1889, 712; Taylor 2010, 84, fig. 27) classified as David Aston's type I (2009, 293–5), belonged to Nesikhonsu. Canopics of this type are described as having a high shoulder and straight sides slanting towards the base. They generally bear an inscription in two to four columns on the front. Aston observed that all published jars of this type are made of travertine. The stoppers are more variable, either made of travertine or plastered wood. The headdresses are either plain or decorated with stripes. In Nesikhonsu's set, the stoppers adopt the animal iconography of the Sons of Horus – baboon for Hapy, hawk for Qebehsenuef, jackal for Duamutef, and human for Imset – perpetuating the tradition attested from the end of the New Kingdom onwards. The jars are fully hollowed out without any trace of their contents, although there are some light stained brown marks on the inside walls. These marks may be the result of secondary deposition (sawdust, mud, or resin) that may have entered the jars subsequent to the burial. Indeed, their position at the top of the jars as well as their colour do not tally with the dark resinous material usually found at the bottom when viscera were contained in the jar.

The four columns of text on Nesikhonsu's canopics are identified as type XIV of Kurt Sethe's typology (1934, 9*), regularly found from the 21st dynasty onwards. They report the words spoken by the Sons of Horus to the Osiris of Nesikhonsu, giving her offerings of incense, cloth, bread, water, and the ability to come and go in the necropolis. They attest to significant changes in the textual content of the Third Intermediate Period canopic jars: the formulae for the protection of the viscera, associated with the Sons of Horus on canopics from the Middle Kingdom onwards (Sethe 1934, 1*–8*), is replaced with offering formulae. This dissociation from exclusive protection of the viscera in the texts may point to an extended use of these objects, apart from that of containers for viscera.

A survey of the funerary material found in the ten other burials of the Royal Cache (Aston 2009, 220–31; Dodson 1994, 78–80, 82–3) reveals that three contained only canopic jars: Isetemkheb D, Pinedjem II, Nesitanebashru. Henettawy A had both canopic jars and figurines of the Sons of Horus, while Nodjmet and Djedptahiuefankh had only figurines. The presence of the organs inside the mummies of Henettawy A and Pinedjem II confirms, in their case at least, that their sets of canopics were actually not intended for the organs. No information, however, is available regarding the contents of the canopics of Isetemkheb D (Dodson 1994, 83, pl. 36a) and Nesitanebashru (Dodson 1994, 83, pl. 36b).

The above observations of the funerary practices in the Royal Cache are summarised in Table 7.1.

Table 7.1: Elements of viscera protection in the Royal Cache. © S. Klein.

	Viscera (mummy)	Canopic jars sets	Figurines of Sons of Horus
Nodjmet (TG 912)	No (CG 61087)	No. But canopic chest	Yes
HPA Masaharta (TG 913)	No (CG 61092)	No	No
Tayuherit (TG 914)	x	No	x
HPA Pinedjem I (TG 915)	x	No	x
Henettawy A (TG 916)	Yes. Fragments of intestine (CG 61090)	Yes. BM EA 51814–51817	Yes (2)
Maatkare A (TG 917)	No (CG 61088)	No	No
Isetemkheb D (TG 918)	x (CG 61093)	Yes. JE 26254 A-D	x
Nesikhonsu A (TG 919)	No (CG 61095)	Yes. BM EA 59197–59200	No
HPA Pinedjem II (TG 920)	Yes (CG 61094)	Yes. Brisco Eyre collection	No
Nesitanebashru (TG 921)	No (CG 61096)	Yes. JE 26256 A-D	No
Djedptahiuefankh (TG 922)	Yes (CG 61097)	No	Yes (1)

Key. No: not attested; Yes: attested; x: no information. TG: tomb group number (Aston 2009).

Taihuty: a case study of the Second Cache

Placed in the courtyard of Hatshepsut's mortuary temple, near the north-eastern corner of the wall (Winlock 1924, 7, fig. 2, 20, n. 5), the Second Cache (also known as Bab el-Gusus) was excavated in 1891 by Eugène Grébaut and Georges Daressy for the Egyptian government. It had been used as a cache for the burials of 153 individuals, all priestly members of Amun's cult in Thebes, in the 21st dynasty (Daressy 1900; Maspero 1915, 274–81; Winlock 1924, 20–9; Aston 2009, 164–98, TG 674–826). Many of these priests, prophetesses, and chantresses of Amun had a considerable number of funerary goods stored with them but, as the cache was hastily emptied (Daressy 1900, 144–5), no records were kept of many of these objects – only the coffins were systematically numbered with Daressy's A-numbers (1907, 4–14) – and their present locations are unknown.

These shortcomings may have naturally impacted Taihuty's burial equipment (A.32) as well, and some of her funerary items may now consequently be lost. Additionally, most of her (known) funerary set is made up of uninscribed and/or reused objects that may have originally belonged to someone else. Therefore, little is known about Taihuty since her outer coffin is the only element bearing her name and title and, to the best of my knowledge, no additional title is recorded anywhere else. She was *šmꜥy.t n Jmn* 'chantress of Amun', a title often, but not exclusively, borne by females related to the priestly lower class in Thebes at the end of the 21st dynasty (Naguib 1990, 235–9).

Taihuty's burial ensemble: features of content

Taihuty's funerary equipment (Elliot Smith 1906a, 156–7; PM I^2, 638; Aston 2009, 168–9) was noted as being 'one of the large series found at Dêr el-Bahari by M. Grébaut in 1891' (Elliot Smith 1906a, 155). The ensemble consisted of a mummiform outer coffin (London BM EA 24793) containing an anonymous inner coffin (London BM EA 24794) and mummy board (London BM EA 24795).[5] Her mummy was covered with an Osiris shroud, mummy braces bearing the name of Pinedjem II, along with a copper hawk pectoral and a heart scarab usurped from Pawah on the chest. The unwrapping of the mummy revealed a copper embalmer's plaque as well as a Thoth plaque and blue glazed *djed* amulets on the left arm, near the elbow. Most importantly, wax figurines of the Sons of Horus were found within the body (Elliot Smith 1906a, 157). A *Book of the Amduat* had also been placed between the legs of the mummy (Cairo SR 15444).

From May 1891 onwards, Daressy and Dr Daniel Fouquet started the examination of the mummies (Daressy 1907, 21–38; Daressy and Elliot Smith 1903), unwrapping most of them. The work was then continued by Elliot Smith, who examined Taihuty's mummy in July 1905 in the presence of Brugsch and Daressy (Elliot Smith 1906a). Taihuty was mummified according to the embalming process typical of the 21st dynasty; inside her body Daressy discovered four wax figurines of the Sons of Horus that he described as '[t]outes ont la forme ordinaire, le corps momifié et les mains sur la poitrine' (Elliot Smith 1906a, 157). His observations were later confirmed by Elliot Smith's study (1906a, 165, pl. 1, *c–f*). Taihuty's viscera had been replaced in the abdomen, along with mummiform figurines of the Sons of Horus depicted with their characteristic animal heads and tripartite wigs. Their fists were closed on their chest in a symbolic gesture of holding attributes. Unusually, two human-headed figures were used, one instead of the expected hawk-headed figure of Qebehsenuef (Elliot Smith 1906a, pl. 8 [6–9]). This seemingly rare feature in the cache may point to iconographic and conceptual shifts, as I discuss below.

Most of the mummies from the Second Cache seem to have been unwrapped, but detailed information regarding the treatment of the viscera is limited to the published results of only four other burials: Nesipakaf (A.23), Nestanebtawy (A.88), Neskhons (A.42), Tauhenut (A.20) (Daressy and Elliot Smith 1903, 156–60). In all of these examples, the organs were replaced inside the body, accompanied by wax figurines of Imset, Hapy, Qebehsenuef, and Duamutef; no canopic jars were associated with the burials. Any sense of broader patterns in the cache relies on the conclusions of Elliot Smith (1906b) who compared the arrangement of the organs in 44 mummies of the same period – practically all of them priests of Amun coming from Bab el-Gusus: 'there is no uniformity in the treatment of the viscera nor in the placing of the organs or the wax figurines [in the mummies of the Second Cache]' (Daressy

[5] Aston (2009, 168) assigns EA 24798 (inner coffin) and EA 24799 (mummy board) to Taihuty. These objects, however, adopt an iconography characteristic of men's coffins. Therefore Niwiński's attribution of EA 24794 and EA 24795, which belonged to a woman, to Taihuty's coffins ensemble is more likely (1988a, 153).

and Elliot Smith 1903, 159–60), 'in about 50% of the mummies examined no funerary figures were found. In many cases this was no doubt due to the damage inflicted on the mummies…before they came into my possession; but in a considerable number of instances no Genii had been put in the body' (1906b, 37). Aston's publication of the 153 burials (2009, 164–98) allows the identification of the mummies, studied by Elliot Smith, that contained figurines. Seventeen individuals,[6] in addition to Daressy and Elliot Smith's four, had wax figurines of the Sons of Horus associated to organs within their bodies; none of them had canopic jars in their funerary set.

Even though the sample is small (48 mummies out of 153 individuals) and the publication fragmentary, a pattern in the practice of viscera protection in the Second Cache seems to arise, wherein figurines of the Sons of Horus appear to be significantly preferred over canopic jars. However, it is worth noting that sixteen canopics were discovered in the cache (Aston 2009, 197), of which only four can be traced (Meretamun: Aston 2009, 175–6, TG 744).

The above observations are summarised in Table 7.2.

Table 7.2: Elements of viscera protection in the Second Cache. © S. Klein.

	Viscera in mummy	**Canopic jars sets**	**Figurines of Sons of Horus**
Taihuty (TG 705)	Yes	No	Yes
Second Cache Bab el-Gusus (153)	Yes. Seemingly all of 48? mummies	Yes (4?/153)	Yes (21/48)

Key. No: not attested; Yes: attested; TG: tomb group number (Aston 2009).

Only a limited number of figurines have been published (Elliot Smith 1906b, 40–1, pls. 17–19) and the scarcity of the related information makes it difficult to produce a large scale analysis of their iconography or position in the body. In a couple of cases from the cache (Taihuty; Nestanebtawy: Aston 2009, 178–9) human-headed figures were used in place of the hawk-headed figure of Qebehsenuef. Contrary to Aston (2009, 169, n. 974) and Elliot Smith (1906a, 182), I do not think this was an unintentional 'mistake' as similar iconography shifts are visible in New Kingdom papyrus' vignettes of *Book of the Dead* 151 (Lüscher 1998, 27–31). For example, in the papyrus of Nakht (London BM EA 10471), the human iconography is used for three of the Sons of Horus with the exception of Hapy, while in the papyrus of Nebqed (Paris Louvre N 3068+N 3113), Duamutef adopts the human-headed figure along with Imset (Lüscher 1998, 29). One hypothesis for the preferential use of the human iconography primarily associated with Imset is that the characteristics of each individual's personality (e.g. Maat) are found in the liver, the organ assimilated to Imset (Meeks 1995; Servajean 2001, 264, n. 21). The protection of these characteristics was perhaps being emphasised through the use of two human-headed figures.

[6] See Aston 2009, 166–89: TG 685, TG 711, TG 716, TG 717, TG 721, TG 727, TG 732, TG 737, TG 738, TG 758, TG 764, TG 779, TG 780, TG 792, TG 800, TG 807, and TG 808.

A second hypothesis is suggested through the formula of Imset on Nesibanebdjedet I's canopic jars (Dodson 1994, 79, 173 [41/1]). By indicating that '[Imset] s'unit au corps divin de Rê…en même temps qu'il s'unit au corps osirien du mort' (Yoyotte 1986, 172), the association of Imset with both Re and Osiris is emphasised. In the context of the development of the solar–osirian cycle (Niwiński 1989; Smith, forthcoming), two figures of Imset were perhaps employed to highlight the association of the deceased with both Re and Osiris.

Discussion

Although tentative – as the picture could be skewed by the statistically small and fragmentary sample, the lack of publication or archaeological record at the time of excavation and/or the modern dispersion of funerary components – these two case studies allow for a picture of the practices of viscera protection in the caches of Deir el-Bahri to be drawn. Additionally, the analysis of these practices provides some preliminary answers to the transformations in funerary material in the 21st dynasty.

The protection of the viscera in Deir el-Bahri

Nesikhonsu A's and Taihuty's mummies reveal similarities in the treatment of the body. Both were mummified following the practice of the 21st dynasty, with the embalming of the corpse in a way that tried to produce a less emaciated appearance. Their viscera, however, were treated differently which, in turn, impacted on the material associated with viscera protection; therefore, the two burial ensembles present disparities. Such dissimilarities also extend to the other individuals from the Royal and Second caches.

In the Royal Cache (see Table 7.1), even though the organs were systematically removed as attested by the embalming wound on the eight mummies examined, they were not necessarily replaced inside the body – five mummies (Nodjmet, Masaharta, Maatkare A, Nesikhonsu A, Nesitanebashru) did not contain viscera. These removed viscera were not systematically placed in canopic jars either given that there are no sets of jars for three of them (Nodjmet,[7] Masaharta, Maatkare A). In three other mummies the viscera were found within the body: for Djedptahiuefankh wax figurines of the Sons of Horus were used; for Pinedjem II canopic jars were associated with the burial; for Henettawy A wax figurines and canopics occurred concurrently. Therefore, canopic jars were present in five tomb groups (Nesikhonsu A, Nesitanebashru, Pinedjem II, Henettawy A, Isetemkheb D). Their examination,[8] however, indicates that at least three of these sets were not used (Nesikhonsu A, Henettawy A, Pinedjem II). Additionally, wax figurines of the Sons of Horus were recovered from three bodies (Nodjmet, Henettawy A, Djedptahiuefankh). These were not used concurrently with the jars, except in the case of Henettawy A who possessed both. Finally, there are no

[7] Nodjmet, however, had a canopic chest (Dodson 1994, 78, pl. 31b) indicating that she may have owned such items.

[8] There is no information available on the contents of Nesitanebashru and Isetemkheb D's canopic jars.

elements for viscera protection, that is canopic jars or wax figurines, in Masaharta's and Maatkare A's burials.

In contrast, in the Second Cache (see Table 7.2), the mummified organs seem to have been systematically replaced within the body – as they were apparently found within all the mummies studied. They were accompanied by wax figurines of the Sons of Horus in approximately half of the cases. No sets of canopic jars were included in the equipment of these 23 individuals but a small quantity, at least four sets, was found in the cache.

These various considerations are summarised in Table 7.3. Although individuals from these caches were buried in the same place at the same time (Deir el-Bahri, 21st dynasty), the practices of viscera protection are substantially different, raising questions as to the reasons for this difference.

Nesikhonsu A and Taihuty were both women living under Pinedjem II's pontificate and were buried in Deir el-Bahri. Considering that the time, place, and gender of both are identical, the only difference between them is, in fact, their priestly status. Nesikhonsu was the wife of the high priest of Amun Pinedjem II, first chief of the musical troupe of Amun-Re, which afforded her a higher priestly status than Taihuty, a chantress of Amun. Interestingly, this difference in status applies more broadly to the individuals buried in these caches; only high priests of Amun and their family were found in the Royal Cache, while the Second Cache is dedicated to priests, prophetesses and chantresses of Amun. Therefore, one could suggest that the differences in practice in Deir el-Bahri are a mark of 'priestly social status': canopic jars were preserved for members of the priestly upper classes whereas wax figurines were in use in 'lower' priestly elites.

Canopic jars and figurines: different aspects of the Sons of Horus?

The process of placing the organs back into the body, associated with the four Sons of Horus through the use of wax figurines wrapped in viscera 'packages', theoretically made canopic jars redundant. However, their ongoing presence in tombs indicates that they remained essential objects, even though they were not systematically used anymore for the purpose of containing and physically protecting viscera. Looking at the caches, it appears that figurines and canopics were not used simultaneously. Therefore, it could be inferred that there was no need for canopic jars when the protection of the organs was assured by the figurines.

Table 7.3: Elements of viscera protection in Deir el-Bahri. © S. Klein.

	Viscera in mummy	Canopic jars sets	Figurines of Sons of Horus
Royal Cache TT 320 (11)	3 out of 8 mummies	Yes (5/11)	Yes (3/8)
Second Cache Bab el-Gusus (153)	Yes. Seemingly all of 49? mummies	Yes (4?/153)	Yes (22/49)

Considering that the canopics were present, even if unused and their protective role apparently taken over by wax figurines, one could ask whether canopics communicated new ideas or whether they were kept simply out of tradition. For basic economic reasons at least, the latter seems unlikely. Pressures on the Theban economy in 21st dynasty meant that no elaborate tombs were built and cemeteries were 'managed' more rigorously, with mummies being hidden in cache tombs (Cooney 2012, 144–7). The range of grave goods is reduced in comparison to earlier periods, implying that only the most meaningful funerary elements would be retained. Perhaps the commissioners of the priestly upper classes were interested in the social prestige they might receive from funerary display. For most of the Third Intermediate Period, richly decorated tombs were replaced by caches devoid of paintings and reliefs. As

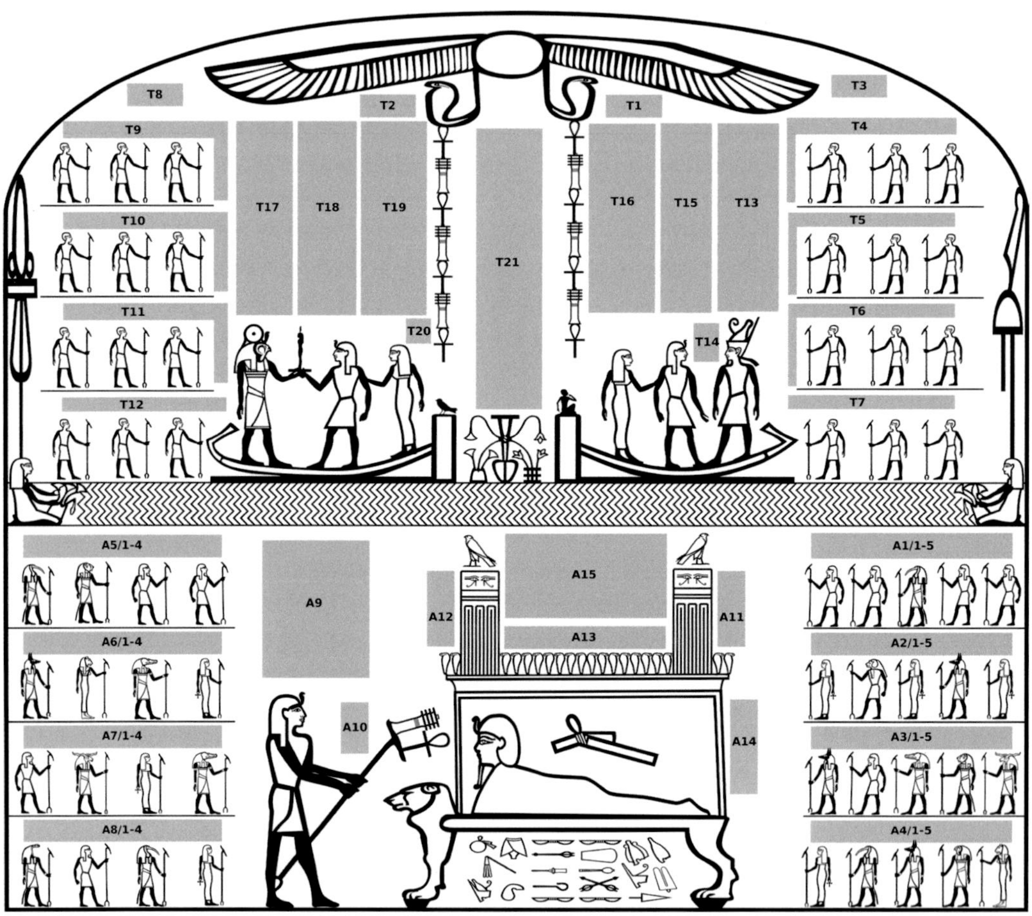

Fig. 7.1: Schematic diagram of the Awakening of Osiris (lower register). The Sons of Horus are depicted in registers A1/1–2 (Duamutef, Qebehsenuef) and A5/1–2 (Imset, Hapy). Roberson 2013, 2, fig. 1 (corrected, reproduced by permission of the author).

Kathlyn Cooney suggested for the coffins (2011, 29), if the tomb owner was not able to display decorated tomb walls, perhaps the canopic jars (alongside the coffins) were meant to fill this role of social display at the funeral.

Additionally, canopic jar texts from the 21st dynasty evolve from asserting protection (Sethe 1934, 1*–8*) to offering formulae (Sethe 1934, 9*), pointing to some conceptual shifts in the ideas they communicate. Therefore, the presence of canopic jars which do not contain viscera anymore in the burial could be understood as a change in the symbolic function of the canopic; it had now assumed an importance quite separate from its role as a container ensuring a physical protection of the organs. This reinterpretation of their conceptual function may relate to changes in the role of the Sons of Horus. One hypothesis, supported by material and textual observations, is that canopic jars are embodiments of the Sons of Horus, acting as protectors of the deceased. In earlier times, the Sons of Horus were prominently assimilated to the organs (Gardiner 1947, 245–50; Servajean 2001), participating in the reconstruction of the body. From the Third Intermediate Period onwards, changes (of use and of texts) seen in the canopics could indicate that the role of the Sons of Horus was extended from specifically protecting the organs to guarding the complete body.

As differing roles of the Sons of Horus may have coexisted, it is feasible that canopic jars and wax figurines performed slightly different functions and thus conveyed different aspects of the Sons of Horus. I suggest that the wax figurines of the four Sons replace the canopic jars and stand for their role as protectors of the organs while the canopic jars transform. They become embodiments of the Sons of Horus and manifest their role as protective deities who watch over the deceased's – assimilated to Osiris – corpse, as depicted in the Awakening of Osiris (Fig. 7.1; Roberson 2013).

References

Aston, D. A. 1994. 'The shabti box: a typological study'. *Oudheidkundige Mededelingen uit het Rijksmuseum van Oudheden* 74: 21–54.

Aston, D. A. 2009. *Burial assemblages of dynasty 21-25. Chronology – Typology – Developments*. Vienna: Verlag der Österreichischen Akademie der Wissenschaften.

Brugsch, E. and Maspero, G. 1881. *La trouvaille de Deir el-Bahri*. Cairo: Imprimerie française F. Mourès.

Cooney, K. 2011. 'Changing burial practices at the end of the New Kingdom: defensive adaptations in tomb commissions, coffin commissions, coffin decoration, and mummification'. *Journal of the American Research Center in Egypt* 47: 3–44.

Cooney, K. 2012. 'Objectifying the body: the increased value of the ancient Egyptian mummy during the socioeconomic crisis of dynasty 21'. In J. Papadopoulos and G. Urton (eds.) *The construction of value in the ancient world*: 139–59. Los Angeles: Cotsen Institute of Archaeology Press.

Daressy, G. 1900. 'Les sépultures des prêtres d'Ammon à Deir el-Bahari'. *Annales du Service des Antiquités de l'Égypte* 1: 141–8.

Daressy, G. 1907. 'Les cercueils des prêtres d'Ammon (deuxième trouvaille de Deir el-Bahari)'. *Annales du Service des Antiquités de l'Égypte* 8: 3–38.

Daressy, G. and Elliot Smith, G. 1903. 'Ouverture des momies provenant de la seconde trouvaille de Deir el-Bahari'. *Annales du Service des Antiquités de l'Égypte* 4: 150–60.

Dodson, A. 1994. *The canopic equipment of the kings of Egypt*. London: Kegan Paul International.

Edwards, A. B. 1882. 'Recent discovery of royal mummies and other Egyptian antiquities'. *Illustrated London News* 80, no. 2231: 113.
Edwards, A. B. 1883. 'Relics from the tombs of the priest-kings at Dayr el-Baharee'. *Recueil de travaux relatifs à la philologie et à l'archéologie égyptiennes et assyriennes* 4: 79–87.
Elliot Smith, G. 1906a. 'An account of the mummy of a priestess of Amun supposed to be Ta-usert-em-suten-pa'. *Annales du Service des Antiquités de l'Égypte* 7: 155–82.
Elliot Smith, G. 1906b. 'A contribution to the study of mummification in Egypt with special reference to the measures adopted during the time of the 21st dynasty for moulding the form of the body'. *Mémoires de l'Institut Égyptien* 5: 3–53.
Elliot Smith, G. 1912. *Catalogue général des antiquités égyptiennes du Musée du Caire. Nos 61051-61100. The royal mummies.* Cairo: Imprimerie de l'Institut Français d'Archéologie Orientale.
Elliot Smith, G. and Dawson, W. R. 1924. *Egyptian mummies.* London: George Allen & Unwin.
Gardiner, A. 1947. *Ancient Egyptian onomastica* II. Oxford: Oxford University Press.
Gardiner, A. 1962. 'The gods of Thebes as guarantors of personal property'. *Journal of Egyptian Archaeology* 48: 57–69.
Gauthier, H. 1914. *Le livre des rois* III, 2, Mémoire publiés par les membres de l'Institut Français d'Archéologie Orientale 19/2. Cairo: Imprimerie de l'Institut Français d'Archéologie Orientale.
Golenischeff, W. 1927. *Catalogue général des antiquités égyptiennes du Musée du Caire. Nos 58001-58036. Papyrus hiératiques.* Cairo: Imprimerie de l'Institut Français d'Archéologie Orientale.
Graefe, E. 2003. 'The Royal Cache and the tomb robberies'. In N. Strudwick and J. Taylor (eds.) *The Theban necropolis. Past, present and future*: 74–82. London: The British Museum Press.
Graefe, E. and Belova, G. 2010. *The Royal Cache TT 320: a re-examination.* Cairo: Supreme Council of Antiquities.
Gunn, B. 1955. 'The decree of Amonrasonthēr for Neskhons'. *Journal of Egyptian Archaeology* 41: 83–105.
Ikram, S. and Dodson, A. 1998. *The mummy in ancient Egypt. Equipping the dead for eternity.* London: Thames & Hudson.
Jansen-Winkeln, K. 2000. 'Zur Geschichte der "Cachette" von Deir el-Bahri'. In R. J. Demarée and A. Egberts (eds.) *Deir el-Medina in the third millennium AD. A tribute to Jac. J.* Janssen: 163–70. Leiden: Nederlands Instituut voor het Nabije Oosten.
Jansen-Winkeln, K. 2006. '*Relative chronology of dyn. 21*'. In E. Hornung, R. Krauss, and D. Warburton (eds.) *Ancient Egyptian chronology*: 218–33. Leiden: Brill.
Kitchen, K. A. 1986. *The Third Intermediate Period in Egypt (1100–650 B.C.)*, 2nd ed. with supplement. Warminster: Aris & Phillips.
Klein, S. 2013. *Une approche de la conception funéraire égyptienne: recherches sur les vases canopes.* Unpublished MA dissertation, École Pratique des Hautes Études.
Lüscher, B. 1998. *Untersuchungen zu Totenbuch Spruch 151*, Studien zum altägyptischen Totenbuch 2. Wiesbaden: Harrassowitz.
Maspero, G. 1889. *Les momies royales de Déir el-Baharî*, Mémoires publiés par les membres de la Mission Archéologique Française au Caire 1/4: 511–787. Paris: Ernest Leroux.
Maspero, G. 1915. *Guide du visiteur au Musée du Caire*, 4th ed. Cairo: Imprimerie de l'Institut Français d'Archéologie Orientale.
Meeks, D. 1995. 'Le foie, Maât et la nature humaine'. In T. DuQuesne (ed.) *Hermes Aegyptiacus. Egyptological studies for BH Stricker*, Discussions in Egyptology Special Number 2: 145–56. Oxford: DE Publications.
Naguib, S.-A. 1990. *Le clergé féminin d'Amon thébain à la 21e dynastie*, Orientalia Lovaniensia Analecta 38. Leuven: Peeters.
Niwiński, A. 1988a. *21st dynasty coffins from Thebes. Chronological and typological studies*, Theben 5. Mainz: Zabern.

Niwiński, A. 1988b. 'The wives of Pinudjem II–a topic for discussion'. *Journal of Egyptian Archaeology* 74: 226–30.

Niwiński, A. 1989. 'The solar-osirian unity as principle of the theology of the "state of Amen" in Thebes in the 21st dynasty'. *Jaarbericht van het vooraziat.-egyptisch Genootschap, Ex Oriente Lux* 30: 89–107.

Reeves, C. N. 1990. *The Valley of the Kings. The decline of a royal necropolis*. London: Kegan Paul International.

Roberson, J. A. 2013. *The awakening of Osiris and the transit of the solar barques. Royal apotheosis in a most concise Book of the Underworld and Sky*, Orbis Biblicus et Orientalis 262. Fribourg and Göttingen: Academic Press Fribourg; Vandenhoeck & Ruprecht.

Servajean, F. 2001. 'Le lotus émergeant et les quatre fils d'Horus. Analyse d'une métaphore physiologique'. In S. H. Aufrère (ed.) *Encyclopédie religieuse de l'univers végétal. Croyances phytoreligieuses de l'Égypte ancienne* II, Orientalia Monspeliensia 11: 261–97. Montpellier: Université Paul Valéry – Montpellier III.

Sethe, K. 1934. 'Zur Geschichte der Einbalsamierung bei den Ägyptern und einiger damit verbundener Bräuche'. *Sitzungsberichte der Preussischen Akademie der Wissenschaften* 13: 211–39.

Smith, M. (forthcoming). *Following Osiris. Perspectives on the Osirian afterlife from four millennia*. Oxford: Oxford University Press.

Taylor, J. 2003. 'The Third Intermediate Period (1069–664 BC)'. In I. Shaw (ed.) *The Oxford history of ancient Egypt*: 324–63. Oxford: Oxford University Press.

Taylor, J. 2010. *Journey through the afterlife. Ancient Egyptian Book of the Dead*. London: The British Museum Press.

Winlock, H. E. 1924. 'The Museum's excavations at Thebes'. *Bulletin of the Metropolitan Museum of Art* 19 (12): 5–33.

Yoyotte, J. 1986. 'Conférence de M. Jean Yoyotte'. *École Pratique des Hautes Études. Section des sciences religieuses. 1986–1987. Annuaire* 95: 168–73.

Chapter 8

The ancient Egyptian Book of the Moon: Coffin Texts spells 154–160

Gyula Priskin
Eötvös Loránd University, Hungary

Introduction

Spells 154–160 of the Coffin Texts (*CT* II 266a–388c) have long been known to form one composition because all of them, according to their titles, promise knowledge of the bas, mostly in connection with different localities (Sethe 1922, 1–4; Lapp 1989, 181–2; Quirke 2003, 173; Hays 2008, 190; Robinson 2008, 128). These spells are also frequently cited in discussions on the lunar concepts of the ancient Egyptians (Parker 1950, 12; Derchain 1962, 24; Leitz 1994, 269–71; Servajean 2003, 446; Lieven 2007, 199; Eaton 2011, 236–40; Arquier 2013, 122–6), yet so far these two noticeable aspects of the spells have not been intertwined more tightly. A careful reading of the texts reveals that – underlying the thematic unity postulated in the first place by the presence of the bas – the real editorial principle of this group of spells is a chronologically ordered account of the phenomena that happen during a lunar month. After the introduction (spell 154) which explains the origins of the month, the subsequent spells represent the successive stages of the monthly cycle: the period of invisibility (spell 155), waxing (spell 156), full moon (spell 157), waning (spell 158), arrival of the last crescent at the eastern horizon (spell 159), and again the conjunction of the sun and the moon, which is when a solar eclipse can occur (spell 160).

While this sense of the spells can, in most cases, be deduced from the already existing and widely used translations of the Coffin Texts (Faulkner 1973, 132–9; Barguet 1986, 571–8; Carrier 2004, 370–97), I am currently working on a new one with an extensive commentary that is to bring out the lunar character of these spells more than any previous rendering has thus far. My analysis relies on the text variant that is found on the coffin of the Hermopolitan official, Sen (B4L^{b} according to the siglum in *CT* II). The reasons for my choice will be the subject of a separate study which is to be incorporated into my monograph on the Book of the Moon, but suffice it to say here that they are based on the impression that spells 154–160 were compiled in their sequence in Hermopolis, the main cult centre of the lunar god Thoth. In support of this claim, I point to the fact that Hermopolis (also often referred to by the site name of its necropolis, Deir el-Bersha) is known to have contributed to the corpus of the Coffin Texts (Gestermann 2008, 201–3), as well as to the fact that some autobiographical tomb inscriptions found there hint at a deep interest in astronomy by the local elite (Willems 2006, 437–9). I have already argued elsewhere (Priskin 2013, 27–8) that at least one of the spells (155) from the Book of the Moon was written in its entirety in Hermopolis. Spells 154, 157, and 158, in contrast, share a number of common traits, such as the prominence of Re within the narrative and the frequent aetiological motif. The most likely scenario, therefore, is that there existed a core text consisting of these spells, possibly as part of the central royal archive at Memphis. At some point in time, this group of spells reached Hermopolis where it was extended by the insertion and addition of four more spells (155, 156, 159, and 160), and thus the Book of the Moon was created. This supposed genealogy of the book, however hypothetical it may appear, is in tune with what we now seem to know about the history of early mortuary texts (see Baines 2008, 26–30; Gestermann 2008, 209–12).

Due to the limitations of this paper, it is impossible to give a thorough and detailed overview of the Book of the Moon here. I can only pick out some of the most salient points that will, nevertheless, acquaint the reader with the way in which the lunar references are generally formulated in these texts to describe the magnificent journey of the moon through space and time.

Spell 154: the origins of the month

Spell 154 is about the origins of the month and explains why months are not of uniform length in nature. Any steadfast observer of the moon is bound to discover that, in some lunations, 30 days elapse between two identical phases of the moon, whereas in other months only 29 do. In the language of modern astronomy we express this irregularity by saying that the synodic month (the period between two successive full moons, or any other phases) lasts an average of 29.53059 days.

> *jw=j rḫ.kw jr.t Jwn.w tmm.t bsj wr-mꜣ.w ḥr=s*
> *ḫb.t r m sn.wt d̠ꜣ.t ꜥ jn ḥtm r jwꜥ Jwn.w jw=j rḫ.kw jry.t ḥnk.t n ṯꜣ.y ḥr=s* (*CT* II 272a–4b)
> I know the eye of Heliopolis into which not even the greatest of seers has been initiated, the diminishing of the part in the senut, and how the destroyer extends the arm against the heir of Heliopolis. I know how a braided lock of hair of a man is made upon it.

The allusion to a lock of hair (*ḥnk.t*) at the end of this passage is juxtaposed later in the text by the mention of a shorn man (*fꜣk*, *CT* II 282c–4b). These images surely evoke the waxing and waning of the moon, stemming from an old concept that likened the different phases of the Earth's satellite to a bald head (the full moon) with hair gradually beginning to cover it (Derchain 1962, 20; Eaton 2011, 236). Another key phrase here is *sn.wt*, the name of the sixth day of the month (Parker 1950, 11; Winter 1970, 152). In later texts, this term was often used interchangeably with *smd.t*, the designation of the fifteenth of the lunar month, on which day the full moon takes place in most lunations (Lieven 2000, 75). The sixth day symbolised the fullness of the moon in Heliopolitan doctrine (Smith 2002, 122) and could be associated with it because of a related mytheme according to which the lunar eye consisted of six parts (Junker 1911, 101; Meeks 2006, 220). The six fractions corresponding to these parts (the dimidiated series starting with ½) fail to add up to a unity by a tiny margin (1/64), such that they expressed the idea of near completeness at the same time (Robins and Shute 1987, 14–15). Furthermore, this arithmetic exercise of the fractions may have actually been connected with the average length of the synodic month (Priskin 2002). The 'diminishing of the part of the senut' would therefore refer to a month that is somewhat shorter than the ideal 30 days, the period that was the basis for the twelve equally measured monthly units of the civil calendar. This length of time is alluded to in spell 154 by the mention of the *mꜥbꜣ*-harpoon, which was written with the number 30 (*CT* II 278a–b; Arquier 2013, 123). The harpoon belongs to He-who-is-in-his-fire, a creature – a snake according to the hieroglyphic determinative – that acts as the enemy of the sun god Re.

> *Rꜥ pw ḥr mdw.t ḥnꜥ Jm.j-whm=f ḥr psš.t Jwn.w*
> *ꜥḥꜥ.n r=f jꜣṯ ḫpr ḫb.t pw m ꜣbd* (*CT* II 274c–6c)
> It was the case that Re had a discussion with He-who-is-in-his-fire over the division of Heliopolis.
> Then his part was injured and that is how the diminishing of the month came into being.

Thus we learn that the reduction in the length of the month resulted from a dispute between Re and He-who-is-in-his-fire. This name must be a designation of the moon in conjunction, that is, when the moon is between the sun and the earth. During this period of lunar invisibility, when the waning crescent can no longer be seen before sunrise at the eastern horizon and the first crescent has not yet appeared in the western sky after sunset, the moon apparently dwells in the vicinity of the sun i.e. in the sun god's fire. In other words, the moon is invisible because it moves conjointly with the sun (for possible iconographic and textual references to this union of the sun and the moon from the New Kingdom onwards, see Depuydt 1998, 76–85). That the name He-who-is-in-his-fire describes the moon in conjunction will further be reinforced by spell 160 in which the serpent will once more make an appearance as a hostile entity towards the moon, this time responsible for a solar eclipse (see below). The ancient Egyptians started the lunar month with the onset of lunar invisibility (Parker 1950, 9–23), so this was the time when the months were really reckoned. Consequently, it is appropriate for the invisible moon to feature in a description that is trying to come to terms with the different lengths of the month. The serpent injures and takes away a part of Re, and the recognition that the moon reflects the light of the sun may lie behind this statement. The motif may also be a distant relative or predecessor of Plutarch's story of how Thoth won a part of each day from the moon through playing draughts to form the five epagomenal days (see Griffiths 1970, 135).

Spell 155: the period of lunar invisibility

The title of spell 155 (*CT* II 290a) leaves absolutely no doubt about which phase of the lunar cycle this text describes because, unlike the other spells, it connects the bas not with a place or cardinal direction, but with *psḏn.tjw*, the invisibility of the moon. Further lunar references of the spell have already been analysed in detail in my recently published article (Priskin 2013), so there is no need to repeat the arguments presented there. It is, however, worth reiterating that the text of the spell closes with an allusion to the end of the period of invisibility.

> *wn n=j ntjw m psḏn.tjw*
> *jw mꜣꜣ.n=j wp.w pr(.w) m sẖ.w n.w Wr.t* (*CT* II 306a–b)
> Open to me, those in the moon's invisibility.
> I have seen the gelder come out of the slaughterhouse of the Great Eye.

Written sources that have come down to us from Graeco-Roman times indicate that the two halves of the lunar cycle were envisioned as bulls with different temperaments (Derchain 1962, 43; Leitz 1994, 268–9; Lieven 2000, 86). The waxing moon was thus seen as a fiery, vigorous bull (*kꜣ psj*), whereas the waning moon was equated with an ox, a castrated bull (*sꜥb*) (Sethe and Firchow 1957, 54). So, when the person responsible for the castration of the lunar bull (*wp.w* 'someone who cuts, a gelder') leaves the slaughterhouse, it means that the period of waning and invisibility is about to end, and the waxing of the moon can begin.

Spell 156: waxing

It is at this point, at the very end of lunar invisibility, that spell 156 joins in and provides an all-encompassing description of the waxing period by identifying two of its key moments.

> *ṯwn šw.t ẖnt qꜥḥ*
> *wbn dšr.t m mntꜣ.t* (*CT* II 312f–14b)
> The feather is thrust into the shoulder,
> and the Red Crown rises in the mentjat-bowl.

It is clear from a number of other sources, including notably other Coffin Texts (spells 6 and 9, *CT* I 16c–19a, 29a–31a), that the feather was a symbol of the first lunar crescent appearing over the western horizon just after sunset (Kees 1980, 282; Goedicke 1989, 61; Willems 2005, 210), which in turn led to its close association with this cardinal direction (Willems 2005; Meeks 2006, 32, 292). In this context, then, the shoulder must refer to the relevant body part of the arching sky goddess, Nut, which is in fact situated in the west. The signification of the Red Crown in the next line is less certain – not negligibly because of the obscurity of the word *mnṯꜣ.t* (Willems 1996, 215) – but it most probably denotes the full moon rising from the eastern horizon (the connotations of the verb *wbn* hint at this meaning). Due to the atmospheric scattering of light, the full moon when close to the horizon – just like the sun near the horizon – may appear to have a red hue (for the association of redness and the full moon, see Goebs 2008, 158–9). The two lines thus demarcate the starting and end points of the waxing period: the first crescent above the western horizon and the full lunar disc over the eastern horizon. Such an interpretation finds strong support towards the final lines of the spell where the same two antithetic lunar events framing the first half of the month are named again in more certain terms (Parker 1950, 12).

> *jw=j rḫ.kw bꜣ.w Ḫmnw*
> *šr.t m ꜣbd pw ꜥꜣ.t m smd.t pw* (*CT* II 322c–4a)
> I know the bas of Hermopolis.
> It is the small eye on the second day of the lunar month, it is the great eye on the fifteenth day of the lunar month.

Spell 157: full moon

Spell 157 introduces a new context into the Book of the Moon with the struggle between Horus and Seth. It is about the two different kinds of injury that the full moon – the intact eye of Horus – can suffer.

> *Rꜥ pw ḏd.n=f n Ḥr.w jmj mꜣꜣ=j jr.t=k ḏr ḫpr nw r=s*
> *mꜣꜣ.n=f s(t) ḏd.jn=f dg r pfꜥ=k ḥbs(.w) m wḏꜣ.t jmj.t*
> *wn.jn Ḥr.w ḥr dg.t r pf ḏd.jn Ḥr.w*
> *mk wj ḥr mꜣꜣ=f ḥḏ.wj ḫpr mꜣ-ḥḏ pw* (*CT* II 334b–8b)
> It was the case that Re said to Horus: 'Let me see your eye because this happened to it'.
> As he looked at it, he said: 'Take a look at this part as your hand covers the sound eye there'.
> And Horus looked at that part and said:
> 'Behold, I see it as altogether white'. And this is how the oryx came into being.

Through a pun between the expressions *ḥr mꜣꜣ=f ḥḏ.wj* and *mꜣ-ḥḏ*, the oryx plays a crucial role in this story. Its connection with the time of the full moon is intimated in some of the inscriptions that accompany the scenes of the slaying of this animal on the walls of Graeco-Roman temples: 'The oryx is burnt and killed as the wedjat-eye is provided with its constituent elements. Moon, come so that you may wander through the sky and your movement could be whole and sound!' (*smꜣ mꜣ-ḥḏ ḏd-mdw mḥ nsr.tw mꜣ-ḥḏ m ds.tw wḏꜣ.t ꜥpr.tw m r.w=s ḥr.j-jꜣb.t m ḫns=k m ḥꜣj.t nm.t=k jr(.t) m ꜥḏ wḏꜣ*; Chassinat 1928, 138–9). Horapollo – the Greek author who penned down often enigmatic descriptions of a series of hieroglyphic signs in the 4th century CE – also connects the oryx with the moon, and most probably with the full moon, when he says that it could foretell the rising of the sun and the moon (Boas 1993, 65–6). He also speaks of this animal as somewhat inimical to the moon (Boas 1993, 65). These two strands of tradition are intermingled in spell 157 of the Coffin Texts as well. The oryx is included in a context that deals with a temporary covering of the moon given that, after Re warned Horus of some overcast part to his celestial eye, Horus replied that it was still shining unblemished. The whole episode must then denote a lunar eclipse during which one part, or the entirety, of the lunar disc is temporarily dimmed as the shadow of the Earth falls on it. Lunar eclipses, as a matter of fact, can only happen during a full moon, at the time of opposition when the Sun, Earth, and moon are aligned.

The second injury involves the pig as a Sethian animal, knocking Horus unconscious, thus presaging the regular monthly waning of the moon.

> *ḏd.jn Rꜥ n Ḥr.w dg m-dj r(rj) pf km*
> *ꜥḥꜥ.n Ḥr.w ḥr dg.t r(rj) pf km*
> *ꜥḥꜥ.n Ḥr.w ḥr kjw.t ḥr qd wr[.t] n jr.t=f nšn.t ḏd=f*
> *m(k) jr.t=j mj sqr pf jrj.n Stẖ r jr.t=j* (*CT* II 338c–41b)
> Then Re said to Horus: 'Now look at this black pig'.
> Horus looked at the black pig.
> Then Horus shouted because of the grave condition of his raging eye, saying:
> 'Behold, my eye is like the injury that Seth has inflicted on my eye'.

The pig was closely associated with the full moon and, once again, there is plenty of evidence from later times that support this notion. A hieroglyphic inscription from the temple of Edfu (Chassinat 1930, 354), as well as the writings of classical authors (Meeks 2006, 219) testify to the fact that the ancient Egyptians sacrificed pigs and consumed pork on the day of the full moon. According to Plutarch, furthermore, Seth discovers the body of Osiris when he is chasing a pig in the light of the full moon (Griffiths 1970, 129). The pig is also portrayed as a threat to the moon – a repugnant animal that is ready to swallow the lunar disc – in, for instance, the Book of Gates (Manassa 2006, 122–5, 137–41) or a 7th century BCE mythological manual from the Delta (Meeks 2006, 14–15, 218–19). As a consequence, we must assume that the mention of the pig in Coffin Texts spell 157 refers to the regular injury suffered by the lunar eye, i.e. the beginning of the monthly waning of the moon.

Spell 158: waning

The period of waning itself is evoked in the following spell through subtle, but still intelligible, allusions.

> *rḫ bꜣ.w Nḫn jw=j rḫ.kw sštꜣ n Nḫn*
> *ḏr.tj Ḥr.w pw jrj.n mw.t=f qmꜣ.tj ḥr mw* (*CT* II 349a–d)
> Knowing the bas of Nekhen. I know the secret of Nekhen.
> It is the hands of Horus that his mother made and that were thrown into water.

From a story that was already known in Middle Kingdom times (Quirke 2004, 181–2), but has survived in its fullest form in a Ramesside papyrus recounting the strife between Horus and Seth (Lichtheim 1976, 219–20), we know that Isis cuts off and replaces Horus' hands because he used them to collect the semen of Seth who had tried to force sexual intercourse with him. At a later point of the narrative, it is Horus' semen that eventually prevails over Seth, leading to the creation of a disc on the head of Thoth that must be the moon itself (Servajean 2004, 125). The hands of Horus being made by his mother therefore surely refers to this mythological episode and symbolises the waning of the moon in the lunar cycle, when it is feeble and vulnerable, but still carries its inherent capacity for rejuvenation. The statement that Horus' hands are thrown into water metaphorically describes the second half of the lunar cycle because the waning crescent, after having risen from the eastern horizon and travelled some distance towards the west, never reaches the western horizon and is never able to set. Each day in the second half of the monthly cycle, the rising sun starts to cancel out the moon's light at dawn and, as the light of the sun intensifies, the lunar crescent fades away into the blue background of the sky; it is, in effect, 'thrown into the celestial waters'.

> *ḏd.jn Rꜥ ḥḏ sꜣ pn n ꜣs.t ẖr jr.t.n mw.t=f r=f ḏs=s*
> *ḥꜣ <jnj> n=j Sbk n pḥ.wj ḥꜣm=f st srd=f st dj=f st r s.t jr.jt*
> *Sbk n pḥ.wj ḏd=f jw ḥꜣm.n=j bꜣ.n=j btktk m ꜥ=j ḥr sp.tj mw*
> *ḥꜣd.n=j m pḥ.wj ḫpr ḥꜣd pw* (*CT* II 350b–3c)
> Re then said: 'This son of Isis was injured because of what his mother herself had done to him. I wish Sobek of the edge of the waters <were fetched> for me so that he could fish them out, grow them and put them back to their right place'.
> Sobek of the edge of the waters said: 'I fished, I scooped (it) up, but (the catch) has slipped from my hands onto the shores of the water.
> Finally, I caught it in the edge of the waters with a cover basket'. And that is how the cover basket came into being.

This passage further refines the description of the waning moon. The crocodile god Sobek is the embodiment of the rising sun (Zecchi 2010, 23) that causes the concealment of the waning crescent. In some of the netherworld books of the New Kingdom, a crocodile gives birth to the morning sun (Piankoff 1953, 67–9). Also, in the much later Book of the Fayum (2nd century CE), Sobek is depicted as the sun dwelling around the liminal zones of the eastern and western horizons (Beinlich 1991, 319, pl. 9); in the context of spell 158 he must be the rising sun in the east (see also spell 160 below). His epithet, 'Sobek of the edge of the waters', also implies that he lingers around the horizon, close to the shore of the celestial waters – just as real crocodiles habitually lurk at the edge of waters waiting for their prey. He tries to fish out the hands but they keep slipping from his grasp. This describes how the dwindling crescent still continues to elude the sun on the successive days of the waning period, even though it rises closer and closer to dawn and travels shorter and shorter distances towards the west. Sobek finally catches his fish (the hands/moon) with a device that is used in shallow waters: a cover basket (a wickerwork basket with no bottom that is placed over a fish, which could thus be grabbed by hand through the upper opening remaining above the level of the water; see Lacau 1954, 137–51). In astronomical terms, this act corresponds to the meeting of the sun and the moon at the eastern horizon, and consequently, to the eventual capture of the moon by the sun i.e. the disappearance of the waning crescent.

Spell 159: the arrival of the last crescent at the eastern horizon

Spell 159 is also concerned with the beginning of the period of lunar invisibility. It further elaborates the theme of the encounter of the moon and the sun at the eastern horizon, in the realm that was known to the ancient Egyptians as the Field of Reeds (*sḫ.t jꜣr.w*) (*CT* II 368c; Hays 2008, 177, n. 14; Taylor 2010, 243).

> *rḫ bꜣ.w jꜣb.tjw jw=j rḫ.kw sbꜣ pw ḥr.j-jb prr.w Rꜥ jm=f m jꜣb.t rs.j=f m š.w ḫbs.w m bw sqdd Rꜥ jm m ṯꜣw mḥ.tj=f nw.yt sr.w m bw sqdd Rꜥ jm m ḫnj* (*CT* II 363c–6a)
> Knowing the bas of the easterners. I know it is the gate in the middle, from which Re emerges in the east. Its south is in the lake of the *ḫbs*-geese, which is the place where Re navigates by sailing; its north is in the waters of the *sr*-geese, which is the place where Re navigates by rowing.

Whereas spell 155 is about the invisible moon in the evening, anticipating the appearance of the first crescent in the west, this spell is connected with the east and the morning sun. Because the moon becomes hidden in the light of the sun, the text refers to it through a description of the latter. The southern and northern limits of the sun's yearly path along the eastern horizon are specified; this part of the text perhaps emphasises the fact that, although the moon slightly strays off the trajectory of the sun (the ecliptic) during its monthly cycle, they are always close enough for the moon to become invisible when the two meet at the eastern end of the sky. The enormous dimensions of the vegetation in the Field of Reeds as described in the second part of this spell – barley five cubits tall, emmer seven cubits (*CT* II 369b–70d) – possibly allude to the closeness of the moon and its beneficial effects on the growth of plants (Smith 2002, 126).

Spell 160: a solar eclipse

The last chapter of the Book of the Moon, Coffin Texts spell 160, describes the situation when the invisible moon in conjunction travels with the sun through the day sky and a solar eclipse occurs.

> *rḫ bꜣ.w jmn.tjw jw=j rḫ.kw [[bꜣ.w jmn.tjw]] ḏw pf n Bꜣḫ.w*
> *ntj p.t tn rhn=s ḥr=f wnn=f ṯḥn ḫt 300 ꜣw=f ḫt 120m wsḫ.t=f*
> *wnn Sbk nb Bꜣḫ.w ḥr jꜣb.t ḏw pf wnn ḥw.t-nṯr=f m ḥrs.t*
> *wnn ḥfꜣ.w ḥr wp.t ḏw pf mḥ 30m ꜣw=f mḥ 3 ḫnt m ḥꜣ.t=f m ds*
> *jw=j rḫ.kw rn n ḥfꜣ.w pf tp ḏw=f Jm.j-whm=f rn=f* (*CT* II 375b–9a)
> Knowing the bas of the westerners. I know [[the bas of the westerners,]] the mountain of Bakhu
> on which the sky leans; it is of crystal, 300 rods in length and 120 rods in width.

> Sobek, the Lord of Bakhu is on the east of the mountain, and his temple is made of carnelian. There is a snake on the top of the mountain, 30 cubits in length and the three cubits of its forepart are of flint.
> I know the name of the serpent dwelling on the mountain: He-who-is-in-his-fire is its name.

The two protagonists of an eclipse are named: Sobek once more stands for the morning sun in the east, whereas the moon reappears as He-who-is-in-his-fire – cast again in the role of the enemy of the solar deity (his name, however, is slightly misspelled on Sen's coffin; for the correct orthography see coffins B17C, B1C, and B3C[a] in *CT* II 379a). The lunar connotations of the passage are also evident from the dimensions: the celestial mountain is 300 rods long (ten times 30), 120 rods wide (ten times twelve), and the lunar serpent itself is meaningfully 30 cubits long. Quite in keeping with the contents of the spell, the three-cubit-long forepart possibly represents the period of invisibility since, for the Egyptians, its maximum length equalled three days (the first crescent could be sighted at the latest on the evening of the third day of the lunar month, see my discussion in Priskin 2013, 36).

> *jr r=f m tr n mšr.w pnᶜ.ẖr=f jr.t=f r Rᶜ*
> *ḫpr.ẖr=f ᶜḥᶜ.w m js.t sg.wt ᶜ3.wt m-ẖnw sqd.wt* (*CT* II 379b–80b)
> Now, as if it was the time of evening, it (the snake) turns its eye against Re,
> and there occurs a stoppage in the crew, and a great astonishment within the journey.

When He-who-is-in-his-fire turns his eye towards Re, i.e. when the moon 'turns its back' on its earthbound observers, the crew of the solar barque stops. The stoppage of the barque (when it grinds to a halt on the sandbank in the Lake of Knives) is associated with a solar eclipse in two Ptolemaic papyri (Altmann 2010, 91–2), and therefore a similar incident must also refer to such an event here. The darkening of the sky that is characteristic of a total solar eclipse is indicated by the statement that the meeting of the serpent and Re happens when the light of day dims (*mšr.w*, 'evening', 'twilight'). According to the rest of the spell, Seth, in his capacity of defender of the solar barque, springs into action and, after he utters a magic spell and displays his strength to repel the lunar serpent, the voyage of the sun continues and Re can set in the west (*CT* II 380c–6c). The moon presumably also emerges from the encounter unscathed, and thus the endless cycle of lunar withering and renewal can be perpetuated.

Conclusion

In conclusion, I would like to stress that not only do the lunar references abounding in spells 154–160 follow a clear chronological pattern, but that they also comprise all the phenomena that can be viewed along the monthly cycle: the period of invisibility, waxing, full moon, a potential lunar eclipse during a full moon, waning, and a possible solar eclipse during invisibility. As a consequence, the Book of the Moon can be said to belong to the rare group of ancient Egyptian literary products that give a systematic treatment of a particular topic (Baines 2007, 41). Admittedly, the allusions to the moon are often rather cryptic and can, in most cases, only be deciphered with the help of later sources – usually of Graeco-Roman date – that are much more explicit with their lunar content. It should not be forgotten, however, that the ancient Egyptian Book of the Moon is not a scientific treatise, but belongs to a collection of mortuary spells that is often characterised by a striving for arcane knowledge (Hays 2008, 190). In accordance with the circumstances prompting the creation of the text, the ultimate purpose of the book was not to disseminate factual information about the moon, but no doubt to equip the deceased with the regenerative powers of this well-observed celestial body. Thus, these spells may be seen as the very first clear-cut evidence for a set of beliefs that became more emphatic at the later stages of Egyptian civilisation, such as when the dead assumed the identity of the moon in some New Kingdom versions of the Book of Going Forth by Day (see the papyrus of Ani, Faulkner 1994, pl. 18), or when the pre-eminent divine actor of resurrection, Osiris, became thoroughly equated with the moon in Graeco-Roman times (Derchain 1962, 46; Koemoth 1996, 203).

References

Altmann, V. 2010. *Die Kultfrevel des Seth. Die Gefährdung der göttlichen Ordnung in zwei Vernichtungsritualen der ägyptischen Spätzeit (Urk. VI)*, Studien zur spätägyptischen Religion 1. Wiesbaden: Harrassowitz.

Arquier, B. 2013. *Le double sarcophage de Mésehti S1C (CG 28118)-S2C (CG 28119). Recherches sur l'organisation du décor iconographique et textuel.* Unpublished PhD thesis, Université Paul Valéry – Montpellier III. [online] ⟨https://tel.archives-ouvertes.fr/tel-00937051/document⟩, accessed 19 January 2015.

Baines, J. 2007. *Visual and written culture in ancient Egypt.* Oxford: Oxford University Press.

Baines, J. 2008. 'Modelling sources, processes, and locations of early mortuary texts'. In S. Bickel and B. Mathieu (eds.) *D'un monde à l'autre. Textes des Pyramides et Textes des Sarcophages. Actes de la table ronde internationale 'Textes des Pyramides* versus *Textes des Sarcophages', Ifao, 24–26 septembre 2001*, Bibliothèque d'Étude 139: 15–41, 2nd ed. Cairo: Institut Français d'Archéologie Orientale.

Barguet, P. 1986. *Les textes des sarcophages égyptiens du Moyen Empire.* Paris: Les Éditions du Cerf.

Beinlich, H. 1991. *Das Buch vom Fayum. Zum religiösen Eigenverständnis einer ägyptischen Landschaft*, Ägyptologische Abhandlungen 51. Wiesbaden: Harrassowitz.

Boas, G. 1993. *The hieroglyphics of Horapollo*, Bollingen Series 23, trans. G. Boas. Princeton: Princeton University Press.

Carrier, C. 2004. *Textes des sarcophages du Moyen Empire égyptien* I–III. Monaco: Éditions du Rocher.

Chassinat, É. 1928. *Le temple d'Edfou* III, Mémoires publiés par les membres de la Mission Archéologique Française au Caire 20. Cairo: Imprimerie de l'Institut Français d'Archéologie Orientale.

Chassinat, É. 1930. *Le temple d'Edfou* V, Mémoires publiés par les membres de la Mission Archéologique Française au Caire 22. Cairo: Imprimerie de l'Institut Français d'Archéologie Orientale.

Depuydt, L. 1998. 'The hieroglyphic representations of the moon's absence (*psḏntyw*)'. In L. H. Lesko (ed.) *Ancient Egyptian and Mediterranean studies in memory of William A. Ward*: 71–89. Providence: Department of Egyptology, Brown University.

Derchain, P. 1962. 'Mythes et dieux lunaires en Égypte'. In *La lune, mythes et rites*, Sources Orientales 5: 19–68. Paris: Éditions du Seuil.

Eaton, K. 2011. 'Monthly lunar festivals in the mortuary realm: historical patterns and symbolic motifs'. *Journal of Near Eastern Studies* 70 (2): 229–45.

Faulkner, R. O. 1973. *The ancient Egyptian Coffin Texts* I: *spells 1–354.* Warminster: Aris & Phillips.

Faulkner, R. O. 1994. *The Egyptian Book of the Dead: the Book of Going Forth by Day.* San Francisco: Chronicle Books.

Gestermann, L. 2008. 'Sargtexte aus Dair al-Biršā. Zeugnisse eines historischen Wendepunktes?'. In S. Bickel and B. Mathieu (eds.) *D'un monde à l'autre. Textes des Pyramides et Textes des Sarcophages. Actes de la table ronde internationale 'Textes des Pyramides versus Textes des Sarcophages', Ifao, 24-26 septembre 2001*, Bibliothèque d'Étude 139: 201–17, 2nd ed. Cairo: Institut Français d'Archéologie Orientale.

Goebs, K. 2008. *Crowns in Egyptian funerary literature. Royalty, rebirth, and destruction*. Oxford: Griffith Institute.

Goedicke, H. 1989. 'Coffin Text spell 6'. *Bulletin de la Société d'égyptologie de Genève* 13: 57–64.

Griffiths, J. G. 1970. *Plutarch's De Iside et Osiride*. Swansea: University of Wales Press.

Hays, H. M. 2008. 'Transformation of context: the Field of Rushes in Old and Middle Kingdom mortuary literature'. In S. Bickel and B. Mathieu (eds.) *D'un monde à l'autre. Textes des Pyramides et Textes des Sarcophages. Actes de la table ronde internationale 'Textes des Pyramides versus Textes des Sarcophages', Ifao, 24-26 septembre 2001*, Bibliothèque d'Étude 139: 175–200, 2nd ed. Cairo: Institut Français d'Archéologie Orientale.

Junker, H. 1911. 'Die sechs Teile des Horusauges und der »sechste Tag«'. *Zeitschrift für Ägyptische Sprache und Altertumskunde* 48: 101–6.

Kees, H. 1980. *Totenglauben und Jenseitsvorstellungen der alten Ägypter. Grundlagen und Entwicklung bis zum Ende des Mittleren Reiches*, 4th ed. Berlin: Akademie-Verlag.

Koemoth, P. 1996. 'Osiris-Lune, l'horizon et l'oeil *oudjat*'. *Chronique d'Égypte* 71 (142): 203–20.

Lacau, P. 1954. 'Le panier de pêche égyptien'. *Bulletin de l'Institut Français d'Archéologie Orientale* 54: 137–63.

Lapp, G. 1989. 'Die Papyrusvorlagen der Sargtexte'. *Studien zur Altägyptischen Kultur* 16: 171–202.

Leitz, C. 1994. *Tagewählerei. Das Buch ḥꜣt nḥḥ pḥ.wy ḏt und verwandte Texte*, Ägyptologische Abhandlungen 55. Wiesbaden: Harrassowitz.

Lichtheim, M. 1976. *Ancient Egyptian literature. A book of readings* II. *The New Kingdom*. Berkeley and Los Angeles: University of California Press.

Lieven, A. von 2000. *Der Himmel über Esna. Eine Fallstudie zur Religiösen Astronomie in Ägypten am Beispiel der kosmologischen Decken- und Architravinschriften im Tempel von Esna*, Ägyptologische Abhandlungen 64. Wiesbaden: Harrassowitz.

Lieven, A. von 2007. *The Carlsberg papyri 8: Grundriss des Laufes der Sterne. Das sogenannte Nutbuch*, CNI publications 31. Copenhagen: Museum Tusculanum Press.

Manassa, C. 2006. 'The Judgment Hall of Osiris in the Book of Gates'. *Revue d'Égyptologie* 57: 109–50.

Meeks, D. 2006. *Mythes et légendes du Delta d'après le papyrus Brooklyn 47.218.84*, Mémoires publiés par les membres de l'Institut Français d'Archéologie Orientale 125. Cairo: Institut Français d'Archéologie Orientale.

Parker, R. A. 1950. *The calendars of ancient Egypt*, Studies in Ancient Oriental Civilization 26. Chicago: The University of Chicago Press.

Piankoff, A. 1953. *La création du disque solaire*, Bibliothèque d'Étude 19. Cairo: Imprimerie de l'Institut Français d'Archéologie Orientale.

Priskin, G. 2002. 'The Eye of Horus and the synodic month'. *Discussions in Egyptology* 53: 75–81.

Priskin, G. 2013. 'Coffin Texts spell 155 on the moon'. *Birmingham Egyptology Journal* 1: 25–63.

Quirke, S. 2003. 'Measuring the underworld'. In D. O'Connor and S. Quirke (eds.) *Mysterious lands*, Encounters with ancient Egypt: 161–81. London: UCL Press.

Quirke, S. 2004. *Egyptian literature 1800 BC. Questions and readings*, GH Egyptology 2. London: Golden House Publications.

Robins, G. and Shute, C. 1987. *The Rhind mathematical papyrus: an ancient Egyptian text*. London: British Museum Publications.

Robinson, P. 2008. 'Book of the Dead chapters 149 and 150 and their Coffin Texts origins'. In K. Griffin (ed.) *Current Research in Egyptology 2007. Proceedings of the eighth annual symposium, University of Wales Swansea, April 2007*: 123–40. Oxford: Oxbow Books.

Servajean, F. 2003. 'L'étoffe *sj3.t* et la régénération du défunt'. *Bulletin de l'Institut Français d'Archéologie Orientale* 103: 439–57.

Servajean, F. 2004. 'Lune ou soleil d'or? Un épisode des *Aventures d'Horus et de Seth* (P. Chester Beatty I R°, 11, 1–13,1)'. *Revue d'Égyptologie* 55: 125–48.

Sethe, K. 1922. 'Die Sprüche für das Kennen der Seelen der heiligen Orte (Totb. Kap. 107–109. 111–116)'. *Zeitschrift für Ägyptische Sprache und Altertumskunde* 57: 1–50.

Sethe, K. and Firchow, O. 1957. *Thebanische Tempelinschriften aus griechisch-römischer Zeit*, Urkunden des ägyptischen Altertums 8. Berlin: Akademie-Verlag.

Smith, M. 2002. *The Carlsberg papyri 5: on the primaeval ocean*, CNI publications 26. Copenhagen: Museum Tusculanum Press.

Taylor, J. H. 2010. 'The perfect afterlife'. In J. H. Taylor (ed.) *Journey through the afterlife. Ancient Egyptian Book of the Dead*: 238–61. London: The British Museum Press.

Willems, H. 1996. *The coffin of Heqata (Cairo* JdE *36418). A case study of Egyptian funerary culture of the early Middle Kingdom*, Orientalia Lovaniensia Analecta 70. Leuven: Peeters.

Willems, H. 2005. 'The feather of the west'. *Revue d'Égyptologie* 56: 208–13.

Willems, H. 2006. 'An astronomer at Deir al-Barsha'. In E. Czerny, I. Hein, H. Hunger, D. Melman, and A. Schwab (eds.) *Timelines. Studies in honour of Manfred Bietak* I, Orientalia Lovaniensia Analecta 149: 433–41. Leuven: Peeters.

Winter, E. 1970. 'Nochmals zum *snwt*-Fest'. *Zeitschrift für Ägyptische Sprache und Altertumskunde* 96: 151–2.

Zecchi, M. 2010. *Sobek of Shedet. The crocodile god in the Fayyum in the Dynastic Period*, Studi sull'antico Egitto 2. Todi: Tau Editrice.

Chapter 9

Hatshepsut's expedition to the land of Punt – novelty or tradition?

Filip Taterka[1]
Adam Mickiewicz University, Poland

Since the rediscovery of the famous Punt reliefs in the temple of millions of years of Hatshepsut at Deir el-Bahari by Auguste Mariette (1877) in the second half of the 19th century CE, scholars have tried to determine the exact location of this mysterious land. Mariette himself proposed to situate it on the African continent south-east of Egypt (1875, 60–6). While this is now the most universally accepted view, other scholars argue that the land of Punt was located on the opposite coast of the Red Sea, i.e. in the Arabian Peninsula. Another source of disagreement is the route the Egyptians took in order to get to Punt. Most specialists claim that it was maritime, but riverine and terrestrial itineraries have been proposed as well (Diego Espinel 2011, 59–120). The aim of this paper, however, is to bring to scholarly attention an aspect of Hatshepsut's Punt expedition that seems to be generally neglected by Egyptologists, namely its ideological and religious background.

As surprising as it might seem, scholars used to underestimate the importance of Hatshepsut's Punt expedition. It is often argued that Hatshepsut's feminine nature precluded her from organising any violent military expeditions; the allure of luxurious products and exotic animals like rhinoceroses, baboons, leopards, cheetahs, or giraffes[2] would have driven her to send a rather insignificant, small-scale foreign expedition of a peaceful character (Winlock 1928, 51; Wilson 1951, 174–6). This view does not withstand criticism however; Hatshepsut did indeed organise military expeditions (Redford 1967, 57–87) and, moreover, took an active part in at least one of these, leading the Egyptian army to victory over Nubian troops, as attested in the inscription of the

[1] I would like to express my deepest gratitude to Dr. Zbigniew E. Szafrański, the director of the Polish-Egyptian Archaeological and Conservation Mission at the Temple of Hatshepsut at Deir el-Bahari, for the opportunity to work on the Punt reliefs in Hatshepsut's temple.

[2] For the fauna of Punt, see Kitchen 1971, 187–8; Meeks 2002, 275–83; 2003, 55–6, complemented by the remarks of Cannuyer 2012, 178, n. 13.

official named Ty (Habachi 1957, 100, fig. 6).[3] Therefore, it is necessary to reconsider our assessment of the female king's Punt expedition (for a detailed analysis see Diego Espinel 2011, 326–90).

The initial question which should therefore be asked is why Hatshepsut organised this expedition in the first place. The scene on the north wall of the Southern Middle Portico of Hatshepsut's Deir el-Bahari temple (also known as the Punt Portico) depicts the enthroned female ruler announcing to her courtiers her decision to send an expedition to the land of Punt (Naville 1898, pls. 85–6). According to the inscriptions accompanying it, she was following a direct order from her divine father Amun-Re (Sethe 1906, 349, l. 16–354, l. 3). This is corroborated by the words of the king of the gods himself, as inscribed in the long text on the west wall of the Southern Middle Portico (Naville 1898, pl. 84):

> I have given to you Punt in its entirety as far as the lands of the gods: the God's Land that has never been treaded and the Terraces of Myrrh which are not known to the people, although it was heard from mouth to mouth as the stories of the ancestors. Although the marvels brought hence were brought already under your fathers, the kings of Lower Egypt, one by one, since the time of the ancestors, for the kings of Upper Egypt, who had come into existence before, in exchange for great payment, no one reached it, except for your emissaries. Now, I will make your troops tread it. I have led them by water and by land, opening for them the secret paths, as I have travelled to the Terraces of Myrrh, the sacred district of the God's Land. It is indeed my seat of my heart's enjoyment. I have made it in order to make my heart happy together with your mother Hathor, the lady of the White Crown, the lady of Punt, the lady of the [sky], Great of Magic, mistress of all the gods. (Sethe 1906, 344, l. 6–345, l. 9. All translations of Egyptian texts contained in this article were made by the author.)

This passage is striking in its presentation of the Punt expedition as a theologically important event and religious duty of the king. This clearly shows that it was not a mere commercial expedition, as it might seem at first glance, but that it was much more important than usually assumed. The cited text makes it clear that the land of Punt, as part of the God's Land (Nutz 2009, 281–8; Cooper 2011, 47–66), was strongly connected with the most important ancient Egyptian deities – namely Amun-Re, king of the gods and Hathor (Meeks 2002, 291–5). The latter was worshipped as the female counterpart of the creator god and was therefore the embodiment of the female principle of nature. The association of Punt with these deities explains why it was not only the most influential civil officials of Hatshepsut's reign who were involved in the organisation of the expedition, but also religious representatives including Hapuseneb, the high priest of Amun in Karnak (Davies 1961, 19–23, pl. 4; Bács 2015, 16, fig. 10a).

From the inscription on the southern wall of the Southern Middle Portico, we are also informed that the female king commanded that a special statue be made and

[3] This is also corroborated by the self-presentation of Djehuty inscribed on the walls of his tomb (TT 11): Sethe 1906, 438, l. 10.

taken to Punt, where it was to stand and serve as the object of cult. The fragmentarily preserved text reads:

> [Now, a seated statue of this god (i.e. Amun-Re) was executed] with its fellow statue of the king of Upper and Lower Egypt ([Ma'at-ka-]Re)|. [Its base was made of one piece of stone in] hard granite, so that the Gre[at] Ennea[d] [which is in P]unt, may be [in the palace around them], [so that] they may endure and la[st] forever and ever up[on their seat] in front of the Terraces of Myrrh [of P]unt, the sacred seat [of the heart's enjoyment, which] the Majesty of this noble god [had made for him]. Her Majesty has made this, whe[n she sent the expedition to this foreign land], as [her father] had foreseen for [her long ago], in order to make this foreign land behold [Her Majesty together with her father, the ruler of Punt, in] the light of every day, because of the [great]ness of his power, because of the excellence of [his] power, because of the [superiority of] his [power], more than all the [go]ds, because of the greatness of his love for [his] daughter [(Ma'at]-ka-[Re])| more than the kings who came into existence since the time of the [ancestors]. (Sethe 1906, 319, l. 12–320, l. 12)

The granite statue of Hatshepsut in the company of her father Amun-Re mentioned in this passage might have shed new light on the exact location of Punt, but it has unfortunately never been found. Nevertheless, its very execution is of utmost importance: by erecting the statue of herself and her divine father in Punt, Hatshepsut emphasised the dominion of the Egyptian ruler over the far side of the world. The statue itself would have also become an object of cult for the foreigners at the same time. It is tempting to suggest that Hatshepsut thereby identified herself with Hathor (Robins 1999, 103–12) who, alongside Amun, was strongly associated not only with Punt itself, but with all foreign lands – especially southern.

After the expedition, led by an official named Nehes (Zivie 1984, 245–52), reached the land of Punt, the Egyptians organised a great feast to which the leaders of the local inhabitants were invited (Naville 1898, pl. 69). This is described in the Deir el-Bahari inscriptions:

> Preparing the tent for the king's messenger with his troops in the Terraces of Myrrh of Punt at the shores of the Great Green in order to receive the elders of this foreign land. They were offered bread, beer, wine, meat, fruits, and everything which is in the Beloved Arable Land (i.e. Egypt), according to what has been ordered in the palace – may he live, may he prosper, may he be healthy! (Sethe 1906, 325, l. 12–17)

Apparently, the feast was not only organised to celebrate the successful arrival of the Egyptian expeditionary force to Punt, but also to emphasise the power of the Egyptian king, who is able to feed both her own subjects and the foreigners at the edge of the then known world (Liverani 2001, 166–9; for the obligation of the Egyptian king to provide food for his subjects, see Taterka 2016).

The aim of the Punt expedition sent by Hatshepsut was to bring back precious and luxurious products (Kitchen 1993, 606; Meeks 2002, 315–18), many of which are represented on the walls of the Deir el-Bahari temple (Naville 1898, pls. 78–81). The accompanying inscriptions describe:

> Loading the ships to the extreme with the marvels of the land of Punt: all beautiful plants of the God's Land, heaps of myrrh-resin of myrrh-trees, with ebony and pure ivory, with green gold of Amu, with the *tj-špss*-plant, with *ẖs'jjt*-plants, with *ihmwt*-spice, incense, black eye-paint, with baboons and other monkeys, hounds, with skins of Upper Egyptian panthers, with servants together with their children. The like of this had never been brought by any king who came into existence since the primeval time. (Sethe 1906, 328, l. 17–329, l. 12)

It seems that the most important of all the products brought from the land of Punt was the *ꜥntjw* 'myrrh' (for the identification of the plant, see Dixon 1969, 55–65; Hepper 1969, 66–72) which gave Punt its name of 'Terraces of Myrrh'. Hatshepsut's expedition brought back not only large quantities of the *ꜥntjw*-resin, to be used in the cult of Amun-Re, but also the trees which produced it. These were meant to be replanted in Karnak in order to 'establish for him Punt inside his House, planting trees of the God's Land at both sides of his temple in his garden, according to what he commanded to happen' (Sethe 1906, 353, l. 2–5). The importance of the *ꜥntjw* can be illustrated by the fact that the store-room for this product – erected by the female Pharaoh in Karnak temple – was unconventionally constructed not of mud brick but of granite, a hard stone with solar connotations (Lacau 1952, 185–90). All this suggests, once again, that there was a direct link between the Punt expedition organised by Hatshepsut and the cult of Amun-Re.

We know, however, that Hatshepsut was not the first (or last) Egyptian Pharaoh who decided to send an expedition to the land of Punt. The first expedition of this kind may have been organised by king Sneferu, the founder of the 4th dynasty. This can be assumed based on the scene from his so-called Valley Temple in Dahshur depicting the king inspecting trees brought back from foreign lands (cedar and *ꜥntjw*-trees; Edel 1996, 200–4), and from evidence found in contemporaneous private tombs (Tallet 2013, 190–8). The first certain and historically attested expedition was sent in the 5th dynasty, in the last year of the reign of king Sahure. This expedition was commemorated on the recently published blocks from the king's causeway (El-Awady 2009, 155–86, pls. 5–7), as well as on the Palermo stone, which informs us that the king's expedition brought back from Punt '80 000 measures of myrrh, 6000 measures of electrum, 2900 measures of malachite, and 23 020 measures of (... a yet unidentified substance...)' (Wilkinson 2000, fig. 3). The reliefs of Sahure's mortuary temple also indicate that this expedition brought back products identical to Hatshepsut's: *ꜥntjw* ready for use and *ꜥnd*-trees.

Later Old Kingdom kings sent expeditions to Punt as well, but their exact number is difficult to determine (for a detailed examination see Diego Espinel 2011, 181–202). From the letter of king Pepy II to Herkhuf, the nomarch of Elephantine in the 6th dynasty, we learn of a past expedition organised in the reign of Djedkare Izezi of the 5th dynasty (Sethe 1933, 128, l. 14–129, l. 1; Verner 2014, 87).[4] Several expeditions were

[4] The expedition was led by an official named Bawerdjeded or Werdjededba (Marcolin and Diego Espinel 2011, 583–5).

sent during the long reign of Pepy II as well, as evidenced by the self-presentations of Pepynakht, called Heqaib (Sethe 1933, 134, l. 13–17), and Khui (Sethe 1933, 140, l. 16–141, l. 3; Newberry 1938, 182–3). An expedition might have also been sent by king Teti, the founder of the 6th dynasty, but this is not certain (Kitchen 1993, 587).

Middle Kingdom rulers continued to organise expeditions to this mysterious land (for a detailed analysis, see Diego Espinel 2011, 246–97). The first one was sent in the 11th dynasty by king Sankhkare Mentuhotep III in regnal year 8, as known from the *graffito* left by the expedition's leader He(ne)nu in the Wadi Hammamat (Kitchen 1993, 589–90). The *graffito* states:

> [My lord – may he live, may he prosper], may he be healthy! – [has] sent [me] to lead the vessels to Punt in order to bring for him the fresh myrrh from the possession of the rulers, having the authority over the Redland thanks to the fear of him throughout the foreign lands. (Couyat and Montet 1912, 82, l. 13–15)

Thanks to the research of the Italian-American mission working at the sites of Mersa/ Wadi Gawasis, we also know that almost every king of the 12th dynasty sent at least one expedition to Punt (Bard and Fattovich 2007; 2010, 33–8; 2012, 21–6; Bard *et al.* 2013, 533–56). We currently know of one expedition under Senwosret I in regnal year 24, Amenemhat II in regnal year 28, Senwosret II in regnal year 1, and Senwosret III, probably in regnal year 5; at least one, but possibly more, under Amenemhat III; and, finally, one under Amenemhat IV in regnal year 8 (Nibbi 1976, 45–56; Sayed 1977, 138–78; Obsomer 1995, 709–16; Mahfouz 2012, 117–32).

However, no evidence of Punt expeditions under Amenemhat I or Sobeknofru has been found to date. This might be due to the haphazard nature of the findings, but other explanations are equally possible. Amenemhat I, as the founder of the 12th dynasty, might have been preoccupied with the need to strengthen the position of the new royal line – although we do know that he was active in Nubia (Žába 1974, 39–44). As for Sobeknofru, the lack of a Punt expedition might have resulted from the brevity of her reign; similarly, the female ruler's inscriptions are also attested in Nubia (Hintze and Reineke 1989, 102 [382], pl. 133). Nevertheless, it seems that sending an expedition to the land of Punt was standard royal practice under the 12th dynasty.

The evidence concerning Old and Middle Kingdom expeditions to the land of Punt is extremely important for the proper interpretation of that of Hatshepsut. It is tempting to suggest that Hatshepsut's expedition was just the final step in the re-establishment of Egypt's past glory in line with the accomplishments of her direct predecessors. Indeed, Ahmose II (recently renumbered by Biston-Moulin[5] (2012, 61–71)) reunified Egypt after the crisis of the Second Intermediate Period (Vandersleyen 1971; Barbotin 2008); Amenhotep I took care of the country's internal stability (Schmitz 1978); and

[5] The recently discovered fragments of a granary door bearing the titulary of the 17th dynasty Senakhtenre revealed that his Birth Name was Ahmose, for which reason the founder of the 18th dynasty should be renumbered to Ahmose II and his 17th dynasty predecessor to Ahmose I.

finally, Thutmose I eliminated Egypt's most dangerous enemies in the south and the north (Baligh 1997, 213–86). Therefore, by organising her Punt expedition, Hatshepsut presented herself not as a unique Pharaoh, but as the legitimate and true heir on the Egyptian throne. As the faithful daughter of Amun-Re, she was able to provide him with all the precious products necessary for his cult, and was also preoccupied, just like her predecessors, with the maintenance of *Maat* – the cosmic order established by the sun god at the creation of the world. It is interesting to note that a similar situation might have occurred in the early Middle Kingdom. It does not seem to be mere coincidence that the first Punt expedition of the Middle Kingdom was organised by Sankhkare Mentuhotep III after the reunification and internal stabilisation of Egypt and, to some extent, defeat of external enemies by king Nebhepetre Mentuhotep II.

The expedition to Punt was thus just another occasion for Hatshepsut to emphasise the legitimacy of her rule over Egypt. It seems that Hatshepsut knew how to use her success to maximum effect, as can be deduced from the inscription accompanying the scene of the offering of the products which were brought back from Punt to Amun-Re (Naville 1898, pls. 82–3). The text reads:

> The king himself, the king of Upper and Lower Egypt (Ma'at-ka-Re)|, takes the measuring stick of electrum and stretches the arm in order to measure the heaps. It is the first time of making good and measuring the fresh myrrh before Amun, lord of the thrones of the two lands, lord of the sky, at the beginning of each harvest which were [brought] as the marvels of the land of Punt. The lord of Khemenu (i.e. Thoth) perpetuated (it) in writing, while the seven-horned goddess (i.e. Seshat) was counting the amounts. [Her] Majesty herself was acting with her arms, putting the myrrh-unguent upon all her limbs: her smell is the divine aroma as her odour mingles with Punt and her skin glitters with electrum, shining like the stars do in the interior of the festival courtyard in front of the entire land. All the people are in jubilation, when they give praise to the lord of the gods and applaud (Ma'at-ka-Re)| in the deeds of her divine nature, because of the greatness of the marvels that happened for her. (Sethe 1906, 339, l. 4–340, l. 6)

The above text is extremely significant for the understanding of the nature of Hatshepsut's Punt expedition. It has already been said that its main purpose on the practical level was to provide *ʿntjw* for the temple of Amun-Re. This was accomplished by bringing back to Egypt not just the substance in question, but also actual *ʿntjw*-trees; an act which constitutes a direct link with the divine cult and creates the religious background of the expedition. If the only concern of the Egyptians was to import *ʿntjw*, they could equally well have done it through Nubia – which they certainly did anyway (Diego Espinel 2011, 292–7). In the Old and Middle Kingdoms, they might have wished to eliminate any intermediaries, but in Hatshepsut's time, Nubia was already a part of the Egyptian empire and therefore no longer an obstacle to their contact with Punt.

Furthermore, it does not seem likely that 31 trees imported from Punt in the reign of Hatshepsut (Sethe 1906, 334, l. 16–17) would have been sufficient for the constant and continuous need for *ʿntjw* in Egypt. The expedition to Punt was thus a symbolic event, and not just a simple commercial undertaking meant to provide Egyptian temples with products necessary for the daily cult. This is illustrated by the actions of Hatshepsut after the return of the expedition. By putting *ʿntjw* on her limbs, she mingled her own royal aroma with the odour of Punt, which, as we know from other texts from the Deir el-Bahari temple, is the smell of Amun-Re himself (Sethe 1906, 220, l. 5–6). That way Hatshepsut emphasised, to some extent, her own divine nature as the female counterpart of the king of the gods. In the texts from the Punt Portico (Sethe 1906, 332, l. 11), furthermore, she is referred to as the female counterpart of the sun (*rʿ.t*).

It should also be stressed that, by organising the Punt expedition, Hatshepsut did not aim to establish a completely new tradition but, quite the contrary, to revive an ancient one which already existed in the glorious times of the Old and Middle Kingdoms. The recently published blocks from the Sahure causeway, showing the king in front of the *ʿnd*-trees, demonstrate that the very layout of Hatshepsut's Punt reliefs and, to some extent, the content of her inscriptions referring to the land of Punt, were also traditional (Breyer 2014, 47–91; contra Callender 2002, 30–2). There are, however, some notable differences in the reliefs. The representations of the Old and Middle Kingdom expeditions seem to be focused mainly on the person of the king. In Sahure's mortuary temple, for example, the king is shown incising the trees in order to obtain the myrrh, probably destined primarily for the royal palace (El-Awady 2009, 160, 169–70, pls. 5–6). The representation of Hatshepsut's expedition, however, is centered mostly on the figure of Amun-Re and his cult, with the female Pharaoh acting as her earthly representative. This may be due to the evolution of Egyptian religious beliefs and of the mutual relations linking the king and the Theban god, but it may well be only an impression due to the incomplete state of evidence at our disposal. Whatever the original purpose might have been, Hatshepsut's Punt expedition appears to have been the final step in the re-establishment of past Egyptian glory – a step that was only possible after re-unification, internal stabilisation, and elimination of external enemies by Hatshepsut's direct predecessors in the 18th dynasty. The Punt expedition is therefore just another element of Hatshepsut's broader programme inspired from ancient traditions (Ćwiek 2014, 61–93) – the aim of which was to bring Egypt back to its full might after the crisis experienced during the Second Intermediate Period. This explains the profound theological and ideological background of the Punt expedition: it was Amun-Re himself who wished to re-establish the glory of Egypt and who was obeyed in his wish by his faithful daughter, Hatshepsut.

Re-establishing contacts with Punt was definitely Hatshepsut's personal achievement, with later kings (Diego Espinel 2011, 439–95, 534–77) continuing to bring luxurious products from Punt, until the reign of Ramesses III in the 20th dynasty at least (Tallet 2013, 198–203), perhaps even later (Meeks 2002, 295–309; Diego Espinel 2011, 579–86). This assumption, however, cannot yet be confirmed given the present state of knowledge.

These preliminary remarks will certainly be developed in the future, thanks to the new project recently undertaken by the Polish-Egyptian Archaeological and Conservation Mission at the Temple of Hatshepsut at Deir el-Bahari. Its aim is to document the Punt reliefs and prepare a full and up-to-date publication of this part of Hatshepsut's temple, and this will surely shed new light on some questions touched upon in this short study.

References

Bács, T. A. 2015. 'Researches in the funerary complex of Hapuseneb, high priest of Amun at Thebes (TT 67): an interim report'. In T. A. Bács and G. Schreiber (eds.) *Current research of the Hungarian archaeological mission in Thebes 2014-2015*, Publications of the Office of the Hungarian Cultural Counsellor in Cairo: 9–21. Cairo: Office of the Hungarian Cultural Counsellor.

Baligh, R. O. K. 1997. *Tuthmosis I*. Unpublished PhD thesis, Yale University.

Barbotin, C. 2008. *Âhmosis et le début de la XVIIIe dynastie*. Paris: Pygmalion.

Bard, K. A. and Fattovich, R. (eds.) 2007. *Harbor of the pharaohs to the land of Punt. Archaeological investigations at Mersa/Wadi Gawasis, Egypt, 2001-2005*. Naples: Università degli Studi di Napoli 'L'Orientale'.

Bard, K. A. and Fattovich, R. 2010. 'Recent excavations at the ancient harbor of *Saww* (Mersa/Wadi Gawasis) on the Red Sea'. In S. H. D'Auria (ed.) *Offerings to the discerning eye. An egyptological medley in honor of Jack A. Josephson*, Culture and History of the Ancient Near East 38: 33–8. Leiden: Brill.

Bard, K. A. and Fattovich, R. 2012. 'Archaeological investigations at Wadi/Mersa Gawasis, Egypt 2006–2007, 2007–2008 and 2009 field seasons'. In P. Tallet and El-S. Mahfouz (eds.) *The Red Sea in pharaonic times. Recent discoveries along the Red Sea coast. Proceedings of the colloquium held in Cairo/Ayn Soukhna, 11th-12th January 2009*, Bibliothèque d'Étude 155: 21–6. Cairo: Institut Français d'Archéologie Orientale.

Bard, K. A., Fattovich, R. and Manzo, A. 2013. 'The ancient harbor at Mersa/Wadi Gawasis and how to get there: new evidence of pharaonic seafaring expeditions in the Red Sea'. In F. Förster and H. Reimer (eds.) *Desert road archaeology in ancient Egypt and beyond*, Africa Praehistorica 27: 533–56. Cologne: Heinrich-Barth-Institut.

Biston-Moulin, S. 2012. 'Le roi Sénakht-en-Rê Ahmès de la XVIIe dynastie'. *Égypte Nilotique et Méditerranéenne* 5: 61–71.

Breyer, F. 2014. 'Vorlagen zur "Punthalle" von Dair al-Baḥrī aus dem Alten Reich. Philologisch-epigraphische, textkritische und ikonographische cruces im Zusammenspiel von Darstellungen und Inschriften'. *Studien zur Altägyptischen Kultur* 43: 47–91.

Callender, V. G. 2002. 'The innovations of Hatshepsut's reign'. *Bulletin of the Australian Centre of Egyptology* 13: 29–46.

Cannuyer, C. 2012. 'Tempête en Nil! Nouvelle note sur le grain qui fit sombrer le navire du *Naufragé*'. In C. Cannuyer and N. Cherpion (eds.) *Regards sur l'orientalisme belge suivis d'études égyptologiques et orientales. Mélanges offerts à Claude Vandersleyen*, Acta Orientalia Belgica 25: 175–84. Brussels: Société Belge d'Études Orientales.

Cooper, J. 2011 'The geographic and cosmographic expression *T3-nṯr*'. *Bulletin of the Australian Centre of Egyptology* 22: 47–66.

Couyat, J. and Montet, P. 1912. *Les inscriptions hiéroglyphiques et hiératiques du Ouâdi Hammâmât*, Mémoires publiés par les membres de l'Institut Français d'Archéologie Orientale du Caire 34. Cairo: Institut Français d'Archéologie Orientale.

Ćwiek, A. 2014. 'Old and Middle Kingdom tradition in the temple of Hatshepsut at Deir el-Bahari'. *Études et Travaux* 27: 61–93.

Davies, N. M. 1961. 'A fragment of a Punt scene'. *Journal of Egyptian Archaeology* 47: 19–23.

Diego Espinel, A. 2011. *Abriendo los caminos de Punt. Contactos entre Egipto y el ámbito afroárabe durante la Edad del Bronce (ca. 3000 a.C.–1065 a.C.)*. Barcelona: Bellaterra.

Dixon, D. M. 1969. 'The transplantation of Punt incense trees in Egypt'. *Journal of Egyptian Archaeology* 55: 55–65.

Edel, E. 1996. 'Studien zu den Relieffragmenten aus dem Taltempel des Königs Snofru'. In P. Der Manuelian and R. E. Freed (eds.) *Studies in honor of William Kelly Simpson* I: 199–208. Boston: Museum of Fine Arts, Boston.

El-Awady, T. 2009. *Sahure - the pyramid causeway. History and decoration program in the Old Kingdom*, Abusir 16. Prague: Charles University in Prague.

Habachi, L. 1957. 'Two graffiti of Sehēl from the reign of queen Hatshepsut'. *Journal of Near Eastern Studies* 16 (2): 88–104.

Hepper, F. N. 1969. 'Arabian and African frankincense trees'. *Journal of Egyptian Archaeology* 55: 66–72.

Hintze, F. and Reineke, W. F. 1989. *Felsinschriften aus dem sudanesischen Nubien* I–II. Berlin: Akademie-Verlag.

Kitchen, K. A. 1971. 'Punt and how to get there'. *Orientalia* 40: 184–207.

Kitchen, K. A. 1993. 'The land of Punt'. In T. Shaw, P. Sinclair, B. Andah, and A. Okpoko (eds.) *The archaeology of Africa: food, metals and towns*, One World Archaeology 20: 587–608. London: Routledge.

Lacau, P. 1952. 'Deux magasins à encens du temple de Karnak'. *Annales du Service des Antiquités de l'Égypte* 52: 185–98.

Liverani, M. 2001. *International relations in the ancient Near East, 1600–1100 BC*. Basingstoke: Palgrave Macmillan.

Mahfouz, El-S. 2012. 'New epigraphic material from Wadi Gawasis'. In P. Tallet and El-S. Mahfouz (eds.) *The Red Sea in pharaonic times. Recent discoveries along the Red Sea coast. Proceedings of the colloquium held in Cairo/Ayn Soukhna, 11th–12th January 2009*, Bibliothèque d'Étude 155: 117–32. Cairo: Institut Français d'Archéologie Orientale.

Marcolin, M. and Diego Espinel, A. 2011. 'The sixth dynasty biographic inscriptions of Iny: more pieces to the puzzle'. In M. Bárta, F. Coppens, and J. Krejčí (eds.) *Abusir and Saqqara in the year 2010* II: 570–615. Prague: Charles University in Prague.

Mariette, A. 1875. *Les listes géographiques des pylônes de Karnak comprenant la Palestine, l'Éthiopie, le pays des Somâl*. Leipzig: J. C. Hinrichs.

Mariette, A. 1877. *Deir-el-Bahari. Documents topographiques, historiques et ethnographiques recueillis dans ce temple pendant les fouilles exécutées par Auguste Mariette-Bey*. Leipzig: J. C. Hinrichs.

Meeks, D. 2002. 'Coptos et les chemins du Pount'. In M.-F. Boussac, M. Gabolde, and G. Galliano (eds.) *Autour de Coptos. Actes du colloque organisé au Musée des Beaux-Arts de Lyon (17–18 mars 2000)*, Topoi Orient-Occident, Supplément 3: 267–335. Paris: De Boccard.

Meeks, D. 2003. 'Locating Punt'. In D. O'Connor and S. Quirke (eds.) *Mysterious lands*, Encounters with ancient Egypt: 53–80. London: UCL Press.

Naville, É. 1898. *The temple of Deir el Bahari* III. *End of northern half and southern half of the Middle Platform*, Egypt Exploration Fund Memoir 16. London: Egypt Exploration Fund.

Newberry, P. E. 1938. 'Three Old-Kingdom travellers to Byblos and Pwenet'. *Journal of Egyptian Archaeology* 24 (2): 182–4.

Nibbi, A. 1976. 'Remarks on the two stelae from the Wadi Gasus'. *Journal of Egyptian Archaeology* 62: 45–56.

Nutz, R. 2009. 'Zur ideologischen Verortung von *Tꜣ-nṯr* und Punt'. *Studien zur Altägyptischen Kultur* 39: 281–8.

Obsomer, C. 1995. *Sésostris Ier. Étude chronologique et historique du règne*, Étude 5. Brussels: Connaissances de l'Égypte ancienne.

Redford, D. B. 1967. *History and chronology of the eighteenth dynasty of Egypt: seven studies*. Toronto: University of Toronto Press.

Robins, G. 1999. 'The names of Hatshepsut as king'. *Journal of Egyptian Archaeology* 85: 103–12.
Sayed, A. M. A. H. 1977. 'Discovery of the site of the 12th dynasty port at Wâdi Gawâsîs on the Red Sea shore'. *Revue d'Égyptologie* 29: 138–78.
Schmitz, F.-J. 1978. *Amenophis I. Versuch einer Darstellung der Regierungszeit eines ägyptischen Herrschers der frühen 18. Dynastie*, Hildesheimer Ägyptologische Beiträge 6. Hildesheim: Gerstenberg.
Sethe, K. 1906. *Urkunden der 18. Dynastie*, Urkunden des ägyptischen Altertums 4. Leipzig: J. C. Hinrichs.
Sethe, K. 1933. *Urkunden des Alten Reichs*, Urkunden des ägyptischen Altertums 1, 2nd ed. Leipzig: J. C. Hinrichs.
Tallet, P. 2013. 'Deux notes sur les expéditions au pays de Pount à la lumière de nouvelles données archéologiques'. *Revue d'Égyptologie* 64: 189–210.
Taterka, F. 2016. 'The role of the pharaoh as the feeder of his people'. In M. Kajzer, Ł. Miszk, and M. Wacławik (eds.) *The land of fertility* I. *South-east of Mediterranean since the Bronze Age to the Muslim Conquest*: 33–50. Cambridge: Cambridge Scholars Publishing.
Vandersleyen, C. 1971. *Les guerres d'Amosis, fondateur de la XVIIIe dynastie*, Monographies Reine Élisabeth 1. Brussels: Fondation Égyptologique Reine Élisabeth.
Verner, M. 2014. *Sons of the Sun. Rise and decline of the fifth dynasty*. Prague: Charles University in Prague.
Wilkinson, T. A. H. 2000. *Royal annals of ancient Egypt. The Palermo Stone and its associated fragments*. London: Kegan Paul International.
Wilson, J. A. 1951. *The culture of ancient Egypt*. Chicago: The University of Chicago Press.
Winlock, H. E. 1928. 'The Egyptian expedition 1925–1927: the Museum's excavations at Thebes'. *The Metropolitan Museum of Art Bulletin* 23 (2): 3–58.
Žába, Z. 1974. *The rock inscriptions of Lower Nubia (Czechoslovak concession)*, Czechoslovak Institute of Egyptology in Prague and in Cairo Publications 1. Prague: Charles University in Prague.
Zivie, A.-P. 1984. 'Un chancelier nommé Nehesy'. In *Mélanges Adolphe Gutbub*, Orientalia Monspeliensia 2: 245–52. Montpellier: Publication de la Recherche – Université de Montpellier.

Chapter 10

Travelling in space and time. The 'west' and 'east' sides of the Harpoon: two geographic divisions of the same nome or two different regions?

Elena Tiribilli[1]
Independent researcher, Italy

Introduction

The origin of the administrative districts of ancient Egypt dates back to the Late Predynastic (*c.*5300–3000 BCE) and Early Dynastic periods (*c.*3000–2686 BCE) (Kaplony 1963, 160–2; Engel 2006, 151–60), when the first standards of Lower and Upper Egyptian nomes appeared on seal impressions. The 22 nomes of Upper Egypt are canonically arranged following a precise geographical order, from south to north. Such an order was already established during the Middle Kingdom, as attested on the southern base of the White Chapel of Senusret I in Karnak (Lacau and Chevrier 1956–1969, 220–30, pl. 3). The numbering of the nomes in Lower Egypt, on the other hand, was less straightforward due to the ramifications, canals, and swamps of the Delta. The situation was further complicated by the fact that its main branches moved over time, which entailed that the nomes' borders changed accordingly. Thus, the number of Lower Egyptian nomes went from sixteen, as attested in the White Chapel of Senusret I (Lacau and Chevrier 1956–1969, 231–7, pl. 42), to seventeen, as attested in the Red Chapel of Hatshepsut (Burgos and Larché 2006, 16–29), and ultimately 20 in the Ptolemaic Period (Rochemonteix and Chassinat 1987, 329–36). Their order and final number were canonised only in the Graeco-Roman Period (Helck 1974, 132–8).

The Western and Eastern Harpoon are always represented in succession in geographic processions and, according to a conventional division created by scholars, they correspond respectively to the seventh and eighth nomes of Lower

[1] The author has made every effort to contact the copyright holders and to obtain their permission for the use of copyright material in this article.

Egypt. However, they were apparently geographically located in diametrically opposite areas of the Delta, with the Western Harpoon in the westernmost part of the Delta (Yoyotte 1991–1992, 625), and the Eastern Harpoon in its southeastern corner (Leclère 2008, 542). The Eastern Harpoon corresponded to the region of the Wadi Tumilat, and its capital was Tell el-Maskhuta. In contrast, the reconstruction of the history of the Western Harpoon is more difficult, and it has scarcely been explored or studied in depth, with a few exceptions (e.g. Yoyotte 1957; 1991–1992; Goddio 2007). The capital and main cities of the nome are unknown, and any attempt at a definitive identification of its territorial boundaries is met with complications (Stanley and Warne 1993, 628–34; 2007, 21–2). For this reason, there is great dissonance among scholars regarding the precise geographical extent of the Western Harpoon, for which two main hypotheses have been advanced: 1) according to a theory first elaborated by Heinrich Brugsch (1880, 1291), and later supported by other scholars (Rougé 1891, 31; Bietak 1975, 169), the nome was located between the Canopic and Bolbitine branches of the Nile, and included modern lake Edku (Fig. 10.1); 2) according to Georges Daressy (1929, 22), Wolfgang Helck (1974,

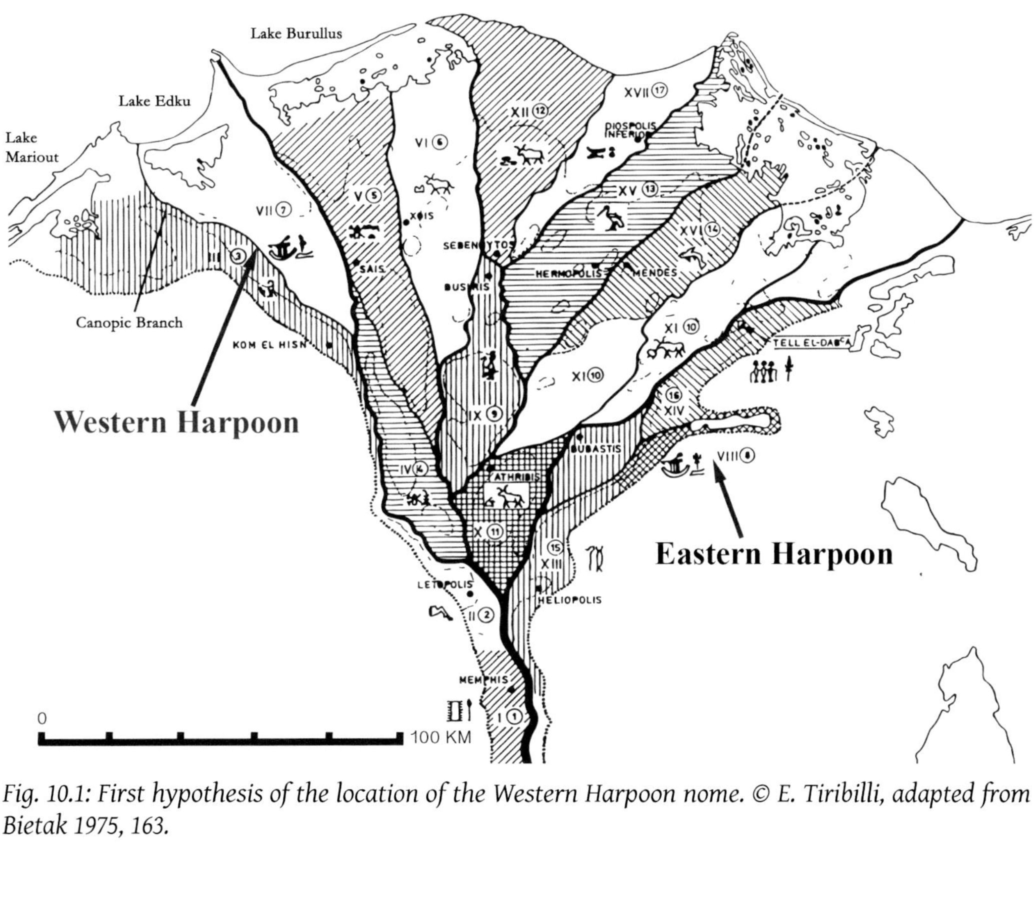

Fig. 10.1: First hypothesis of the location of the Western Harpoon nome. © E. Tiribilli, adapted from Bietak 1975, 163.

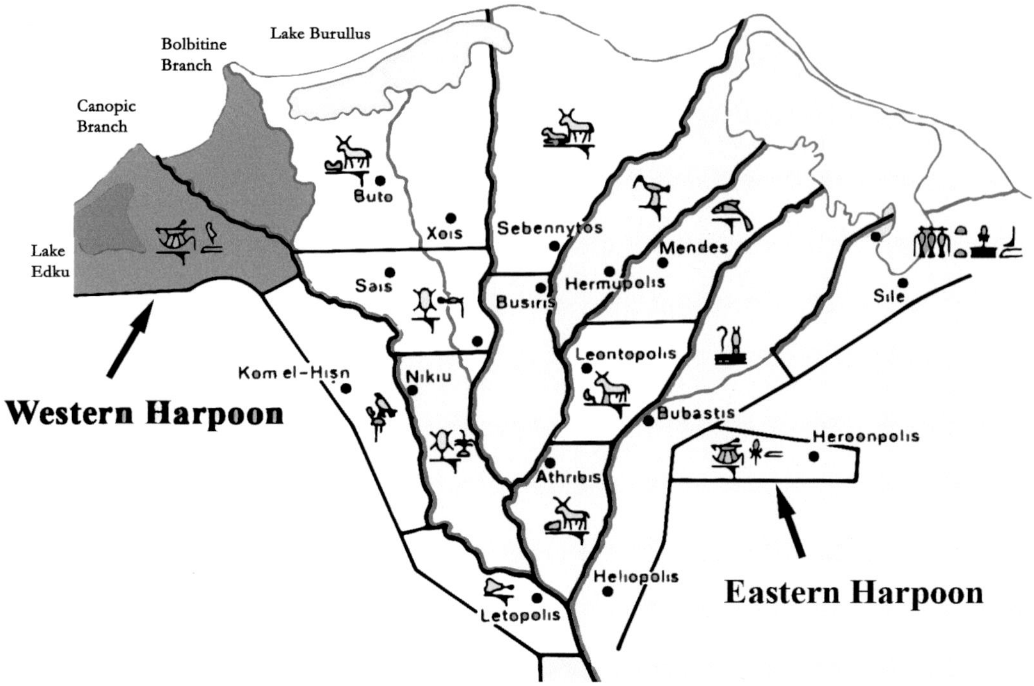

Fig. 10.2: Second hypothesis of the location of the Western Harpoon nome. © E. Tiribilli, adapted from Helck 1974, fig. 5.

fig. 5), and Jean Yoyotte (1991–1992, 65), the nome was instead located between the Libyan desert and the Rosetta branch, and included lake Mariut, the coastal area of Alexandria, and the bay of Aboukir (Fig. 10.2).

The Western and Eastern Harpoon shared a common origin, at least during the earlier epochs of ancient Egyptian history. Between the 4th dynasty and the beginning of the 5th, only a single 'Harpoon' nome is known, without the specification of 'Eastern' or 'Western'. Later, at the end of the 5th dynasty, a nome called 'Harpoon, west side' is attested, while a 'Harpoon, east side' is found only from the 6th dynasty onwards. The aim of this paper is to examine the relationship between the Western and Eastern Harpoon nomes through an analysis of the available material and textual documentation[2] in order to explore the movement of these two nomes across time and in geographical space.

A single Harpoon nome: attestations from the Prehistoric Period to the 5th dynasty

According to the traditional interpretation, the standard of the Harpoon nome usually consists of a harpoon tied to a boat with some ropes (Montet 1957, 69). The

[2] All the documents presented in the article are numbered and listed in Table 10.1, at the end of this paper.

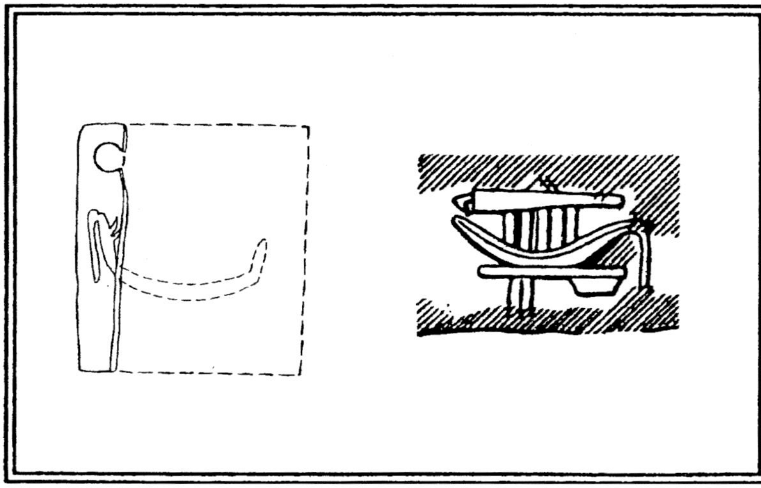

Fig. 10.3: Fragment of label (K 561) from tomb U-k 1 in Cemetery U at Abydos. Kahl 2003, 130.

symbol of the nome, the harpoon, could provide a close link to the geographical landscape of the Delta and to a common activity in this region: hunting with a harpoon.

The earliest attestation of the Harpoon nome, according to Günter Dreyer, might be a small fragmentary label from tomb U-k 1 in Cemetery U at Abydos (doc. 1). He interpreted the partially preserved image as the bow of a boat from which hangs a rope, and thus as a possible representation of the standard of the Harpoon nome (Dreyer 1998, 132–4; Kahl 2003, 128). This, however, is hypothetical, given that the majority of the image is missing (Fig. 10.3).

Some scholars have suggested that the *verso* of the Narmer Palette (doc. 2) bears an early version of the writing of the Harpoon nome's standard (e.g. Goedicke 1966, 22, n. 1; Martin-Pardey 1975, 23; Laurent 2009, 20). This interpretation remains doubtful as the hieroglyphic group consisting of a harpoon (Gardiner T 21) and a lake (Gardiner N 21) could indicate any geographical area in the western Delta rather than a specific nome (Fig. 10.4).

The first reliable source relating to the Harpoon nome dates to the 4th dynasty and is found in the tomb of the official Metjen (doc. 3), who lived in the reign of Sneferu (Urk. I, 1, l. 15; Goedicke 1966, 18–22, pl. 5; Gödecken 1976, 105–12; Strudwick 2005, 192–4). Among his administrative titles related to Lower Egypt, two refer to the Harpoon nome: *ḥḳꜣ-ḥw.t-ḥn.(t)*(?) 'administrator of the estate Henet(?)' and *ꜥḏ-mr Wꜥ-m-ḥwy* 'nome official of the Harpoon nome'. The first administrative title, *hḳꜣ-ḥw.t* 'administrator of the estate', is much discussed by scholars. Widely attested from the end of the 2nd dynasty onwards, it is closely linked to royal rural territories, which were usually administrated by people connected with the royal family, as in the case of Metjen (Piacentini 1994, 239). The presence of the title *ḥḳꜣ-ḥw.t* in association

Fig. 10.4: Detail of the verso of the Narmer Palette. Quibell 1898, pl. 13.

with the Harpoon nome could indicate that this region was already administratively active by the end of the 3rd dynasty. Indeed, in the late 4th and early 3rd millennia BCE, numerous rural territories were acquired in the eastern and western Delta, so that new lands could be integrated into the state administration (Junker 1939, 64; Moreno García 1996, 124). However, the spelling of the toponym *ḥn(.t)*(?), after the title *ḥḳꜣ-ḥw.t*, is far from being clear as it is a *hapax* (Gauthier 1927, 100–1; Goedicke 1956, 18–24; 1963, 88–97). The second title, *ꜥḏ-mr* 'nome official', on the other hand, was very common in Lower Egyptian nomes during the Old Kingdom. It designates the administrator in charge of royal property in the Delta or the desert (Wb I, 240 [7–9]; Jones 2000, 354 [1316], 355 [1321]).

In addition, an ostracon (doc. 4) dated to the late 4th to early 5th dynasties contains other titles linked to the Harpoon nome (Goedicke 1968, 27, pl. 5 [2]). It consists of two parts made of limestone: one is inscribed, and the other, left blank, is of roughly the same shape and presumably intended to protect the inscription. The text is well preserved: *ḫrp-ʿpr(.w) Nfrḫw ḫry-ʿ Wʿ-m-ḥwy ʿrḳ-in.t ḥm-nṯr Ḫnmw Iṯt sꜣ sḳd Tti* 'The director of the crew, Neferkhu's subaltern from Arek-inet in the Harpoon nome, son of the priest Khenemu and of Itjet, the oarsman Teti'.

In the 5th dynasty, the Harpoon nome is mentioned on a stone fragment belonging to the 'Palermo Stone' (doc. 5) and is listed under the section of Sahure's rural estates (Urk. I, 244; O'Mara 1979; Wilkinson 2000; Strudwick 2005, 65–74). On the second register it reads: *[nsw.t bi.ty] (Sꜣḥw-Rʿ)| ir.n=f m mnw=f n Ḥw.t-Ḥr m (Sꜣḥw-Rʿ)| ḫʿ bꜣ Wʿ-m-ḥwy ꜣḥ.t stꜣ.t 2 ḫꜣ[.wj 1/4]* '[The king of Upper and Lower Egypt] (Sahure)|, he set up a monument to Hathor, in the pyramid "the soul of (Sahure)| shines", (in) the Harpoon nome, two arouras, [two] *kha*, [and ¼] of land'. Although difficult to interpret due to the lacunas in the text, the size of land and architectural activity performed by Sahure seem to indicate a particular interest in the region of the Harpoon nome.

Finally, the first geographic procession, which depicts the standard of the Harpoon nome, is a block fragment from the temple of Niuserre at Abu Ghurab (doc. 6; Bissing 1955, 319–38; Kees 1956, 33–40; Fischer 1959, 129–42). It consists of a procession of offering bearers (Baines 1985, 83–115) personifying the nomes of Lower Egypt, but without the hieroglyphic inscriptions that are the norm from the New Kingdom onwards. The first register contains the emblem of the Harpoon, and is preceded by the sixth nome of Lower Egypt, Xois.

The analysis of this first set of documents offers some preliminary conclusions: 1) the first sources, dating to Predynastic and Early Dynastic periods, do not provide any evidence that the Harpoon was an administrative nome at that time (docs. 1–2); 2) the first administrative titles related to the Harpoon nome appeared from the 4th dynasty onwards and some documents attest to cultivation and architectural activity. These elements might indicate that the Harpoon had become an administrative nome by then, and that a part of its land was reclaimed (docs. 3–5); 3) these sources show that, until the reign of Niuserre at least, the Harpoon nome was one unit and that a separation of the territory between 'west' and 'east' sides had not occurred yet (docs. 3–6).

The appearance of the Harpoon 'west side': attestations in the late 5th and 6th dynasties

In the late 5th and 6th dynasties, the documentation mainly consists of the processions of the funerary domains, i.e. lists of rural properties depicted on the walls of royal and high elite tombs (Walle 1957, 288–96; Jacquet-Gordon 1962; Moreno García 2008). At Saqqara, 43 funerary domains are represented in the tomb of Akhethetep (doc. 7), an official who probably lived during the reign of Unas (Davies 1901, pls. 10, 13, 15; Jacquet-Gordon 1962, 388–9, 393–4; Ziegler 2007). There, the Harpoon nome is mentioned eight times in connection with lands associated with several kings of the 5th dynasty, and is indicated each time by the expression *gs imy wr*, 'west side'. The use of the term *imy wr* derives from nautical jargon, where it was often used to refer to the 'west' (Wb I, 73 [6–9]).

One procession of funerary domains is also carved on the walls of the funerary temple of Pharaoh Unas at Saqqara (doc. 8; Jacquet-Gordon 1962, 169–70). At the time of Helen Jacquet-Gordon's study, some of the reliefs were still *in situ*, while others had already been moved to the magazines of the Supreme Council of Antiquities in Saqqara. The Harpoon 'west side' appears seven times there, but the images of the procession are currently unpublished and Jacquet-Gordon did not provide information about the hieroglyphs used to indicate the geographic orientation 'west'.

On the southern walls of the funerary chapel of Ptahhetep II (doc. 9), the son of the Akhethetep mentioned above, three out of the 20 female offering bearers of Upper and Lower Egypt belong to the Harpoon nome. In this instance, the figures do not present any geographic orientation (Quibell *et al.* 1898, pl. 35; Davies 1900, 40, pl. 4, fig. 22; Jacquet-Gordon 1962, 400–1; Harpur and Scremin 2008, 55 [73], 284–5, 355, fig. 4).

The nome of Harpoon 'west side' continues to occur in inscriptions of the 6th dynasty. A rural property in the tomb of Khnementi in Giza (doc. 10) is related to Harpoon 'west side' (Reisner and Fisher 1914, 248–9; Reisner and Smith 1955, 53–4; Jacquet-Gordon 1962, 310–12). In this inscription, the geographic orientation 'west' is designated with *gs i3b.t*, which is a more traditional term to indicate the 'west'. The appearance of a Harpoon 'west side' in the inscriptions implies the existence of a Harpoon 'east side'.

The first attestation of a Harpoon 'east side' is found in the southern side of the corridor walls of the tomb of Mehu (doc. 11), an official who lived during the reign of Teti (Jacquet-Gordon 1962, 419–26; Altenmüller 1998, 128 [26–7]). In the procession visible in this tomb, the toponym *Smn.t Issi* 'the establishment of Isesi', refers to a rural property belonging to the Harpoon 'east side'. On the same wall, eight estates of the Harpoon 'west side' are depicted. From this moment onwards, the Harpoon nome is always divided between an 'east' and a 'west' side. For instance, on the walls of the mastaba of Kairer (doc. 12; Jacquet-Gordon 1962, 428–9), two territories of Harpoon 'west side' are preserved. In a roughly contemporary building, the funerary temple of Pepy II (doc. 13), on the other hand, three territories belonging to Harpoon 'east side' are mentioned with *gs i3b.t* (Jéquier 1940, pl. 25; Jacquet-Gordon 1962, 189).

From the above documentation we can assume that: 1) from the 5th dynasty onwards, the Harpoon nome has probably been a real administrative centre, as attested by the presence of numerous rural territories managed by the royal administration (docs. 7–12); 2) it is likely that, at the end of the 5th dynasty, the size and the importance of the Harpoon nome increased, leading to a separation of the nome into two parts, the Harpoon 'west side' (docs. 7–8, 10–12) and 'east side' (docs. 11, 13); 3) the rural estates of the Harpoon 'west side' were more numerous (26) than those of the Harpoon 'east side' (4); 4) from the 6th dynasty onwards, the designation of

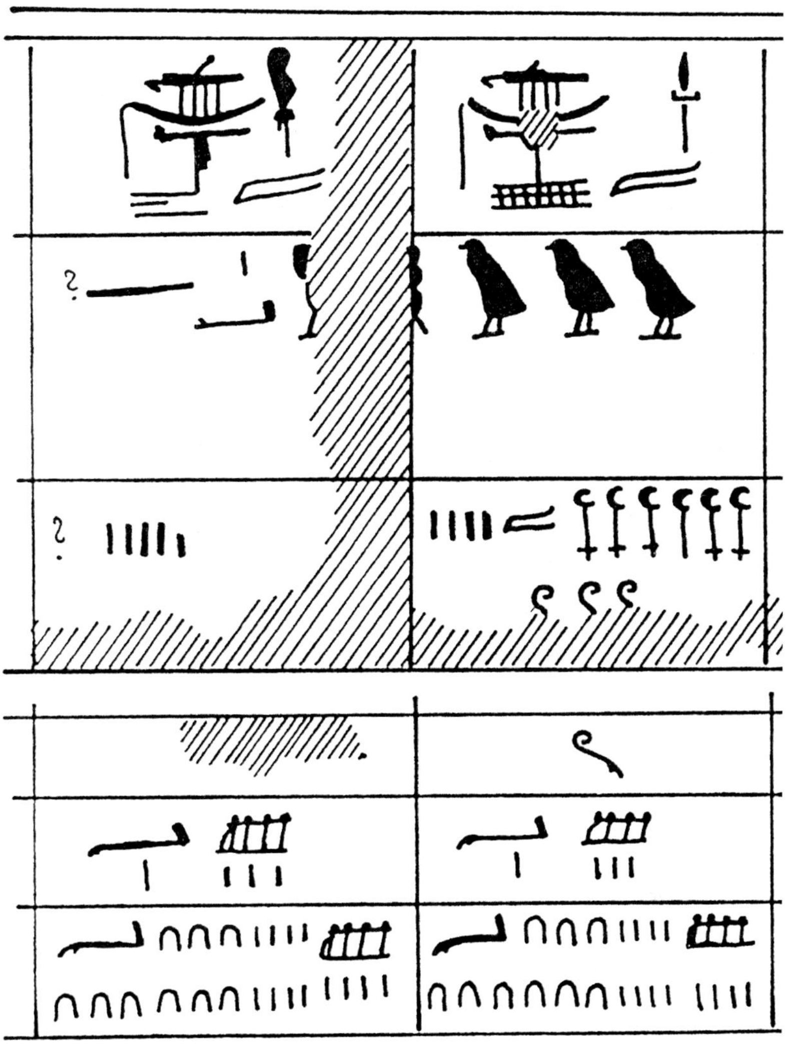

Fig. 10.5: Part of the north 'soubassement' of the White Chapel. Schlott-Schwab 1981, pl. 6.

the geographic orientation 'west' changed from *gs imy wr* (doc. 7) to *gs imn.t* (docs. 10–12). There could be a link between the modification of the terms used to indicate 'west' and the appearance of the Harpoon 'east side'.

The Harpoon 'west' and 'east' sides: two geographic divisions of the same nome or two different regions?

From the data presented in this paper, it is possible to infer that, until the end of the 5th dynasty, there was only one region of the Delta called 'Harpoon', which was only later geographically divided into 'west' and 'east'. The hypothesis that the two nomes originally represented a single administrative region seems to be rooted in the inscriptions of the White Chapel of Senusret I in Karnak (doc. 14; Lacau and Chevrier 1956–1969, pl. 42). The northern base of the chapel is divided into sixteen columns; each contains one of the sixteen nomes of Lower Egypt and is divided into six registers where the main deity, the capital, and some geographical measurements are listed (Graefe 1973, 72–6; Schlott-Schwab 1981, 31–7, pl. 6; Leitz 2006, 409–27). The Eastern and Western Harpoon are set side by side with each register separated by a vertical line; nevertheless, the second register does not present any partitioning line and the two nomes share the same god, *Wꜥ-m-ḥww* (Yoyotte 1957, 82). Similarly, the register which provides the area measurements *sṯꜣ.t* reports the same value for both the Harpoon 'west' and 'east' sides: 98 cubits and four palms, equivalent to 2700 sq. m (Fig. 10.5). The same list is preserved on a block fragment from Amenhotep I's Alabaster Chapel in Karnak (doc. 15; Varille 1943, 16; Schlott-Schwab 1981, pl. 9; Laurent 2009, 30, fig. 3b). As in the White Chapel, there is no partitioning line between the Eastern and Western Harpoon in the register dedicated to the main deity of the nome (Fig. 10.6). However, based on the available documentation, it is impossible to determine whether the earlier Harpoon nome was originally situated in the western or eastern Delta, and when the Harpoon 'west' and 'east' sides started to designate the regions located in the north-west and south-east of the Delta, respectively.

Current interpretation

Véronique Laurent, who studied the sacred geography related to the Eastern Harpoon nome, considered that the Harpoon 'east side' was an eastern extension of a previous nome simply named 'Harpoon', located in the north-west of the Delta. In her opinion, at some point in history, the Harpoon 'east side' was probably absorbed by either the Harpoon 'west side' or Sais and disappeared as a result (Laurent 2009, 48). This fusion

Fig. 10.6: Fragment of the Alabaster Chapel of Amenhotep I. Laurent 2009, 30.

could have been due to a natural phenomenon (e.g. the loss of a natural boundary) which made unnecessary the distinction of 'east' (Laurent 2009, 48).

The political situation of the Third Intermediate Period required the eastern boundaries of Egypt to be fortified, and, at the same time, an open access route towards the Sinai and the Gulf of Suez to be available (Goedicke 1987, 83–98). For these reasons, the Saite pharaohs started to reclaim lands and build canals in the Wadi Tumilat region (Thiers 2007, 107–17). The rise in the importance of this area would have led to the need to 'sacralise' a region lacking a previous religious background. The old and disused name of 'Eastern Harpoon' would have been 'recycled' by the priests in the pre-Saite or Saite periods, thus providing the Wadi Tumilat area with a name full of religious significance given its roots in a mythical past (Laurent 2009, 48–9). Indeed, the Saite period was a time of canonisation and codification of the 'materia sacra' that priests had produced in earlier periods.

Two documents of the Late Period provide particular insight into the religious transformations of the Lower Egyptian nomes, including the 'new' Eastern Harpoon. First, the inner part of the coffin lid of Pasheri(en)aset (doc. 16), probably dating to the 26th dynasty, presents a list which includes the marshlands (*pḥw*) of the eighteen nomes of Lower Egypt and four of the so-called 'additional districts' (Barguet 1962, 7–20). This source could reveal important changes in the religious geography of Lower Egypt, since the inscription includes the first attestation of the marshlands related to the Eastern Harpoon – the eighteenth nome of Lower Egypt – as well as of the four additional districts. Second, the decoration of the southern base of the temple of Hibis in Kharga oasis (room K 2), dated to the Persian king Darius I (doc. 17; Davies 1953, pl. 25; Cruz-Uribe 1988, 103–4), once again shows a geographic procession of the eighteen nomes of Lower Egypt and four 'additional districts'. According to Laurent, some depictions on the south wall of the same temple (Cruz-Uribe 1988, 33–4) could furthermore be evoking the mythology connected with the Eastern Harpoon nome (Laurent 2009, 38–9). Indeed, a disk, containing two goddesses and a god on a boat above the sledge *tm* (Gardiner U 15), is depicted on this wall (Laurent 2009, 39). Comparing this illustration with other examples, the sledge *tm* might be a cryptogram referring to Atum. The god depicted inside the disk could therefore be Atum, the main deity of the ancient Tjeku, the capital of the Eastern Harpoon (Tefnin 1994, 78). The two goddesses, on the other hand, might be the 'two sisters' (*sn.ty*) who often appear associated with Atum, the god of Tjeku, in Ptolemaic and Roman inscriptions (e.g. Cauville 1997, 333–4).

The introduction of the 'additional districts' and the eighteenth nome of Lower Egypt in the textual documentation is incontrovertible evidence of religious elaborations carried out during the Late Period. Moreover, it seems that, before this period, the Eastern Harpoon nome lacked any kind of mythological background. These elements would then confirm that the religious and mythological beliefs of the region of Wadi Tumilat, together with other modifications of the sacred geography of Lower Egypt, were created at the beginning of the Late Period. Although the reconstruction of Laurent is very alluring, according to the available documentation there seems to be no reason to assume that the earlier Harpoon nome was located in the north-western Delta rather than in the south-east.

Another possibility: a symmetrical and notional reconstruction?

The 'formation' of a Harpoon 'west side' and of a Harpoon 'east side' could be due to a purely theoretical need to create two mirroring entities in accordance with the symbolic and religious construction of symmetrical pairs, a diagnostic feature of ancient Egypt. To a Harpoon 'west side', documented in the oldest sources, a counterposed Harpoon 'east side' would have been quickly added on the south-eastern side of the Delta, in accordance with a principle that displays religious and theoretical purposes more than administrative ones.

A similar symmetrical and artificial construction is probably attested for another pair of Lower Egyptian nomes, 'Southern Neith' (*Nt rsj*) and 'Northern Neith' (*Nt mḥtj*), corresponding respectively to the fourth and fifth nomes of Lower Egypt in the Middle Kingdom (Rochemonteix and Chassinat 1987, 330, 15–17, 331, 1–9), while Old Kingdom sources exclusively mention a 'nome of Neith' (Dhennin 2009, 86–91). A clear distinction between 'Southern Neith' and 'Northern Neith' first appears in the White Chapel of Senusret I (Lacau and Chevrier 1956–1969, pl. 42). In this case, it seems evident that there originally was only one administrative region which was later divided into two distinct nomes in order to create symmetrical entities. Are we, in the case of the Harpoon 'west side' and 'east side', again confronted with a purely notional reconstruction of the Delta undertaken by priests who redesigned Egypt's religious geography and topography? The archaeological evidence does not particularly support this possibility. Indeed, the stela of Pithom, dated to Ptolemy II, is the oldest document according to which the territory of Tell el-Maskhuta, in the south-eastern side of the Delta, belonged to the Eastern Harpoon nome (Thiers 2007).

Conclusion

Both of these reconstructions are convincing but, due to the scarcity of the documentation from the Western Harpoon region and to insufficient evidence for the Wadi Tumilat region before the Ptolemaic Period, it is not possible to propose a satisfactory hypothesis for the location of the original Harpoon nome. The localisation of the Western and Eastern Harpoon nomes before the Ptolemaic Period therefore remains an open question. It is very likely instead that, during the Late Period, the Harpoon 'west' and 'east' sides ceased to represent a single administrative region, and started to designate two different nomes, the Western and Eastern Harpoon.

Table 10.1: List of documents presented. © E. Tiribilli.

Doc. no.	Type of document	Present location	Text	Date (BCE)	Main bibliography
				Predynastic Period	
1	Fragment of a label, tomb U-k 1, Umm el-Qa'ab	Unknown (K 561)	—	Naqada IIIa2 (3200–3000)	Dreyer 1998, 132–4
				Early Dynastic Period	
2	Narmer Palette, Hierakonpolis	Egyptian Museum, Cairo (JE 32169)	—	1st dynasty, Narmer (3000–2890)	Goedicke 1966, 22, n. 1; Martin-Pardey 1975, 23
				Old Kingdom	
3	Inscription of Metjen tomb, Saqqara	Ägyptisches Museum und Papyrussammlung, Berlin (No. 1105)	*ḥkꜣ-ḥw.t-ḥn(.t)*(?) *ꜥḏ-mr Wꜥ-m-ḥwy*	4th dynasty, Sneferu (2613–2589)	Urk. I, 1, l. 15; PM III², 493–4
4	Ostracon, Saqqara (?)	Rijksmuseum van Oudheden, Leiden (J 427)	*ḫrp-ꜥpr(.w) Nfrḫw ḫry-ꜥ Wꜥ-m-ḥwy ꜥrḳ-in.t ḥm-nṯr Ḫnmw Itt sꜣ sḳd Tti*	Late 4th–Early 5th dynasty (2494–2345)	Goedicke 1968, 27, pl. 5 [2]
5	Palermo Stone, Memphis (?)	Museo archeologico Salinas (no. 5416)	*[nsw.t bi.ty] (Sꜣḥw-Rꜥ) ir.n=f m mnw=f n Ḥw.t-Ḥr m (Sꜣḥw-Rꜥ) ḫꜥ bꜣ Wꜥ-m-ḥwy ꜣḥ.t stꜣ.t 2 ḫꜣ[.wj 1/4]*	5th dynasty, Sahure (2487–2474)	Urk. I, 244
6	Block fragment, Abu Ghurab	Egyptian Museum, Cairo (JE 34189)	—	5th dynasty, Niuserre (2494–2345)	PM III², 320, 322, 324
7	Mastaba of Akhethetep, Saqqara	Saqqara	**(6)** *Mr Mꜣꜥ.t ([Iss]i)* **(7)** *Ḥw.t N(y)-[wsr-rꜥ]: mr Mꜣꜥ.t N(y)-[wsr-rꜥ]* **(8)** *Mr Mꜣꜥ.t (Issi)* **(9)** *Ḏbꜣ.t ([Wsr-kꜣ=f])* **(27)** *Ḥw.t N(y)-wsr-Rꜥ: mr Mꜣꜥ.t ꜥnḫ N(y)-wsr-Rꜥ* **(28)** *Mr Mꜣꜥ.t ꜥnḫ (Issi)* **(29)** *Ḏbꜣ.t (Wsr-kꜣ=f)* **(30)** *Mr Mꜣꜥ.t ꜥnḫ (Issi)*	5th dynasty, Unas (2375–2345)	PM III², 156, 160

(Continued)

(Table 10.1 Continued)

Doc. no.	Type of document	Present location	Text	Date (BCE)	Main bibliography
8	Funerary temple of Unas, Saqqara	Warehouses of SCA in Saqqara (?)	**(1)** *Ḥw.t Wnis: [s]n.t* (?) *Wnis* **(2)** *Ḥw.t Wnis: n(y) ir.t Wnis Ḫnty-Ṯnnt* **(3)** *Ḥw.t Wnis: […] Wnis* **(4)** *Ḥw.t Wnis: ḏfꜣ Wnis* **(5)** *Ḥw.t Wnis: n(y) ḏbꜣ.t Wnis* **(6)** *Ḥw.t Wnis: ḏfꜣ Wnis* **(7)** *Ḥw.t Wnis:[…] s […]*	5th dynasty, Unas (2375–2345)	PM III^2, 420
9	Chapel of Ptahhetep II, Saqqara	Saqqara	**(7)** *Nfr ꜥnḫ (I-kꜣw-Ḥr)* **(8)** *Mr Mꜣꜥ.t (Issi)* **(12)** *Ḥw.t Sꜣḥw-Rꜥ mr nfr.t Sꜣḥw-Rꜥ*	6th dynasty, Teti (2345–2323)	PM III^2, 156, 160–1, 163
10	Mastaba of Khnementi, Giza	Giza	**(4)** *Mn ḏfꜣ (Tti)*	6th dynasty, Teti (2345–2323)	PM III^2, 35
11	Mastaba of Mehu, Saqqara	Saqqara	**(28)** *Smnt (Issi)* **(29)** *Ḥw.t Tti: nfr mnw (Tti)* **(30)** *Sḫmḫ-ib (Tti)* **(31)** *Mr Ḏḥwty ꜥnḫ (Tti)* **(32)** *Sḏfꜣw (Tti)* **(33)** *Mr Mnw ꜥnḫ (Tti)* **(34)** *Ḥw.t Wnis: sḏfꜣw Wnis* **(35)** *Mr Mnw ꜥnḫ (Wnis)* **(36)** *Smn.t (Ini)*	6th dynasty, Teti (2345–2323)	PM III^2, 619
12	Mastaba of Kairer, Saqqara	Saqqara	**(7)** *Ḥw.t Tti srwḏ Rꜥ Tti* **(8)** *Ḥw.t Wnis srwḏ Rꜥ Wnis*	6th dynasty, probably after Teti (2345–2323)	PM III^2, 631
13	Funerary temple of Pepy II, Saqqara	Saqqara	**(30)** *Ḥw.t Nfr-kꜣ-Rꜥ: šnꜥ Ptḥ Nfr-kꜣ-Rꜥ*	6th dynasty, Pepy II (2278–2184)	Jéquier 1940, pl. 25; Jacquet-Gordon 1962, 189

				Middle Kingdom	
14	White Chapel of Senusret I, Karnak	Open air Museum, Karnak	—	12th dynasty, Senusret I (1956–1911)	Lacau and Chevrier 1956–1969, pl. 42
				New Kingdom	
15	Alabaster Chapel, Karnak	Open air Museum, Karnak	—	18th dynasty, Amenhotep I (1525–1504)	Varille 1943, 16; Schlott-Schwab 1981, pl. 9; Laurent 2009, 30, fig. 3b
				Late Period	
16	Lid coffin	Musée du Louvre (E. 21611)	—	26th dynasty(?) (664–332)	Barguet 1962, 7–20
17	Temple of Hibis, Kharga oasis (room K2 and south wall)	Kharga oasis	—	27th dynasty, Darius I (522–486)	Davies 1953, pl. 25; Cruz-Uribe 1998, 33–4

References

Altenmüller, H. 1998. *Die Wanddarstellungen im Grab des Mehu in Saqqara*. Mainz: Zabern.

Baines, J. 1985. *Fecundity figures. Egyptian personification and the iconology of a genre*. Warminster: Aris & Phillips.

Barguet, P. 1962. 'Une liste des pehou d'Égypte sur un sarcophage du Musée du Louvre'. *Kêmi* 16: 7–20.

Bietak, M. 1975. *Tell el-Dab'a* II. *Der Fundort im Rahmen einer archäologisch-geographischen Untersuchung über das ägyptische Ostdelta*. Wien: Verlag der österreichischen Akademie der Wissenschaften.

Bissing, F. W. von 1955. 'La chambre des trois saisons du sanctuaire solaire du roi Rathourès (Ve dynastie) à Abousir'. *Annales du Service des Antiquités de l'Égypte* 53: 319–38.

Brugsch, H. K. 1880. *Dictionnaire géographique de l'ancienne Égypte. Supplément*. Leipzig: J. C. Hinrichs.

Burgos, F. and Larché, F. 2006. *La chapelle rouge. Le sanctuaire de barque d'Hatshepsout*. Paris: Culturesfrance.

Cauville, S. 1997. *Le temple de Dendera. Les chapelles osiriennes*. Cairo: Institut Français d'Archéologie Orientale.

Chevereau, P.-M. 1989. 'Contribution à la prosopographie des cadres militaires de l'Ancien Empire et de la Première Période Intermédiaire'. *Revue d'Égyptologie* 40: 3–36.

Cruz-Uribe, E. 1988. *Hibis temple project* I. *Translations, commentary, discussions and sign list*. San Antonio: Van Siclen.

Daressy, G. 1929. 'Ménélaïs et l'embouchure de la branche canopique'. *Revue de l'Égypte ancienne* 2: 20–51.

Davies, N. de G. 1900. *The mastaba of Ptahhetep and Akhethetep at Saqqareh* I. *The chapel of Ptahhetep and the hieroglyphs*, Archaeological Survey of Egypt 8. London: Egypt Exploration Society.

Davies, N. de G. 1901. *The mastaba of Ptahhetep and Akhethetep at Saqqareh* II. *The mastaba. The sculptures of Akhethetep*, Archaeological Survey of Egypt 9. London: Egypt Exploration Fund.

Davies, N. de G. 1953. *The temple of Hibis in el Khargeh oasis* III. *The decoration*, Publications of the Metropolitan Museum of Art Egyptian Expedition 17. New York: Metropolitan Museum of Art.

Dhennin, S. 2009. *De Kôm Abou Billou à la Ménoufieh. Recherche historique et archéologique dans le Delta égyptien*. Unpublished PhD thesis, Université Charles de Gaulle – Lille III.

Dreyer, G. 1998. *Umm el-Qaab* I. *Das prädynastische Königsgrab U-j und seine frühen Schriftzeugnisse*. Mainz: Zabern.

Engel, E.-M. 2006. 'Die Entwicklung des Systems der ägyptischen Nomoi in der Frühzeit'. *Mitteilungen des Deutschen Archäologischen Instituts, Abteilung Kairo* 62: 151–60.

Fischer, H. G. 1959. 'Some notes on the easternmost nomes of the Delta in the Old and Middle Kingdoms'. *Journal of Near Eastern Studies* 18 (2): 129–42.

Gauthier, H. 1927. *Dictionnaire des noms géographiques contenus dans les textes hiéroglyphiques* IV. Cairo: Imprimerie de l'Institut Français d'Archéologie Orientale pour la Société royale de géographie d'Égypte.

Goddio, F. 2007. *The topography and excavation of Heracleion-Thonis and East Canopus (1996–2006)*. Oxford: Institute of Archaeology, University of Oxford.

Gödecken, K. B. 1976. *Eine Betrachtung der Inschriften des Meten im Rahmen der sozialen und rechtlichen Stellung von Privatleuten im Ägyptischen Alten Reich*. Wiesbaden: Harrassowitz.

Goedicke, H. 1956. 'The Pharaoh *Ny-swtḥ*'. *Zeitschrift für Ägyptische Sprache und Altertumskunde* 81: 18–24.

Goedicke, H. 1963. 'Ein geographisches Unicum'. *Zeitschrift für Ägyptische Sprache und Altertumskunde* 88: 83–97.

Goedicke, H. 1966. 'Die Laufbahn des *Mṯn*'. *Mitteilungen des Deutschen Archäologischen Instituts, Abteilung Kairo* 21: 1–71.

Goedicke, H. 1968. 'Four hieratic ostraca of the Old Kingdom'. *Journal of Egyptian Archaeology* 54: 23–30.

Goedicke, H. 1987. 'Papyrus Anastasi VI 51-61'. *Studien zur Altägyptischen Kultur* 14: 83–98.

Graefe, E. 1973. 'Einige Bemerkungen zur Angabe der *sṯ3t*-Grösse auf der weissen Kapelle Sesostris I'. *Journal of Egyptian Archaeology* 59: 72–6.

Harpur, Y. and Scremin, P. 2008. *The chapel of Ptahhotep: scene details.* Reading: Oxford Expedition to Egypt.

Helck, W. 1974. *Die altägyptischen Gaue*, Beihefte zum Tübinger Atlas des Vorderen Orients 5. Wiesbaden: L. Reichert.

Jacquet-Gordon, H. K. 1962. *Les noms des domaines funéraires sous l'Ancien Empire égyptien*, Bibliothèque d'Étude 34. Cairo: Institut Français d'Archéologie Orientale.

Jéquier, G. 1940. *Le monument funéraire de Pepi II* III. *Les approches du temple.* Cairo: Institut Français d'Archéologie Orientale.

Jones, D. 2000. *An index of ancient Egyptian titles, epithets and phrases of the Old Kingdom.* Oxford: Archaeopress.

Junker, H. 1939. '*Pḥrnfr*'. *Zeitschrift für Ägyptische Sprache und Altertumskunde* 75: 63–84.

Kahl, J. 2003. 'Die frühen Schriftzeugnisse aus dem Grab U-j in Umm el-Qaab'. *Chronique d'Égypte* 78: 112–35.

Kaplony, P. 1963. *Die Inschriften der ägyptischen Frühzeit*, Ägyptologische Abhandlungen 8. Wiesbaden: Harrassowitz.

Kees, E. 1956. 'Zu den Gaulisten im Sonnenheiligtum des Neuserrê'. *Zeitschrift für Ägyptische Sprache und Altertumskunde* 81: 33–40.

Lacau, P. and Chevrier, H. 1956–1969. *Une chapelle de Sésostris Ier à Karnak.* Cairo: Institut Français d'Archéologie Orientale.

Laurent, V. 2009. 'À la recherche du Harpon de l'Est'. *Chronique d'Égypte* 84: 20–49.

Leclère, F. 2008. *Les villes de Basse Égypte au Ier millénaire av. J.-C.*, Bibliothèque d'Étude 144. Cairo: Institut Français d'Archéologie Orientale.

Leitz, C. 2006. 'Die Große Ägyptens nach dem Sesostris-Kiosk in Karnak'. In G. Moers, H. Behlmer, K. Demuß, and K. Widmaier (eds.) *Jn.t dr.w. Festschrift für Friedrich Junge* II: 409–27. Göttingen: Seminar für Ägyptologie und Koptologie.

Martin-Pardey, E. 1975. *Untersuchungen zur ägyptischen Provinzialverwaltung.* Hildesheim: Gerstenberg.

Montet, P. 1957. *Géographie de l'Égypte ancienne* I. *To-Mehou. La Basse Égypte.* Paris: Imprimerie nationale.

Moreno García, J. C. 1996. 'Administration territoriale et organisation de l'espace en Egypte au troisième millénaire avant J.-C.: *grgt* et le titre *ꜥ(n)ḏ-mr grgt*'. *Zeitschrift für Ägyptische Sprache und Altertumskunde* 123: 116–38.

Moreno García, J. C. 2008. 'Estates (Old Kingdom)'. In E. Frood and W. Wendrich (eds.) *UCLA Encyclopedia of Egyptology.* Los Angeles. [online] ⟨http://escholarship.org/uc/item/1b3342c2⟩, accessed 10 December 2015.

O'Mara, P. F. 1979. *The Palermo stone and the archaic kings of Egypt*, Studies in the Structural Archaeology of Ancient Egypt 1. La Canada: Paulette Pub. Co.

Petrie, W. M. F. 1900. *The royal tombs of the earliest dynasties* I. London: Egypt Exploration Fund.

Piacentini, P. 1994. 'On the titles of the *ḥk3w ḥwt*'. In S. Allam (ed.) *Grund und Boden in Altägypten (rechtliche und sozio-ökonomische Verhältnisse)*: 235–50. Tübingen: Selbstverlag.

Quibell, J. E. 1898. 'Slate palette from Hieraconpolis'. *Zeitschrift für Ägyptische Sprache und Altertumskunde* 36: 81–4.

Quibell, J. E., Paget, R. F. E., and Pirie, A. A. 1898. *The Ramesseum and the tomb of Ptah-hetep.* London: B. Quaritch.

Reisner, G. A. and Fisher, C. S. 1914. 'Preliminary report on the work of the Harvard-Boston expedition in 1911–13'. *Annales du Service des Antiquités de l'Égypte* 13: 227–52.

Reisner, G. A. and Smith, W. S. 1955. *A history of the Giza necropolis* II. *The tomb of Hetep-heres, the mother of Cheops*. Cambridge: Harvard University Press.
Rochemonteix, M. and Chassinat, É. 1987. *Le temple d'Edfou* I, 3, Mémoires publiés par les membres de la Mission Archéologique Française au Caire 10, 2nd ed. revised and corrected. Cairo: Institut Français d'Archéologie Orientale.
Rougé, J. 1891. *Géographie ancienne de la Basse-Égypte*. Paris: Rothschild.
Schlott-Schwab, A. 1981. *Die Ausmasse Ägyptens nach altägyptischen Texten*, Ägypten und Altes Testament 3. Wiesbaden: Harrassowitz.
Stanley, J.-D. and Warne, A. G. 1993. 'Nile Delta: recent geological evolution and human impact'. *Science* 260: 628–34.
Stanley, J.-D and Warne, A. G. 2007. 'Nile delta geography at the time of Heracleion and East Canopus'. In J.-D. Stanley, A. Bandelli, M. P. Bernasconi, T. Jorstad, R. Melis, N. Pugliese, G. Schnepp, and A. G. Warne (eds.) *Geoarchaeology*: 5–22. Oxford: Institute of Archaeology, University of Oxford.
Strudwick, N. C. 2005. *Texts from the pyramid age*. Leiden: Brill.
Tefnin, R. 1994. 'Amenophis III sur son traîneau: mise en abyme et/ou cryptogramme?'. *Göttinger Miszellen* 138: 71–80.
Thiers, C. 2007. *Ptolémée Philadelphe et les prêtres d'Atoum de Tjékou. Nouvelle édition commentée de la 'stèle de Pithom' (CGC 22183)*. Montpellier: Université Paul Valéry – Montpellier III.
Van de Walle, B. 1957. 'Remarques sur l'origine et le sens des défilés de domaines dans les mastabas de l'Ancien Empire'. *Mitteilungen des Deutschen Archäologischen Instituts, Abteilung Kairo* 15: 288–96.
Varille, A. 1943. *Karnak* I, Fouilles de l'Institut Français d'Archéologie Orientale 19. Cairo: Institut Français d'Archéologie Orientale.
Wilkinson, T. A. H. 2000. *Royal annals of ancient Egypt. The Palermo Stone and its associated fragments*. London: Kegan Paul International.
Yoyotte, J. 1957. 'Le Soukhos de la Maréotide et d'autres cultes régionaux du dieu-crocodile d'après les cylindres du Moyen Empire'. *Bulletin de l'Institut Français d'Archéologie Orientale* 56: 81–95.
Yoyotte, J. 1991–1992. 'Égyptologie'. *Annuaire du Collège de France* 92: 625–45.
Ziegler, C. 2007. *Le mastaba d'Akhethetep*. Paris: Musée du Louvre.
Zivie, A.-P. 1975. *Hermopolis et le nome de l'Ibis. Recherches sur la province du dieu Thot en Basse Égypte* I, Bibliothèque d'Étude 66. Cairo: Institut Français d'Archéologie Orientale.